Speaking for Myself

Speaking for Myself

Faith, Freedom,
and the Fight
of Our Lives
Inside the
Trump
White House

Sarah Huckabee Sanders

ST. MARTIN'S
GRIFFIN
NEW YORK

Published in the United States by St. Martin's Griffin, an imprint
of St. Martin's Publishing Group

Designed by Meryl Sussman Levavi

The Library of Congress has cataloged the hardcover
edition as follows:

Names: Sanders, Sarah Huckabee, author.
Title: Speaking for myself : faith, freedom, and the fight of our
    lives inside the Trump White House / Sarah Huckabee Sanders.
Other titles: Faith, freedom, and the fight of our lives inside the
    Trump White House
    Identifiers: LCCN 2020026251 | ISBN 9781250271334
    (hardcover) | ISBN 9781250275233 (signed edition) |
    ISBN 9781250271341 (ebook)
Subjects: LCSH: Sanders, Sarah Huckabee. | United States—
    Politics and government—2017- | Presidents—United
    States—Staff—Biography. | Presidential Press Secretaries—
    United States—Biography. | United States—Politics and
    government—2017–2019. | Press and politics—United
    States—History—21st century.
Classification: LCC E912 .S265 2020 | DDC 352.23/2748092
    [B]—dc23
LC record available at https://lccn.loc.gov/2020026251

ISBN 978-1-250-81713-6 (trade paperback)

First St. Martin's Griffin Edition: 2021

10 9 8 7 6 5 4 3 2 1

For my husband, Bryan, without whom this book and this wonderful life would never have been possible. I couldn't nor would I want to do any of it without you. No one can annoy me more or make me happier than you!

And to our three beautiful, wild, and crazy kids, Scarlett, Huck, and George: you provide endless content, keep me humble, and have shown me how to love bigger than I thought possible.

You are each the best part of me. I love you!

Contents

1

Kill 'Em All

It was Christmas night 2018, and our home in Arlington, Virginia, was filled with the aromas of the traditional "Sanders Christmas Dinner"—plates of marinated-overnight, slow-cooked beef brisket, hash brown casserole filled with cheese just the way our three kids like it, spaghetti squash, Brussels sprouts with crisp bits of bacon, sautéed mushrooms, and warm buttered bread. We topped it off with my bourbon chocolate pecan pie, made famous by CNN's April Ryan after she went on an angry tirade doubting I made it. April should have known better than to question the authenticity of a southern woman's pie!

Around the table my husband, Bryan; our children, Scarlett, Huck, and George; my mother- and father-in-law in from Kansas City; Bryan's sister Virginia, an elementary school teacher from Denver; Bryan's brother David, who is completing his postdoc in neuroscience at Princeton; and David's girlfriend Mel were all scrunched together. They'd come in to celebrate a relaxing Christmas with us. It was great to actually use our dining room for once, which during my two and a half years in the White House was more commonly used as a storage room, while we ate meals in the kitchen either reheated out of the freezer or picked up at a nearby Chick-fil-A.

After dinner we cleared the dishes, threw away the last of the mounds of torn wrapping paper, and laughed at the new basketball goal "Santa" had brought but that our kids never actually received, because Bryan destroyed it during the "easy-to-assemble" process on Christmas Eve. Maybe one of these years Bryan will start putting the kids' gifts together before midnight on Christmas Eve, but after seven Christmases with our kids and many near-traumatic Christmas mornings later, I won't hold my breath (I still love him anyway).

As we read books, said goodnight prayers, and tucked in our worn-out kids, who in their excitement had woken up way too early to open presents, I glanced at the time and announced, "I hate to do this, but I'm going to have to leave because something has come up." My in-laws weren't used to the kind of "somethings" that those of us working at the White House had become familiar with and assumed I must be kidding. After all, it was late on Christmas, and we were three days into what became the longest government shutdown in US history. They only realized I was serious when I said, "It's not an emergency, but I'm not able to discuss it and I'm afraid I have to leave right now." I sincerely apologized because I knew I wouldn't be back before their departure the following morning. I said my good-byes dressed in Lululemon yoga pants and a casual pullover, which prompted Bill, my normally not-so-fashion-conscious father-in-law, to ask, "Should you change before going in? If not, I hope you keep a change of clothes at the office!" I assured him I did and said not to worry, but if he had only known the real purpose for my abrupt departure, he would have been worried. I didn't show it, but I wasn't as calm as I was letting on. I understood the gravity of what I would be doing for the next several hours.

For the first time in nearly two years I drove myself to Joint Base Andrews–Naval Air Facility, a massive military complex covering nearly seven square miles of land. Among its many missions, it is home to Air Force One. En route, I made multiple calls to my good friend and occasional Air Force One spades partner, White House Deputy Chief of Staff Dan Walsh. Walsh was a retired officer in the United States Coast Guard, former presidential military aide at the White House, and former White House military office director. Aside from his distinguished career in the military and being one of the most knowledgeable people in the country about White House operations, Walsh is a really fun person to be around and someone all of us counted on. In the midst of some of our hardest days I was often in Walsh's West Wing office venting, laughing, then walking out with a reminder of why we showed up to our jobs every day.

Walsh was in charge of planning and executing the highly classified and top-secret mission of the next forty-eight hours, and I wanted to make sure I was going in the right direction. This was one time that being late wouldn't be optional—or forgiven. Too many people were involved and were unable to disclose to their families on Christmas Day what duty was calling so urgently. After making fun of me for being "directionally challenged" Dan talked me through each turn. Because I was paying more attention to his precise directions than to other vehicles, I came close to getting killed twice. In what seemed like a longer than usual commute, I pulled up to the designated gate and went through several tightly controlled military checkpoints. They instructed me to follow an unmarked car to a parking lot where a small but familiar senior White House staff gathered.

I spotted Walsh and Dan Scavino, one of my closest friends at the White House, fellow road warrior, and senior advisor to the president. Scavino had worked for the president longer than anyone else in the White House and spent more time with him than just about any other administration official. He was the ultimate Trump insider, and far more influential than the media gave him credit for being (probably because he didn't leak to them). Scavino was my confidant, social media coach, and sounding board, and became like a brother to me over the three and a half years I worked for the president on his campaign and in the White House. We often spent our time on the road watching videos of one another's kids, teasing our friend and colleague Stephen Miller, and working side by side to execute tasks the president assigned us. Stephen was known to many for his hard-line stance against illegal immigration and combative (and often wildly entertaining) media appearances. But the Stephen I got to know during my time in the administration was one of the funniest, most passionate, and thoughtful people in the building. No one on staff could articulate the president's vision and agenda better than Stephen, and his role was so much greater than just a speechwriter or policy advisor. Both Stephen Miller and Dan Scavino were irreplaceable in President Trump's inner circle.

Though all of us had traveled dozens of times on Air Force One from Andrews, this night was different. We stood quietly and nervously outside in the pitch-black and the freezing cold awaiting instructions. After a few minutes of anxious chatter, we loaded onto small unmarked black buses and drove to a section of Andrews that I had never seen.

Air Force One, a gigantic Boeing 747, was still in the hangar. Normally when we were traveling with the president on Air Force One, we would pull onto the tarmac and see the iconic light blue and white plane lit up like a night game at a major league baseball stadium. This was the first time we had ever seen Air Force One in the hangar.

The buses pulled into the building and the massive doors closed behind us. Each of us grabbed our small carry-on bags containing only a few personal items—we wouldn't be gone long—and boarded Air Force One using the small built-in stairs under the plane instead of the large ones they typically pull up to the side door.

Meanwhile, President Trump and First Lady Melania quietly snuck out of the White House through a secret exit and were driven by United States Secret Service from the White House to Andrews.

Just before midnight the president and first lady boarded Air Force One with no fanfare and no photos capturing the pair. Later, aboard the plane, the president walked down the corridor from his office to the conference room and told us in the way only he can about their great escape from the White House: "I'm feeling my way off the White House grounds with no lights, stumbling around . . . ," making wild hand motions to drive his point home. "Having no motorcade is kind of cool, almost makes you feel normal again." (The Secret Service was quick to reassure us the first couple was 100 percent safe throughout their departure.) For the president, this was the most normal ride he had taken in nearly two years, while for the rest of us—even after all our time at the White House—nothing about the last couple of hours on this Christmas night felt normal at all.

Air Force One pulled out of the hangar and powered down the runway, lifting off into the midnight sky. The windows through which we'd ordinarily watch Washington disappear were closed, the plane's exterior lights turned off, and our normally functioning phones and computers shut down. We were off the grid.

On board were the president, First Lady Melania Trump, Acting Chief of Staff Mick Mulvaney, Deputy Chief of Staff Dan Walsh,

National Security Advisor John Bolton, Senior Advisor Stephen Miller, Senior Advisor Dan Scavino, Communications Director for the First Lady Stephanie Grisham, Chief of Staff to the First Lady Lindsay Reynolds, presidential aide Nick Luna, Deputy Press Secretary Lindsay Walters, a few other White House staff, members of the press, and an army of US Secret Service agents loaded down with enough advanced weaponry to invade a small country.

So far, so good.

Earlier in the week I had met with all of the Washington bureau chiefs for the five major television news outlets that are each part of the traveling presidential press pool. The press pool is a rotating group of thirteen journalists who travel with and cover the president everywhere he goes. They take videos and pictures of his every move, document his every word, and provide pool reports that go to thousands of journalists providing a second-by-second, minute-by-minute, hour-by-hour historical account of just about everything the president does. They ride in every motorcade and aboard every Air Force One flight, and attend just about every event on the president's schedule. The name of the pool comes from the space where the White House press briefings are typically held—it used to be where the White House swimming pool was, but now is home to the James S. Brady Press Briefing Room, named after President Ronald Reagan's press secretary who was shot during the assassination attempt on the president.

Walsh and I had sat down with the DC bureau chiefs for ABC, CBS, NBC, CNN, and FOX in a secure room in the Eisenhower Executive Office Building, a large French–architecturally styled building adjacent to the White House that spans the equivalent of nearly a dozen football fields. The Eisenhower Executive Office Building used to house nearly the entire federal government, including the Department of State and Department of War, but thanks to the ever-expanding size of our federal government can now only accommodate the majority of the president's staff who don't have offices in the West Wing of the White House.

We confiscated each participant's phone before the meeting started and put them in protected lockers. We then walked them through the plan for the following week. We explained how important it was that this information not leak, and that doing so could put their team as well as the president and his team in danger. Everyone in the room understood the risks and in this moment we were all working together. They—along with the print reporters and photographers in the pool we later briefed about the trip—agreed to the terms and we spent the next several days in communication about the details and logistics. No one ever leaked it—perhaps another first for this White House. Prior to boarding Air Force One on the day of the trip we again confiscated the phones and equipment of every member of the press pool to make sure no one inadvertently jeopardized the trip. They reluctantly turned them over.

Air Force One is a plane like no other in the world. It serves as a functioning Oval Office and Situation Room in the sky for the president when he travels, and includes security features that make it nearly impossible for an enemy to attack it. Air Force One is divided into several sections. In the back you have the thirteen members of the press pool and one White House press staffer called a wrangler, who is always with the press to help them move from place to place, as well as members of the Air Force One crew. Just in front of them are members of the Secret Service, and then a staff cabin usually filled with support staff and special guests traveling with the president—but on this flight the only people in this entire section were the much larger than usual contingent of heavily armed Secret Service agents. There is a fully equipped office and a large office-sized copier and printer that took a lot of abuse from Stephen Miller and Staff Secretary Derek Lyons—a confidante, constant collaborator, and although never the loudest guy in the room typically one of the smartest—due to its endless paper jams and breakdowns. Just to the left of the office is where the White House photographer, stenographer, and the White House IT and communications team sit. This group helps keep track of the historical account of everything the president does and keeps the president and staff around him in touch with the rest of the world wherever we go. A few feet in front of them is another section for White House staff and the Military Aide, who carries the nuclear football and keeps track of every contingency plan for the president at all times. There are five Mil-aides always assigned to the president—one from each branch of the military. They are the cream of the crop from their respective branches—tough, smart, strategic, and if available always my spades partners on Air Force One. A short walk down the hall brings you to a large conference room where the president has meetings, cabinet members or elected officials sit, staff watch movies, news, and sporting events, play cards, eat meals, and on long overseas trips is where you will find many members of the staff asleep on the floor or on one of the two highly coveted couches. At the front of the plane there is a small senior staff cabin, kitchen, medical unit, and the president's office and bedroom.

On Christmas night on Air Force One we were gathered in the conference room trading stories about leaving our families so confused about our abrupt departure for a secret destination. As we engaged in mostly fun and lighthearted chatter Walsh and Tony Ornato, the head of the president's protective detail in the US Secret Service and someone we had all come to love, admire, and depend on, walked in. Tony was the man most responsible for keeping the president and his family safe, and he is a hero in more ways than one. On another trip we made, to the UK, Tony was walking across a crowded bridge in London on his way to meet the rest of us for dinner and passed by a young girl who appeared distressed. The girl looked at Tony, and he noticed a look of despair in her eyes as she turned and hurled herself off the bridge into the water a hundred feet below. Tony looked over the edge, ready to jump in after her, but he determined he probably couldn't survive the fall, sprinted across the bridge, threw his body through a locked door of a building, and ran down several flights of stairs to the main floor of the building level with the river, where he was able to follow her body as it drifted downstream and radio local authorities the exact location to find her and pull her out. The girl miraculously survived. Afterward Tony said he just did what anybody else would do in that situation.

Tony and Walsh had come by to give us some additional details and guidance for when we arrived. They briefed us on the dangers of being in a war zone and Tony said, "If at any time you hear a loud whizzing or whistling sound it means we're under attack—and you need to take cover immediately." He explained there are bunkers all around—"just run to one of them and jump in." The night had just gotten real. While we knew it could be dangerous this was when the fear really set in.

For a moment I was pretty terrified. Tony and Walsh could sense it and tried to put me at ease. I told Walsh not to leave my side while we were on the ground and make sure I knew where I was supposed to be if something happened. Given that he was in charge of executing the entire operation I knew it was an unfair request, but he reassured me he wouldn't let me out of his sight.

We sat down to dinner in the Air Force One conference room. Undoubtedly the best food and service you'll find anywhere on a plane is on Air Force One, thanks to the amazing work of members of the US Air Force. Every time you board the plane you have an assigned seat with an Air Force One seat card with your name on it, to let you know where your seat is for that leg. Each meal is served on Air Force One china—ivory plates with a gold band around the edge and the Presidential Seal at 12 o'clock, and napkins with the seal. There is a set meal for each flight and that night we had traditional lasagna, Italian salad, cappuccino cheesecake, and our choice of beverage.

After dinner I walked up to the president's cabin, where the president is usually working and rarely sleeps. He typically carries ten to fifteen (I believe the record is twenty-one) file boxes full of newspapers, magazines, articles, briefing papers, and other documents to go over while we are in the air. Sometimes he will read or see something that catches his eye and will call one of us up to discuss it.

Tonight was no different. The president asked me about the press traveling with us and whether news of the trip had leaked. I reassured him all was clear. During our conversation the first lady and Stephanie Grisham walked in from the president and first lady's bedroom behind his office.

This was the first time I had seen the first lady since I released a statement announcing her plans to return from Mar-a-Lago to Washington to be with the president on Christmas due to the shutdown. The first lady is strong, smart, independent, funny, and incredibly warm. She gets no credit for the great job she has done nor for how tough she is. I have often said if the first lady—an immigrant who has lived the American dream—was married to a Democrat president she would be one of the most celebrated first ladies in history. One thing I know to never do is to speak on her behalf. She has a very capable team and likes to handle her own statements and releases. Unfortunately, that hadn't crossed my mind when the president had called me a few days before the trip and told me to release a statement letting the world know his plan to stay in Washington during the shutdown and the first lady's plan to join him. After I released the statement I heard from Grisham, who let me know they were not too thrilled I'd done it without giving them the heads-up. I knew I had messed up, but figured in time everyone would forget about it. Wrong again. At Andrews, Grisham had once again given me a hard time about my statement.

So when I saw the first lady in the president's cabin on Air Force One I tried to lightheartedly clear the air: "I got in a little trouble with your team for the statement announcing your return to Washington. . . ." I smiled, pointed at her husband, and said, "Just so you know, he made me do it."

The president said, "Oh, come on! It was a beautiful statement . . . I love how we made it sound like you needed to rush back to be by my side." He laughed hysterically, and (a bit nervously) so did I. The president didn't let up: "Melania . . . you have the best life. How could you ever go on without me?"

"Actually, Donald . . . you'd be the one who could never go on without me. You'd be a total mess. Leaving me message after message, begging 'Call me back! Call me back! Please, Melania, call me back!'" In triumph, she laughed. The president did, too, loving the banter and knowing she was right. (Message for the husbands out there: your wife always is.) The president needs Melania and frankly so does the country. The president is more relaxed around the first lady and the staff is always glad when she travels with him. We were especially thankful she was here tonight. She was such a positive force and had far more influence than most realized.

We spent the next several hours talking, working, playing cards, and trying to sleep.

Nearly twelve hours later in the pitch-black of the night, with no lights on the plane or the runway, we landed at Al Asad Airbase in the war-torn Anbar province of western Iraq. We quickly unloaded into vehicles and as we drove away and looked back Air Force One was barely visible in the desert darkness.

The president and first lady entered the dining hall filled with a hodgepodge of Christmas decorations. Hundreds of troops had gathered, thinking they were about to be joined for dinner by some of the generals leading the battle against ISIS. Instead, they got their commander in chief. The room erupted. The men and women of our armed forces were spending Christmas away from their families and instead spending it with the First Family.

The president and first lady went by each table individually thanking the troops and wished them a Merry Christmas. A member of the US Army told the president he rejoined the military because of him, and the president said, "And I am here because of you." When the president moved to the next table, the soldier walked over to me and said, "Thank you, Sarah. I love the way you handle yourself. You have a tough job."

I politely corrected him and said, "Thank you, but what I do is nothing compared to the sacrifice you make. You're halfway around the world risking your life for the rest of us. That's a tough job."

The US Army soldier silently reached up, tore the Brave Rifles patch representing the 3rd Armored Cavalry Regiment from his arm, and handed it to me. "We're in this together. It's an honor to meet you."

Overwhelmed with emotion and speechless, I just hugged him. I probably held on for longer than I should have, and walked away with tears in my eyes more grateful than ever for the brave men and women of our armed forces. Their selfless sacrifice represents the best of America. I still can't think about this night and not feel the tears well up, and it's a memory I will cherish for the rest of my life. I keep the patch on my desk in my office to remind me of their sacrifice. I later found out that the 3rd Armored Cavalry Regiment in Iraq had been led by my good friend General H. R. McMaster from 2004 to 2005. He said it was one of his greatest achievements in the military.

Standing outside a massive hangar packed with American heroes, the president wore an army green bomber jacket and signature red tie. Alongside the president stood the first lady, in a mustard-colored jacket and army green pants. They walked into the hangar and up onto the stage with a gigantic camo net and American flag backdrop as hundreds of troops shouted "USA! USA! USA!" I looked around. Every race, ethnicity, socioeconomic background, and political party must have been represented in the room but in that moment everyone was united as Americans.

After being on the ground for well over an hour there had still been no leaks, but it was time to tell the world. The reporters traveling with us were desperate to file their stories and it was killing them to have to wait. We had made it nearly impossible for anyone to post on social media, text friends, or send emails by shutting down all the cell signals at the base. We finally opened the signal and as the president addressed the troops I announced: "President Trump and the first lady traveled to Iraq late on Christmas night to visit with our troops and senior military leadership to thank them for their service, their success, and their sacrifice."

Just six days before the trip, on December 19, the president declared that US forces would withdraw from Syria. The president's decision was met with immense pushback, including from some Republican lawmakers and even some officials inside the administration, like Secretary of Defense Jim Mattis. The president had campaigned on and long pledged to get America out of endless wars and bring our troops home, but some Republicans apparently didn't expect him to follow through and actually do it.

I have sat with the president in the Oval Office as he made calls to family members after their sons were killed in action. As a mom, I imagined being on the other end of that line. It is heart-wrenching, each call more difficult than the last, and you can see the physical and emotional toll it takes on the president. He's said it's the hardest part of the job. After one of these calls, the president hung up, looked at me, and said, "My, Sarah, it's so awful. These beautiful kids never come back. Their parents are so crushed. I never want another brave American to be killed in somebody else's civil war."

These were some of the rare instances I saw the president fully let his guard down, show his heart, and be completely vulnerable. President Trump isn't perfect, he isn't always easy, but he loves the American people and is willing to fight for them even if that means fighting alone.

Unfortunately, the right answer to ending the long wars in Afghanistan, Iraq, and the broader Middle East wasn't always clear.

President Trump strongly opposed the war in Iraq. But he also understood the dangers of pulling out. After all, it was the disastrous withdrawal of American forces by President Obama and Vice President Biden that gave rise to the ISIS caliphate in the first place.

At the height of its power during the Obama administration, the ISIS caliphate controlled territory the size of Florida or New York. ISIS terrorists raped women and children, crucified Christians and other religious minorities, and slaughtered and dumped the bodies of innocent civilians in mass graves. President Obama's reference to ISIS as the "JV team" notwithstanding, ISIS directed or inspired terrorist attacks around the globe, including the senseless and vicious murder of forty-nine people inside a gay nightclub in Orlando in June 2016.

Fast-forward two years under the leadership of President Trump, and our great military was crushing ISIS, their caliphate in ruins. But as President Trump addressed US troops at Al Asad, thousands of ISIS terrorists still held territory deep inside Syria, refusing to surrender.

The president entered a tent where two large eight-foot tables were pushed together to create a meeting space. At the table were some of the top American military officials leading the fight against ISIS. President Trump took a seat at the head of the table. The first lady and Bolton joined him. Scavino, Miller, Walsh, Grisham, Luna, and I stood next to the table and listened as a decisive moment in the battle against ISIS and the future of America's role in the Middle East unfolded.

After introductions, the president got straight to the point: "What do you need to win?" None of the military leaders at the table pushed back on the president's decision to pull troops out of Syria; instead, they recommended using troops from Iraq to complete the mission.

Major General J. Daniel Caine said, "This base is closer to what's left of ISIS than our base in Syria. We can finish off the caliphate easier and faster from here."

The president, anxious to bring our brave men and women home, asked, "How long will it take?"

"A matter of weeks."

Stunned, the president asked, "Then why haven't we done it yet?"

"Mr. President, those are not our orders from our commanding officer."

"They are now!"

The president unleashed our military to finish off the ISIS caliphate, and if necessary, kill 'em all.

It was classic Trump.

The president loves talking to people in the trenches doing the actual work to find out the solution to a problem. I suspect it's from years of talking to foremen and workers at job sites around the world. Over the course of the last three years I've watched the president go straight to the source for ideas, whether it's defeating ISIS or building the wall. The president is a hands-on, all-in person, and it works.

On March 20, 2019, on the South Lawn of the White House just before leaving for Ohio, the president showed reporters a map with

all of the territory ISIS once controlled across Iraq and Syria alongside a new map, showing the ISIS caliphate in control of no territory
whatsoever. Thanks to the strong leadership of President Trump and
our courageous armed forces, millions had been liberated and the
evil ISIS caliphate had been wiped off the face of the earth.

Leaving Iraq on Air Force One en route home, I called Bryan,
and the kids to tell them I was safe and I loved them. I got a few
hours of sleep on the floor in the conference room of the plane
before we touched down back at Andrews right as the sun was coming up. In less than forty-eight hours, I had gone from opening
gifts with my family under the Christmas tree to Iraq and back. I
drove home exhausted yet exhilarated from the trip, thankful to
God for the courageous heroes of our military who keep us free.
I knew my kids would just be getting up, and with no energy to
make them breakfast I hit the McDonald's drive-through and arrived back home to Bryan and the kids with Egg McMuffins and
pancakes, concluding just another not-so-normal day in the life of
working for President Trump.

It was moments like this, in the quiet of the morning, that I
wondered how I'd made it so far, and prayed I'd always remain
grateful for the opportunity and live up to the responsibility that
came with it.

2

Arkansas

In May 1996, the Whitewater scandal threatening the Clinton presidency upended Arkansas politics. Arkansas's Democratic governor Jim Guy Tucker was convicted of fraud as part of Ken Starr's investigation into the Clintons, and announced he would resign effective July 15. My family at the time was living in Texarkana—a two-hour drive south of Little Rock, the state's capital—but the Whitewater scandal upended our lives, too.

My dad had been a pastor and had run a small Christian communications business for most of my early life until he got involved in politics. In 1992, he resigned as the pastor of Beech Street Baptist Church, a traditional Southern Baptist church in Texarkana, to run against Democratic US senator Dale Bumpers. Senator Bumpers had been in office for decades and was widely popular, while my dad was virtually unknown in political circles.

Republicans in Arkansas had only won three statewide races

since Reconstruction in the 1870s, and 1992 was definitely not the year to be a Republican on the ballot in my state. Arkansas governor Bill Clinton won the presidency, and my dad lost his Senate race. He got 40 percent of the vote, which was better than many expected a Republican could do, but nowhere near enough to win. My parents put everything, including mortgaging our home, on the line for that race. We had worked hard and campaigned all over the state. It was a devastating loss and a hard time for our family.

God closed the door on the US Senate but opened another. Bill Clinton's rise from governor to president meant Democratic lieutenant governor Jim Guy Tucker became governor, and there was a special election held to fill the vacancy for lieutenant governor. My dad threw his hat in the ring against Nate Coulter, senator Bumpers's campaign manager and an attorney for President Clinton. Despite an all-out effort run out of the Clinton White House to defeat him, my dad pulled off a huge upset and narrowly won the race, 51 to 49 percent. The Clinton White House and their Democratic allies back in Arkansas weren't too happy about the result, to put it mildly.

As a way to welcome my dad to the capitol as the new lieutenant governor, the Clinton Democratic machine zeroed out his office budget and literally nailed his door shut. For fifty-nine days my dad wasn't allowed to physically occupy his office in the capitol simply because he was a Republican. John Fund, a reporter for *The Wall Street Journal* at the time, didn't believe this could actually happen in America and flew to Little Rock to see for himself. He was astonished to report that it was in fact true.

Three years later, in the summer of 1996, Arkansas Democrats' worst nightmare was coming true: a small-town former pastor with no money or ties to the political establishment named Mike Huckabee (a "deplorable," as Hillary Clinton might put it) was now going to be the Republican governor of President Bill Clinton's home state, Arkansas.

Unfortunately, my worst nightmare—moving away from home at thirteen years old from the small town I loved to the state capital the summer before my freshman year of high school—was also coming true.

I was happy in Texarkana. I had gone to preschool and kindergarten there at the church where my dad was the pastor. We rode to school each morning together and I played in his office until it was time to go to class. I had my own "office" under the credenza of my dad's desk where I kept paper, markers, tape, and a pair of scissors so I could work each morning alongside him. I loved being around my dad, and made many masterpieces and memories working under his desk at Beech Street.

My brothers and I enjoyed being the "pastor's kids" and running wild around the church. We played hide-and-seek in the Sunday school classrooms, snuck into the fellowship hall for ice cream, and on more than one occasion may have taken a swim in the baptistry. When my dad had had enough of us, we'd ride our bikes around our neighborhood and make forts in the woods behind our house with the dozens of other kids who lived on our street. We even created a neighborhood newspaper, which we printed on the computer we got for Christmas when I was eight. I was responsible for a couple of sections of the newspaper each week and I am proud to report we never printed any fake news!

Life in Texarkana wasn't grand, but it was good. So when it came time to move to the governor's mansion in Little Rock, I said to my parents, "I'm thirteen and old enough to take care of myself. I'll just stay here and live with some friends instead." That didn't go over too well, and soon I was packing up, saying good-bye, and taking every chance I got to let my parents know how much they were "ruining my life!"

Meanwhile, Governor Jim Guy Tucker spent his final days in office appointing hundreds of Democrats to state boards and commissions and spending the last of the entire year's budget to make sure my dad knew he wasn't welcome in the state capital.

July 15 finally came. A Republican hadn't been governor of Arkansas in many years so hundreds of people traveled from all corners of the state to Little Rock. It was a big deal. My mom picked out outfits for each of us. Many years later I still have not forgiven her for the one she chose for me—a red, white, and blue one-piece suit complete with shorts and shoulder pads. Clearly she was trying to ruin my social life in Little Rock before we'd even unpacked!

We left our hotel room and went to the capitol, where we sat in my dad's lieutenant governor's office waiting to receive Tucker's resignation letter making it official. Surrounded by a few staffers and friends my dad instead got a phone call. On the other end of the line was Tucker. I was right next to my dad's side throughout the call. I distinctly remember telling the room to be quiet as my dad listened to the voice on the other end. At that moment, Governor Tucker had already announced his resignation effective July 15. Hundreds of my dad's supporters filled the halls of the capitol awaiting the swearing-in and inauguration. Our family had sold our house and packed everything we owned in Texarkana onto moving trucks to be delivered to the Governor's Mansion the next day. And I had sacrificed all of my dignity wearing that red, white, and blue monstrosity my mom forced me to put on for the big day.

We definitely weren't prepared when Governor Tucker—five minutes prior to his scheduled resignation—informed my dad that he had changed his mind and would not officially step down after all. Governor Tucker said that the Arkansas law stating that a convicted felon could not serve as governor was vague, so he'd wait out a court ruling on his appeal.

My dad said, "This is unacceptable. The law is clear. I'll be taking over as governor today." He set the receiver down and an Arkansas constitutional crisis began. Two men were claiming to be governor of the same state at the same time.

My dad acted quickly. He first called on friends of Governor Tucker's in the heavily Democratic state legislature and implored them to go to Tucker and tell him to do the right thing and resign. To our surprise, many agreed. Bobby Hogue, the Speaker of the house—a longtime Tucker ally—pressured the governor to step down. "We told him a lot of us who have been very trusting supporters of his and had stayed with him through the hard times could not stay with him any longer today. In the history of the state of Arkansas, we certainly hope we never see another day like today."

The halls of the capitol were pure chaos—hundreds, maybe thousands, of people were crammed into every opening around the building cheering, yelling, pushing to try and figure out what was happening. Our family was escorted from my dad's office through the halls of the capitol to the House Chamber for a joint session to address the members of the legislature and I got lost in the shuffle. It was so loud no one could hear me crying out for help. They went ahead and I fell back. Thankfully since my dad had been lieutenant governor for a few years I knew my way around and had made friends with some of the ladies who cleaned the building. Ann Baker was a young African American woman with two young kids who worked hard, didn't take any nonsense from anyone, and loved to talk. Ann knew everyone and everything going on in the capitol. We would sit on the benches in the lobby area of the women's restrooms, and visit, and I'd usually bring her treats from the office supply. If you ever wanted to know anything about anyone, Ann was your source.

I spotted Ann and she grabbed me and pulled me aside. "What are you doing out here in this mess by yourself?" I told her what happened and she wasn't having it. She told me to follow her and dragged me right through the middle of the crowd to state trooper Joel Mullins, who had come back to find me. Ann told me to stay with the group from now on, but if I needed her, I knew where to find her. It wasn't long before Ann had a new job at the Governor's Mansion and I got to see her more often. I made it to the chamber just in time for my dad's speech to the members. Shortly after, he addressed the entire state.

My dad, calm in the midst of the crisis, delivered an unscripted, statewide-televised address calling on Governor Tucker to resign or be impeached. "This is not a time to draw sides. This is a time for us to draw together. We will show the people of America that in this state we still believe in some old-fashioned values of doing what's right."

More Democratic leaders started to fall in line behind my dad. The Democratic attorney general—and friend of Tucker's—Winston Bryant announced he was filing a lawsuit to have Tucker removed as governor. Within an hour of my dad's live address to the state, Governor Tucker surrendered. He sent a letter to the Democratic secretary of state Sharon Priest stating, "This is to inform you that I hereby resign the office of governor effective at 6:00 p.m., July 15, 1996—Governor Jim Guy Tucker."

At approximately 7 that evening, much later than planned, my dad was officially sworn in as the 44th governor of Arkansas. After a day of uncertainty and chaos, my dad and the rule of law had prevailed. Our family would be moving into the Governor's Mansion in Little Rock after all, and our lives would never be the same.

The Arkansas Governor's Mansion is a Georgian colonial home set on nine acres in the heart of the Quapaw Quarter historic district of downtown Little Rock. The neighborhood includes more than two hundred properties on the National Register of Historic Places. Although most of these homes were built in the mid-1800s, the Governor's Mansion wasn't completed until 1950. If you ever watched the sitcom *Designing Women,* you might recognize the mansion as one of the homes in the opening shot of the show. The Governor's Mansion is beautiful and welcoming, but for any tenant, most of the home is part of the "public space," meaning there are always people there. On more than one occasion I came downstairs to a group of strangers on a tour or there for an event in my PJs!

When you walk in the front door to the mansion, you are met by a grand staircase that winds through all three floors. To the right is the formal dining room and the residential kitchen and to the left is the formal living room and East Conference Room (not to be confused with the West Conference Room, because there isn't one—never figured that one out). Upstairs on the third floor is the private quarters for Arkansas's First Family and straight out of the back door is the Janet Huckabee Grand Hall. The hall was named after my mom because she tirelessly raised all of the funds and managed the addition of the Grand Hall in 2003. The seven-thousand-plus-square-foot hall is the star of the home and not just because my mom made it happen. The hall can comfortably seat two hundred people and host receptions for closer to four hundred. There is a commercial-grade kitchen and multiple offices for the mansion staff. Each side of the hall has a huge fireplace and right in the center is my favorite part—the fifteen-foot Arkansas State Seal inlaid in the hardwood floor and carved from fifteen native woods from the state of Arkansas. Directly above the seal hangs the "Arkansas Chandelier," which has twenty-five lights and twenty-five stars to signify Arkansas becoming the twenty-fifth state. The runner on the staircase into the hall has the name of every governor to live in the mansion in ascending order (my kids thought it was pretty cool to take a picture on the step with "Papa's" name on it).

In total the house has just over thirty thousand square feet. The grounds are impeccable and the trustees do an amazing job maintaining them. P. Allen Smith, a world-renowned gardener from Arkansas, helped design the garden outside the Grand Hall. There is also a vegetable garden and an herb garden started by

Betty Bumpers that the National Herb Society maintains. The Governor's Mansion was doing farm-to-table long before it was the in thing to do!

I remember the first day I walked into the Governor's Mansion, which would be our family's home for the next decade (to this day, it's the home I lived in longer than any other). It was overwhelming. Everything seemed bigger, grander, and more intimidating than any place I'd ever visited, much less called home.

When we first walked through the huge front door all the mansion staff, state police, and trustees had gathered in the formal dining room to greet us. The dining room was covered in gold, blue, and white hand-painted silk wallpaper and a table that seated twenty-four. On one wall was a large china cabinet that contained more than sixty pieces of silver service that was used on the USS *Arkansas* in both World War I and World War II. My favorite piece and one that was used often was a large silver punch bowl made from three thousand silver dollars donated from kids around the state. It had the Arkansas State Seal on the front of it. Over the table was an odd-looking chandelier that had a large teardrop-shaped hollow bowl in the middle of it. I later learned the story of that chandelier that I would tell on hundreds of tours I led through the mansion over the course of the next ten and a half years. The legend has it that former US senator Mark Pryor (whose dad was governor when he was a boy) and his brother were filling one of the upstairs bathtubs up as high as they could to float a toy boat. The bathroom happened to be above the dining room and when it flooded, the water seeped down into the dining room causing the chandelier bowl to fill up and eventually come crashing down.

But on my first day in the Governor's Mansion I didn't know any of these stories or the people standing in the room who would later share them with me. I was nervous and felt totally out of place.

My first week at school was rough. It was awkward enough being the new kid dropped off by an unmarked state trooper car. And it didn't make it any less embarrassing that my mom rode along each morning in the front passenger seat to keep me company. But things eventually changed. Kids got to know me as Sarah instead of the governor's daughter and I started making friends. Once we settled in life got better, if never quite normal.

I found that the state troopers were a lot of fun to be around. The guardhouse is where all of my dad's security detail worked and I would often go over and see them and other staff working there. I perfected my spades game and learned to play a decent hand of blackjack hanging out in the guardhouse. The troopers even taught me how to drive (I don't blame them for my lack of reversing skills, Lord knows they tried). Most importantly, they always made my family feel safe. They were good people and we spent so much time together they all became like an extension of our family. The troopers spent holidays and vacations with us as well as accompanying us on trips to the ER and everything in between.

The mansion staff took care of everything, from the grounds and meals, to scheduling and organizing hundreds of events each year. The chefs taught me how to cook and let me sit in the kitchen and taste the amazing dishes they prepared for guests.

The trustees were inmates in the state prison system, most of whom were serving life sentences. Arkansas has a program like a few other states that allows inmates to earn work opportunities for demonstrating good behavior. The most highly coveted jobs for trustees were at the Governor's Mansion. The dozen or so trustees assigned to the mansion maintained the gardens, worked events, and helped me perfect my free throw. My mom was a high school basketball star and although I would never be a star, I loved to play. In the afternoons as they wrapped up their work and waited on the vans to take them back to "The Hill" they called home, we would play basketball together in the driveway.

I suspect most parents wouldn't like the idea of their teenage daughter playing basketball with convicted murderers. But the men selected for this program had already served decades of their life sentences and consistently demonstrated good behavior and remorse for their crimes. Sadly, the best most of them could hope for in this life was to earn the right each day to continue in the trustee program. No trustee ever wanted to risk the alternative—returning to "normal" life in a maximum-security prison. Besides, there were always plenty of troopers around.

It would have been much easier for my parents to tell me to play it safe and stay away from the trustees, but I'm glad they didn't. They wanted us to understand that God unconditionally loves and forgives us and that nobody is unworthy of our compassion or beyond the redemptive power of God's grace.

It's been said that God's grace "is getting what we don't deserve, and not getting what we do deserve." Growing up around the trustees taught me a life-changing lesson about grace. I have since made it a point to focus on people's good qualities, and not dwell too much on their flaws—we all have them.

My dad had a long list of his best moments and proudest achievements as governor, but the list of the worst parts of the job was short and never changed.

I still vividly remember the first death-row execution involving my dad when he was lieutenant governor. I was sitting in Miss Lowe's seventh-grade biology class at North Heights Junior High in Texarkana, Arkansas, on April 19, 1995, when I was unexpectedly called to the office. I was happy for the excuse to get out of class, but when I got to the door the office assistant told me to go back and grab my backpack because I was being checked out for the day. At this I became concerned something bad must have happened to someone in my family. I quickly grabbed my things and returned to the office where a state trooper I didn't recognize was waiting for me. When my brother David, two years older than me and in ninth grade at the same junior high, walked into the office my heart sank. I was sure someone in my family had been hurt. The trooper told us there was something going on and we needed to leave. I was about to walk out with him when David stepped in. Since we were kids David has always been a protective older brother. He may have teased me relentlessly, super-glued my hands together, and coaxed me to jump from our roof to see if I could fly as little kids, but if anyone else dared mess with me, he was the first to step in and stand up for me. No way was he getting into a car with someone we didn't know or letting me do so either.

David told the trooper we weren't leaving until we talked to our parents. About that time the chief of the Texarkana police department, who we knew and went to our church, came in and told us it was okay and that he would take us home.

When we pulled up to our house there were a few cars we didn't recognize. I stayed next to David, holding on to him tight as we opened the door and walked inside. We found our parents and they apologized for scaring us and told us to get our things together because we needed to leave the house immediately. They weren't sure how long but told us to pack for a week.

As we gathered our things, my dad explained that someone had bombed the Alfred P. Murrah Federal Building in Oklahoma City—168 people had been killed, including 19 children.

On that exact same day in Arkansas a man named Richard Wayne Snell, a white supremacist convicted of killing an African American state trooper as well as a gas station worker he assumed to be Jewish, was scheduled to be executed by lethal injection. Snell had attempted to bomb the same Federal Building in Oklahoma City in the 1980s, so authorities were now investigating whether the attack was linked to Snell's execution.

My dad sat us down and said, "Sometimes in my job I have to

make tough decisions, and sometimes the only decision is to do nothing, whether people like it or not."

In Arkansas, the lieutenant governor fills in for the governor and carries out his duties when the governor is out of the state, which meant there were times my dad could have stayed Richard Wayne Snell's execution, but didn't.

Governor Tucker didn't either, and Snell's final words before his execution that day were a threat against Governor Tucker. "Look over your shoulder; justice is coming. I wouldn't trade places with you or any of your cronies. Hell has victories. I am at peace."

This execution would be the first our family experienced, but sadly not the last. My dad went on to oversee seventeen executions over the course of his governorship, more than any governor in the state's history, mainly because the Supreme Court had lifted the prohibition of capital punishment and many of those backed-up cases fell on his desk. When I think back to those dark, painful days, I remember how each decision weighed so heavily on my dad. I was just a kid, and our home—the Governor's Mansion—was put on lockdown as each death-row inmate was administered a lethal injection. My dad often said that executions were the hardest decisions he made as governor because it's the one thing you do that you can never undo.

In January 1999, my mom was in Oklahoma doing an event with her close friend and Oklahoma first lady Cathy Keating. My dad was at a reception down the street from the Arkansas Governor's Mansion. I remained in the main house alone and members of my dad's state police detail were in their office next door. Earlier in the day I'd seen reports for bad weather, but didn't really think much of it. My dad told me to keep an eye on it and he would be back in a few hours. My brothers were off to college so it was just me. A couple hours later Derek Flowers, a state trooper assigned to my dad, called me and said I needed to immediately go down to the basement and wait there until I heard back from him. I didn't really want to but figured I could watch TV for a bit there and then go over to the guardhouse and see what the guys were up to.

As I sat in the basement, the lights flickered and then went out. The generator was getting ready to kick in, but it was scary sitting there all by myself in the dark, so I decided I'd walk over to the guardhouse. As I got to the top of the double-wide grand staircase that opens to the foyer and main entrance of the mansion, all the lights went off and alarms started blaring. The massive, oversized front door to the house ripped open, sending a huge round entry table with a vase and flowers crashing to the floor. A horrific bang-ing noise echoed through the house and I could feel the wind on my face. I froze in fear. I was terrified. I knew I wasn't safe in the entryway, so I started to run toward the door that led to the guardhouse. Instead I ran into Derek, who was on his way to me. He scooped me up in his arms and ran me into the guardhouse and dumped me in the bathtub, and then used his body as a shield over mine, as a giant tornado roared through our neighborhood.

The crashing started to fade away and Derek stood up and helped me to my feet. Only after checking that I was okay did he then start to lecture me about listening when told to stay put some-where. We came out of the guardhouse and the sky was eerily quiet except for a steady but light rainfall. The sky appeared as if nothing had just happened. Everything else around us told a different story. More than fifty huge trees were down all over the mansion grounds, completely uprooted, leaving deep holes in the earth where they once stood. One tree that was torn down had held the tree house that I occasionally played in, which had been built for Chelsea Clin-ton when her dad was governor. Several state police vehicles were destroyed, and one of our neighbors' roofs was in our backyard.

I knew my dad was at an event just a few blocks away. I was so worried. I kept trying to call his cell phone but all the lines were down. Derek was trying to keep me calm and get in touch with the troopers who accompanied my dad. They were having some success with police radios but it was too hard to get a clear signal. I told Derek I was going to walk down there. He told me that I was not. Derek was a big guy, probably six-foot-six, and no way was I going to be able to force myself past him. I was scared and I wanted my dad. A few minutes later his large black Suburban came barreling up to the gate.

The generator was working but for some reason the electric gate was not. My dad and the trooper with him got out and I ran to the gate. My dad climbed over the gate and I fell into his arms. He told me it was going to be a long night as there was a lot of damage across the state and the storm wasn't over.

It turned out that my cell phone was one of the few that worked and so I started helping track calls and requests for my dad. Because our own neighborhood had been hit so hard he wanted to go out now and check on people and see how he could help. He traded his suit jacket for a rain jacket and I asked if I could come with him. He said I could and off we went, house to house, helping pull tree branches off people's cars and mostly making sure folks were okay.

My dad gave everyone we met the number to his office to call if they needed anything. The neighborhood grocery store had been hit hard. We drove toward the store and you could see dozens of people gathered trying to figure out what was going on. The troopers with us connected with law enforcement running the rescue efforts. The store was completely demolished and several people were trapped inside. First responders were working hard trying to get everyone out. They worked while we waited and my dad fielded calls from his staff and reporters from my phone. The last person to be retrieved from the rubble was the sixty-seven-year-old pharmacist at the grocery store, who had serious injuries. He was rushed to the hospital and died the next day.

The tornado that nearly made a direct hit on the Governor's Mansion was an F3, and in addition to the pharmacist, killed two more Arkansans. A total of nine people were killed in the wake of that tornado.

My dad spent the next couple of hours mobilizing people on his staff to start doing damage assessments and working through how to get the thousands of people without electricity back up and running as quickly as possible. He was always compassionate and focused on taking care of people. It was in moments like this when he showed why he was a great leader. He often told me that being a leader is not about handling all the things you know are coming, like healthcare or tax policy, but about stepping up in a crisis you can never plan for.

There were unsettling days and difficult decisions, but also proud ones that inspired me and helped me understand what leadership really means.

A five-minute drive from the Governor's Mansion is Little Rock Central High School. On September 23, 1957, nine African American students—who later became known as the Little Rock Nine—attempted to enter the halls of Central High, following the Supreme Court's landmark *Brown v. Board of Education* decision of 1954 ruling against segregation in public schools.

The Little Rock Nine—Elizabeth Eckford, Melba Pattillo Beals, Minnijean Brown, Ernest Green, Gloria Ray Karlmark, Carlotta Walls LaNier, Thelma Mothershed, Terrence Roberts, and the late Jefferson Thomas—faced a mob of thousands of angry white students and parents screaming at them. Governor Orval Faubus—a Democrat segregationist—called in Arkansas's National Guard and stood in the doorway of the school alongside the Guard to prevent the students from entering. The nine brave students didn't make it through the first day.

Elizabeth Eckford, one of the Little Rock Nine, later said, "They moved closer and closer. . . . Somebody started yelling. . . . I tried to see a friendly face somewhere in the crowd—someone who maybe could help. I looked into the face of an old woman and it seemed a kind face, but when I looked at her again, she spat on me."

The nine courageous students were violently assaulted—one girl even had acid thrown into her eyes. The hatred on display was pure evil and a horrific moment in our nation's and state's history.

The fallout made national headlines, and President Eisenhower told Governor Faubus to stand down. Governor Faubus ignored the president's request, so President Eisenhower ordered more than one thousand troops from Fort Campbell, Kentucky, to intervene, and federalized the entire Arkansas National Guard (about ten thousand troops), thereby stripping Governor Faubus of his power to keep the school segregated.

America was in the midst of a defining struggle for civil rights and Little Rock's Central High was at the center of it all.

Of the nine students only Ernest Green graduated from Central—he was the first African American to graduate from a white high school in Arkansas. His perseverance that year earned him the attention of Dr. Martin Luther King Jr., who attended his graduation with his family.

Forty years later as a tenth-grade student at Central High, I stood on the front steps and cheered alongside thousands of students, parents, and dignitaries from around the world as President Bill Clinton and my dad, Governor Mike Huckabee, held open the doors of Central High for the Little Rock Nine—the same doors that had been previously closed to them because they were black.

My dad addressed the crowd and said, "What happened here forty years ago was simply wrong. It was evil and we renounce it. . . . We come to confront the pain of the past, to celebrate the perseverance of some very courageous people."

Our student body president, Fatima Makendra, an African American girl, also spoke. I was blown away to watch her stand in front of the world and speak out for civil rights. It was a reminder to all of us there that day and to the millions watching on television how far America and Arkansas had come.

The Little Rock Nine bravely advanced racial equality in America, and today Central High is one of the most racially diverse and high-achieving schools in the state. I loved my experience there. My time at Central exposed me to people with all different backgrounds, lifestyles, and viewpoints. While there were some difficult times (it *was* high school) and some very dark times in our school's past, I am very proud to have graduated from Little Rock Central High.

One of our great Central High traditions is for incoming seniors to do a citywide caravan to cement their place as the new senior class, while the outgoing seniors are taking their final exams. For our big day, we dressed in black and gold—as a rite of passage all the new senior girls wore gold lamé skirts (still not sure why that was the fabric of choice to show we were better than the underclassmen)—and decorated our cars in black and gold paint and streamers. From the War Memorial Stadium parking lot in midtown Little Rock, we launched our caravan, hundreds of cars deep, blaring music and driving past all of our rival high schools. Students from other schools launched water balloons at us as we passed by, hanging out of the windows or in our case the side of my best friend Jordan Jones Rhodes's Jeep Wrangler. The caravan is supposed to wrap with one pass by Central, which is risky because you're skipping school to participate in the parade. As you do a loop someone stops and puts a chain around the fence of the senior parking lot to lock the seniors in so they can't get out. It rarely takes long for the seniors to break the chain and leave the lot, so we decided to do something to make it a little more challenging.

A couple of my friends and I pooled money together and bought a broken-down station wagon for $250 from somebody in a neighborhood none of our parents would have approved of us being in, and had it towed to the home of our friend Nathaniel Wills, who also happened to be our class president. We then took a chainsaw to the roof and sawed it off to make it a station wagon convertible, and painted it black and gold. The hood was a solid shiny gold with big black lettering that read "LRCH Class of 2000." We then towed the car to the meet-up parking lot and all of the class of 2000 signed the hood in black Sharpie, towed it along our caravan route, and finally parked it at the gate of the senior lot exit. They were furious and we were victorious. It was a strong start for the class of 2000!

We had a great class—there were around six hundred of us, but it felt small. Our class was poised at the start of a new century and we wanted to show how far we had come. For the first day of school, classes ahead of us had held many different small senior breakfast events to kick off the school year. The class of 2000 decided we didn't like all the cliques kicking off the year apart and so we held one massive breakfast and invited every member of the class of 2000. We worked it out that each student would pay a minimal amount to cover the cost of the food and opened up the Governor's Mansion to our entire senior class wearing black and gold. We wanted our class to feel united as we faced our senior year. Only forty-two years earlier, the man who occupied the Governor's Mansion had stood in the door at Central to prevent black students from entering, and now here we were—a majority of our classmates black—gathered in the place he used to call home, singing our alma mater. It was a moment I was proud to help make happen.

The first test every incoming student takes at Central is to recite the alma mater, and I still remember it to this day. (Sadly my kids are not impressed when I sing it for them!)

Hail To The Old Gold,
Hail To The Black,
Hail Alma Mater,
Naught Does She Lack
We Love No Other,
So Let Our Motto Be,
Victory, Little Rock Central High !!!!

The Governor's Mansion would later be the location for our senior homecoming dinner as well, and one of my friends there was Sarah Tucker, former governor Jim Guy Tucker's daughter, whose room was now mine and who had become a friend and my running mate at Arkansas Girls State. Despite the bruising battles between our dads, who had once claimed to be governor at the same time, we had become friends in a sea of hundreds of students and didn't let the politics get in the way. Something we could probably use a lot more of in America.

That same room that both Sarah Tucker and I called ours was also the childhood bedroom of Chelsea Clinton. It's wild to think that I got ready for prom in the same place Chelsea got ready for her dad's announcement for the presidency at the Old State House just down the street!

Leigh Scanlon Keener and Jordan Jones Rhodes, two of my oldest and closest friends I love and have always been able to count on, I met at Central. Now our kids are friends and are growing up together. I feel pride every time I drive by the school, see a kid wearing Central High clothing, or notice a post about the historic school on social media. Central High helped me to grow as a person, accept the differences of the people around me, and celebrate the fact we lived in a country where we could all succeed no matter how or where we started. There is still much work to do to close the racial divide in America. My faith teaches me that God created every human being to have dignity and purpose and to be loved. We need to be a country that values every human life and never tolerates racism or senseless violence. That starts by teaching our kids to love one another as God loves us, and remind them about the courage and the strength shown by those who have come before us, like the Little Rock Nine.

Later in my senior year of high school I enrolled at the University of Arkansas, but at the last moment instead chose to go to my dad's alma mater—Ouachita Baptist University in Arkadelphia. At Ouachita Baptist I met Lauren Brown, who quickly became one of my best friends and college roommates. Lauren and I were both political science majors who cared more about the boys than the classes. She is a planner, type A and a perfectionist, and I'm spontaneous and rarely organized. It was a perfect balance. After Lauren and I finished our sophomore year at OBU, we moved to Little Rock for the summer to work on my dad's reelection campaign for governor. We were field staffers responsible for traveling the state, recruiting volunteers, and advancing and staffing my dad at campaign events. We spent most of the summer crisscrossing the state together, attending every parade and festival Arkansas has to offer. In Arkansas, we celebrate everything from watermelons to pink tomatoes—even bricks—at festivals. We race chuck wagons, toads, turtles, and cardboard boats, to name just a few. And we hunt most everything, including raccoon—which you can and must eat in order to not offend your hosts at the Gillette Coon Supper.

I spent most of my childhood on the Arkansas festival circuit campaigning with my dad and I loved it. It gave me a chance to see every part of the state, meet interesting people, and spend quality time with my family. Arkansas has a beautiful landscape of mountains, lakes, and rivers, and is an outdoorsman's paradise. The Mississippi Delta in the eastern part of the state is the duck hunting capital of the world, and the Ozark and Ouachita mountains in the northwest offer world-class fly-fishing, kayaking, hiking, and mountain biking.

Back then as a college student and seasoned campaign volunteer, my role had slightly progressed from envelope stuffing, and Lauren and I were organizing and executing a statewide RV tour for my dad. It was early one morning, several days into the multiweek tour, and we had just finished with the first event of the day in Mountain View, a small town nestled in the Ozark Mountains, famous for being the folk music capital of the world. Every weekend you can still find folk musicians gathered all around the town square playing live music for anybody who wants to hang out and listen. I was driving Lauren's maroon 1998 Toyota Camry because we had discovered she was a better navigator than driver.

It had been raining that morning and the curvy mountain roads were wet. Just as we came around the bend of one of the sharper turns the car started to hydroplane. I tightly gripped the wheel and nervously turned it to keep us on the road but overcorrected and sent us into a tailspin right off the side of the cliff. We flipped multiple times and crashed sideways into a tree jutting out the mountainside, crushing the roof of the car and shattering all the windows. It happened so fast. I hung sideways from my seatbelt and Lauren was pinned on the floor.

We were stuck against a tree on the side of the cliff. We asked each other a dozen times if the other was okay, if we were hurt or bleeding. We were in shock, and had no idea what to do. We searched for our cell phones but naturally there was no service in our location deep in the Ozarks.

We could not see the road, only rock and sky and valley below us. The realization was beginning to set in that no one might ever find us here. At that moment we began to hear voices. At first I believed it must be angels who had come to take us to heaven because there was simply no way we had just survived that crash. But neither of us appeared to be injured. We again heard voices—not the voices of heavenly angels—but two good ol' boys in a pickup truck. The driver of the truck had happened to look in his rearview mirror at the moment we'd gone off the edge, and had turned his truck around to search for any survivors of the crash.

The men shouted down to us and in desperation we shouted back for help. They climbed down onto our sideways car and peered in at us through the shattered window. Hanging sideways by my seatbelt off the side of the cliff I can safely say I'd never been so happy to see a stranger in all my life. They pulled Lauren out first. I waited for a few minutes but for what felt like hours until they came back to rescue me.

The men pulled me out of the wreckage and back onto the road, where I was reunited with Lauren. We were banged up, but miraculously we had survived.

The Highway Patrol arrived not long after and radioed the state troopers with my dad not far away. They made it there quickly and the moment I saw my dad I fell apart.

We found out later that another car had gone off the cliff at nearly the exact location as we did and all the passengers had been killed. The tree on the side of the mountain had saved us, but we were also told that if our car had hit that tree six inches in the other direction we would have been killed on impact.

A few years later my friend, college roommate, and fellow survivor Lauren married my brother David. Our kids are now in the same grade at the same school in Little Rock and they're best friends. None of us would be here if we hadn't survived that wreck thanks to God and two angels in a pickup truck. I often look back on that day in the Ozarks. For me it is a reaffirmation of God's grace, and a reminder to try harder every day to live a life worthy of having been saved.

3

Winning

After graduating from Ouachita Baptist University in 2004, I accepted a job in the Bush administration. Like most recent college grads new to Washington, DC, I moved there ready to change the world. I quickly found out the most I'd be changing in my early days at the Department of Education were coffee filters and other people's schedules, but I loved it anyway. I lived with my brother John Mark, who worked for Arkansas's only Republican congressman, John Boozman, and managed to scrape by on a low income in one of America's most expensive cities, thanks in part to my dad regularly buying my dinner when he was in town as chairman of the National Governors Association.

Midway through President George W. Bush's second term I called my dad. He was considering making a run for president and I told him he should let me run his political operation. The Republican nomination in 2008 was wide open, but the field included some well-known and well-funded potential candidates: Senator John McCain (AZ), former governor Mitt Romney (MA), former mayor Rudy Giuliani (NY), Senate Majority Leader Bill Frist (TN), and Senator George Allen (VA), to name a few. In 2006, my dad had been governor for a decade, but had very little name recognition or a fund-raising base outside of Arkansas. I didn't care. I knew my dad would make a better candidate and better president than anybody else and I believed I could help him win. After two years in Washington, I returned home to Arkansas.

It was tough going at first. We focused on Arkansas donors we had long-standing relationships with to give to my dad's political action committee (PAC) and fund his travel—mostly to Iowa, the first-in-the-nation caucus state. In those early days in 2006, I was the only full-time staffer for the PAC. I was twenty-four years old, but I was my dad's scheduler, driver, advance team, digital director, press secretary, political director, and of course, his daughter. I was working more hours in a day than I ever had, but having the time of my life. After several months we raised enough funds to start hiring a staff. One of our first hires was Chip Saltsman to be the campaign manager. Chip was the former chairman of the Tennessee Republican Party and Senate Majority Leader Bill Frist's political consultant, until Frist unexpectedly decided not to run for president. Chip was nothing like my dad. He was a hard-charging, foul-mouthed, dip-chewing, blue-blooded southerner, but he turned out to be exactly what we needed. Chip pushed my dad when he didn't want to be pushed, said no when others around him were afraid to, but ultimately and most importantly let my dad be himself. Chip rubbed some people the wrong way. They didn't like his direct and often abrasive approach, but he and I worked well together, and he was a strong leader for our team.

The Iowa straw poll in the summer of 2007 was the first big

test for the Republican candidates for president. My dad needed a strong finish there or our money was going to dry up. He had a few breakout moments in the early debates, but our campaign attracted a tiny fraction of the money, staff, endorsements, and media attention of other candidates. In the months leading up to the straw poll we relocated most of our small staff to Iowa. Our campaign was so strapped for cash we piled everybody into low-rent apartments off the interstate in Des Moines, where our neighbors were mostly migrant farmworkers. I lived in a two-bedroom, one-bath apartment with seven guys. Thankfully I had one of the two bedrooms to myself, while the seven guys shared the other bedroom and alternated shifts between the couch and the blow-up mattress in the living room. The blow-up mattress had a hole in it, so the guys would bring home bumper stickers every night from the office to plug the hole. It never worked. Every morning, whoever slept on the blow-up mattress woke up to find himself lying on the floor—the mattress once again deflated. But we made the most of a bad situation. We got up early and worked hard all day toward one goal: getting Iowans to the straw poll for my dad.

In the summer of 2007, we barnstormed Iowa in the personal RV of one of our friends from Texas. My dad was able to eat, sleep, do interviews, make donor calls, and prep for events in the RV, which allowed us to do a half-dozen or more events every day. We generally held events in people's homes or the Pizza Ranch. Every town in Iowa had a Pizza Ranch, and every Pizza Ranch had cheap pizza and a free private room to do events. We'd do our best to turn ten or twenty people out, but if nobody showed up, there were always folks already there willing to listen to my dad for free pizza, which guaranteed he'd never have to speak to an empty room. The Pizza Ranch is now a hot spot on the Iowa political circuit, but we were doing it before it was cool!

Straw poll day in August 2007 finally arrived. Governor Mitt Romney was the clear front-runner in Iowa, after dumping millions of dollars into paid advertising, staff, and organization. Romney was a good husband and father, a successful businessman, had turned around the Salt Lake City Winter Olympics, and was elected governor of Massachusetts, a blue state. He had a compelling story to tell and a lot of money to tell it. Senator John McCain and former mayor Rudy Giuliani conceded Iowa to Romney, focusing instead on New Hampshire and later states on the primary calendar. The real fight in the Iowa straw poll was for second place—to be the main alternative to Romney in the upcoming caucus.

The other contenders in the straw poll spent millions of dollars on big, professionally catered parties and popular bands to draw crowds to their tents in the parking lot of the Hilton Coliseum arena at Iowa State University. Our operation was more church potluck than presidential campaign, led by a ragtag army of young staffers and volunteers who believed in my dad. We found our food vendor at a street festival in Des Moines one Saturday morning—a couple of guys who made barbeque sandwiches from the back of their pickup truck. My brother David and my lifelong friend Chris Caldwell chopped Hope watermelons with machetes for dessert. David was my protective older brother and someone I loved to be around who could always make me laugh. He was a key part of my dad's success in nearly everything he's done since leaving the governorship. Chris Caldwell's dad, Rick, was my dad's roommate in college. Chris and I had worked together on many campaigns and he is one of my first calls when I need help. He has a larger-than-life personality and is someone I can always count on. Our entertainment was my dad's band—Capitol Offense—featuring former staffers from the governor's office. Our tent was loaned to us by a family friend and our tables were collected from garages of volunteers from the Des Moines area. My Aunt Pat, her husband, Jim, and my cousin Katie Beth, along with other family friends, drove up from Arkansas to run the check-in tables. The other campaigns spent hundreds of thousands of dollars renting buses to bring their supporters from all over the state to Ames for the event. We couldn't afford buses, but heard that many of the Sam Brownback for President campaign buses were empty, so we told our supporters to take a free ride on them instead.

The candidates delivered their speeches in the arena and Iowans cast their votes. The moment of truth arrived and just as everyone expected, Romney won. But out of nowhere and to the surprise of the media, my dad finished second. It was the story of the night. I will never forget the media surrounding my dad in the arena after the results were announced. It was surreal to watch reporters largely ignore Romney, the winner, and focus instead on my dad, the runner-up.

We returned to Arkansas to map out the next couple of months, focus on fund-raising, and lay out our strategy for winning the Iowa caucus. We needed someone in Iowa to manage the day-to-day operations and our team, so Chip asked me to come off the road with my dad and run Iowa. I accepted on one condition—I wasn't going to live with seven guys anymore and needed my own apartment. He agreed and off I went to Iowa full-time in September 2007 to manage my dad's caucus campaign.

After our better-than-expected straw poll finish, my dad was still the underdog in Iowa. Romney was spending an unprecedented amount of money on paid advertising and organization and we couldn't keep up. It was David versus Goliath, but the momentum was slowly shifting in our favor. A key turning point was the launch of our first TV ad in Iowa, featuring Chuck Norris.

The Chuck Norris ad, produced by my dad's longtime media

consultant Bob Wickers, opened with a narrator who said, "An important policy message from Governor Mike Huckabee," and then cut to my dad and Chuck Norris together.

"My plan to secure the border? Two words: Chuck. Norris," said my dad.

"Mike Huckabee is a lifelong hunter, who'll protect our Second Amendment rights," said Chuck.

"There's no chin behind Chuck Norris's beard, only another fist."

"Mike Huckabee wants to put the IRS out of business."

"When Chuck Norris does a push-up he isn't lifting himself up, he's pushing the earth down."

"Mike's a principled, authentic conservative."

"Chuck Norris doesn't endorse. He tells America how it's gonna be. I'm Mike Huckabee and I approve this message. So did Chuck. . . ."

The ad ended with Chuck Norris punching his fist into the camera as he says, "Chuck Norris approved."

I know I'm biased, but "Chuck Norris approved" was the best ad of the 2008 presidential campaign. The only problem was we had no real money to put behind it. Thankfully, the ad went viral, getting millions of views online, and the cable TV news networks did our job for us rebroadcasting it again and again for free. My dad's campaign—outspent at least 10:1 by the Romney campaign in Iowa—started getting attention, raising more money online and surging in the polls.

The Romney campaign took notice, and launched an onslaught of negative ads in Iowa attacking my dad as a liberal. My dad responded with a positive ad titled "Believe." He said, "Faith doesn't just influence me, it really defines me. I don't have to wake up every day wondering 'what do I need to believe?'"

My dad didn't mention Romney's name in the ad and didn't have to. Most Republicans in Iowa and across the country by that point knew that Romney—despite his impressive record in business and saving the Winter Olympics—had flip-flopped on nearly every major issue during the campaign. At one point Romney even proclaimed himself to be "a lifelong hunter," only to later admit he'd only hunted "varmints" once or twice as a kid. When asked about it my dad said, "That would be like me claiming to be a 'lifelong golfer' because I played putt-putt a couple of times." Romney was trying to be someone he wasn't, and that hardly ever works in politics—or in life, for that matter.

The tide was turning in Iowa, and in the weeks leading up to the caucus, polls showed the race to be a dead heat. The Iowa caucus was scheduled for January 3, 2008, but with the race so close, some of our team decided not to go home for Christmas. Instead we stayed in Iowa and worked through the holidays to be prepared for when my dad and the other staff returned. As the candidate's daughter no one expected me to stay, but I was the leader of the team and there was no way I was going to abandon my team in Iowa away from their families on Christmas. My parents told me to come home. I ignored them and instead helped organize a Christmas dinner at the guys' apartment (they had a working TV, I didn't). We went to a Christmas Eve service at a nearby church, drew names for gifts with a $20 limit, and all made something to bring to dinner. It was the first and only Christmas I spent away from my family, but it's one I will always cherish. We crowded into a tiny apartment without a kitchen table, exchanged one gift each, and drank cheap champagne—laughing, telling stories, and missing our families.

That evening Chip landed in Des Moines and I picked him up at the airport. It was late on Christmas night and the only place open was IHOP. We went there and over pancakes I gave him a status report and the plan for the next few days ahead of the caucus. It wasn't the Christmas I was used to but that didn't matter. Christmas isn't about the big meal, the gifts, or the family traditions, but the loving sacrifice of our Creator.

On caucus night, our staff and volunteers deployed all across Iowa. Chuck Norris attended one of the biggest caucus locations in the state to speak on my dad's behalf before votes were cast. A woman approached Chuck with tears in her eyes and said, "I'm a Mike Huckabee supporter. For months I've been asking my husband to join me at the caucus to vote for Mike Huckabee, but he stayed home tonight to watch *Walker, Texas Ranger* instead." We all had a good laugh at that poor man's expense.

My parents were in Blackhawk County in the eastern part of the state. The votes were coming in fast and it was time for my dad to be back in Des Moines, but there was a massive snowstorm, and their car got stuck. They flagged down a kid in a pickup truck to take them to the airport. In the air with no cell service, the AP called Iowa for my dad—a decisive nine-point victory and a tremendous upset that shocked the media and political establishment. As soon as my parents landed we called and delivered the good news and they came straight to our victory party where I met them at the back entrance. We embraced in a huge celebratory hug, and for a brief moment we were on top of the world.

In the weeks leading up to the caucus hundreds of volunteers poured in from all over the country. Two of the volunteers joined us from Senator Sam Brownback's office in Washington. They drove to Iowa during the Senate's winter recess to help for a few weeks. I had not met either of them, but had heard positive things, including from my brother David. He told me if we won Iowa, we would need more staff and these two would be good to add to the team. We didn't have any money to pay them so I didn't think much about it until the next day when these two guys walked into my office and asked me what I needed them to do. They were both pretty good-looking and one of them caught my attention right away. My brother was right—they would DEFINITELY be a good addition to the team!

After my dad won Iowa, we hired both and nicknamed them K1 and K2 (short for Kansas 1 and Kansas 2). K1 and I became friends right away. As the campaign's national political director, I was responsible for the travel schedule so of course that meant I assigned K1 to all the same places I'd go. One night during a freezing cold stop in Milwaukee, Wisconsin, a few staffers and reporters traveling with us walked to a hole-in-the-wall neighborhood bar close to the hotel. After dinner and a few Pabst Blue Ribbons, K1—always the perfect gentleman—walked me back to the hotel and right there in the lobby looked me in the eye and said, "This is going to happen, but you first need to break up with your boyfriend." I was taken aback, but liked his confidence, so the next day I did exactly that.

After Iowa, my dad won seven other states, but as we approached the Texas primary, Senator McCain had built a substantial lead in the delegate count. Texas, with its massive haul of delegates, became a must-win state for my dad. The polls in Texas weren't looking good, and the team was down. In Houston during a rally, I drove to a famous pie shop and ordered thirty pies for our staff and volunteers. I picked up the pies, but needed to quickly get back to the campaign bus, or I would miss my ride to the airport to fly out with my dad to the next rally. I was driving way too fast and got pulled over. The police officer approached the car, and I said, "Officer, please forgive me. This is a rental car. I have no driver's license or insurance on me, but I do have thirty pies that I need to get to Governor Mike Huckabee and Chuck Norris right away." The story was so preposterous the officer let me go without a ticket and even gave me an escort back to the rally site in exchange for a picture with my dad and Chuck.

Days later Senator McCain clinched the nomination in Texas.

We'd lost the race and I'd lost my job in a matter of hours. I went back to an empty and quiet house in Little Rock. My phone wasn't ringing, I wasn't buried in emails. I was no longer in the center of the political universe. In the blink of an eye it was all over.

K1 moved back to Kansas City, six hours from Little Rock, and I had no idea if it was going to work out. But K1 was determined. After a few months of long-distance dating, K1—also known by his real name, Bryan Sanders—realized he couldn't spend another day apart from me. He packed all his belongings including his big, wild black Lab Slugger into his black Chevy Tahoe and moved to Little Rock. Bryan fell in love with me and the South, and adopted everything from bourbon and grits to Razorback football and duck hunting. As the next summer approached, Bryan and I planned a big party to bring together our friends and family from across the country for the first time at his family's ranch in Kansas.

The Pottawattamie Ranch has been in the Sanders family for more than half a century. An hour's drive south of Kansas City, the ranch is where four generations of the Sanders family enjoyed weekends and holidays and celebrated birthdays, graduations, and weddings. It's where Bryan learned to hunt and fish and drive a truck, and he loves talking about the history of the place.

The entrance to the ranch is just outside of Lane, Kansas (population 227). As you pull into the long gravel driveway, there's a beautiful old rock farmhouse that was built by the abolitionist Judge James Hanway during "Bleeding Kansas"—a violent struggle between free state and pro-slavery forces that preceded the Civil War. Across from the farmhouse is a red-roofed barn, and beyond it, rolling hills of tall prairie grass rising up to woods and down a ravine to the Pottawattamie River. There on the banks of the Pottawattamie River early in the morning of May 25, 1856, is where militant abolitionist John Brown—given safe haven on the property by Judge Hanway—brutally murdered five pro-slavery men in retaliation for the pro-slavery forces' attack on Lawrence, Kansas, a few nights before. John Brown's "Pottawattamie Massacre" deeply divided the nation—he was a hero to many in the North, but a wanted villain in the South. Brown, a Christian who had memorized the Bible, said, "I have only a short time to live, only one death to die, and I will die fighting for this cause. There will be no peace in this land until slavery is done for." On October 18, 1859, John Brown was captured at Harpers Ferry, West Virginia, trying to ignite an armed slave revolt. Lieutenant colonel and future general Robert E. Lee led the counterassault. In his final words before his execution—attended by John Wilkes Booth—Brown wrote: "I, John Brown, am now quite certain that the crimes of this guilty land will never be purged away but with blood." His words were prophetic. Less than two years later the Civil War—America's bloodiest—began.

In the summer of 2009, I had to remind Bryan to focus less on John Brown and more on getting ready for our guests flying in for our "Party on the Pottawattamie." Bryan and I know how to throw a party and this weekend was no exception. We made "Party on the Pottawattamie" shirts and cups, opened the pool, smoked barbeque, and had enough guns and four-wheelers and music and cold beverages to keep everyone entertained. On Saturday, Bryan said a few of his friends had forgotten some fishing gear at one of the ponds, and asked me to drive with him to go clean up. When he passed by the pond and kept going into one of the fields, I knew something was going on. The first thing that crossed my mind—having not yet taken a shower and wearing a dirty T-shirt and no makeup—was *Oh dear God, please don't let this be the moment he proposes to me!*

As Bryan drove us through the field toward a big oak tree on a hill overlooking the old rock farmhouse, he told me about the importance of this ranch to his family. He stopped the truck and there under the big oak tree was a blanket and bottle of champagne. We got out of the truck and he got down on one knee and said, "Sarah,

I love you with all my heart and always will—unconditionally. Will you marry me?" I said yes, we kissed, and Bryan fired off the champagne cork into the tall prairie grass next to the tree. I explained to him that I actually wanted to keep that cork, so Bryan spent the first ten minutes of our engagement hunting through the tall grass for it. Little did I know our forty or so friends and family down at the farmhouse—who had known all along about Bryan's plan to propose that weekend—had been watching from a distance with binoculars. Their initial reaction to seeing Bryan stomp around in the grass was that I must have said no. For the next hour as we laughed, talked about our future, and drank champagne under the big oak tree, our friends and family were in a state of panic, questioning whether they would need to change their flights and go home early. We returned to the farmhouse and shared the good news, to their great relief, and had a beautiful night celebrating under the stars in the clear Kansas sky.

A few years later, a thunderstorm blew through Lane, Kansas, and lightning struck the field Bryan proposed to me in, setting it ablaze. After the fire burned out, in the midst of the devastation, our big oak tree was still standing.

Bryan and I got married on May 25, 2010—my parents' anniversary—on Saint John, US Virgin Islands, in the funky little town of Cruz Bay that Kenny Chesney sings about. My dad performed the wedding at a tiny old church, which had no air-conditioning, on what turned out to be a scorching hot day. In front of our fifty or so family and close friends, I walked down the aisle with my dad toward Bryan. He had on a full tux I'd made him wear and my first thought was, *Is he going to die of heat exhaustion at the altar?* I had never seen a man sweat like that before! I probably should have been concerned about his safety, but at the time I was mostly just annoyed that he was going to ruin all of our wedding pictures! The only break from the unbearable heat and humidity that day was a big rainstorm that forced us to abandon our plans to have a seated candlelight dinner in the gorgeous open-air sugar mill ruins at Caneel Bay (one reason I chose to do my wedding in Saint John in the first place) and instead move the dinner and party inside the resort. I wasn't happy, but everyone else was thrilled to be indoors with air-conditioning. After the party, Bryan and I said good-bye to our family and friends and escaped to our bungalow on the beach and decided to go for a swim. Once we were in the clear Caribbean water under the moonlit sky I remembered why we chose this beautiful destination for the biggest day of our lives. But this moment of romantic bliss was abruptly interrupted when Bryan said, "Um . . . Sarah . . . I may have just lost my ring." He turned and ran back to our bungalow and came back with two flashlights. As we stood there in our bathing suits on our wedding night with flashlights in hand desperately searching for Bryan's lost ring, our guests descended on the beach for the after-party. Knowing he'd never hear the end of it from his friends, Bryan said, "Sarah, don't you dare say a word about the ring," to which I replied, "And what exactly would you like me to say? That we're just out for a crab hunt on our wedding night?" Within minutes dozens of our wedding guests had joined us in the water with flashlights. The after-party was now a search party. We didn't find the ring, and the next morning Bryan had to explain to my dad—who had talked at length at our wedding ceremony the night before about the significance of the rings—that he'd already lost his! My mom spent the entire next day in snorkel gear trying to find it but she didn't have any luck either. So off we went on our honeymoon in Saint Lucia, a ring on my hand and nothing on his, where I had to explain to everyone we met that "Yes, this is my husband. We're on our honeymoon. Don't be alarmed he's not wearing a ring—he lost it on our wedding night."

After the honeymoon, Bryan and I returned to the States, but to different ones. No, I didn't divorce him! Bryan went to Alabama where he was the campaign manager, pollster, and media consultant for Robert Bentley, and led Bentley's campaign to a shocking come-from-behind upset victory to win the governorship. I went back home to Arkansas where I was campaign manager for John Boozman in his race against incumbent Democratic US senator Blanche Lincoln, the chair of the Agriculture Committee. John Boozman was a late entry to the 2010 Senate race—seven other Republican candidates had already announced and been running their campaigns for months. But Boozman was a popular and well-respected congressman from the most Republican part of the state. His family and mine had been close for years and there was no question that we'd be supporting him. Earlier in the year John had asked me to run his campaign and I told him I couldn't because I was getting married in a few months. In fact if he didn't get a majority of the vote in the eight-candidate Republican primary, he'd be forced into a runoff and I would have to be gone for nearly two weeks in the middle of it for our wedding and honeymoon. He assured me it would be fine and I agreed, joking that I would only do it if he would work hard enough to avoid a runoff.

We went to work and assembled a great team. One of my best hires was a kid from Texas referred to me by Jim Terry, a seasoned Washington political operative who volunteered on my dad's presidential campaign and became a friend. We loved Jim. He became such good friends with our crew that he relocated permanently from Washington to Little Rock and ended up being our next-door neighbor. I'll never forget the first call I had with the kid Jim recommended I hire. He had a big voice and even over the phone you could tell he had a strong presence. He was out working on his family's farm when he took the call. I could hear goats and cows in the background during our interview. He seemed like a political novice but I liked him and offered him the job right then on the phone without ever meeting him in person. I had a feeling and I was right. From the day Colton Burran showed up he fit right in. He was notoriously cheap and loved taking dares for money—he once let another one of the staffers punch him in the stomach as hard as he could after he drank an entire bottle of Pepto-Bismol. Our office was more Animal House than campaign headquarters, but the team worked as hard as they played so I was okay with it.

John came through on his end of the deal and won his primary outright—no runoff. Bryan and I got married, and I returned to Arkansas to focus on the general election. John Boozman went on to defeat Senator Blanche Lincoln 58 to 37 percent, the largest margin of victory against any US Senate incumbent in decades. A lot of the campaign staff moved to Washington, but Colton stayed in Arkansas. He was far from home and those of us who stayed in Arkansas adopted him into our families like he was a younger brother. One night sitting at home I got the call no one ever wants to receive. Colton had been out four-wheeling in the Ouachita mountains, taken a turn too fast, and hit a tree. Colton was killed instantly. He had been at our house the night before, and was the last to leave. Now he was gone. Colton's parents asked me to speak at his funeral. It was something I had never done before and I was anxious about it. When we arrived in the small town of Brownfield, Texas, at the Baptist church where Colton and his family were members, there wasn't an open seat to be found. The entire town showed up, heartbroken. I was nervous that my comments wouldn't do justice to Colton's life. But as I sat there thinking about it, I realized I was looking at it all wrong. It wasn't up to me to give Colton's life purpose—God had already done that. And by the number of people present that day I knew Colton had fulfilled it. My job was simply to remember the Colton we loved and remind everyone there grieving to live life like he had.

Colton lived his life fun and fast, but he also lived it with purpose. He was an example for all of us about what it means to live out your faith. He may have seemed like a younger brother to us, but it was Colton teaching us something far more important. It was his relationship with our Creator that helped the rest of us find some peace when he died. We knew his life wasn't over, but just beginning in a much better place.

In 2011, Bryan and I went with his parents to Turkey and Greece. I hadn't felt great ahead of the trip, so before we left I took a pregnancy test. It was negative, so I didn't think much more about it. We arrived in Istanbul and spent a few days getting lost in the winding streets of the ancient city, playing backgammon, and drinking tea before we boarded a ship to the Greek isles. Bryan and I love adventure and to get off the beaten path, so at each stop Bryan rented four-wheelers for us to explore little towns and remote beaches. It was beautiful and fun and romantic, but I still wasn't feeling any better. I figured some of it was jet lag, some of it was probably motion sickness from the ship. One day after Bryan forced me to climb to the top of a mountain, I hit a wall. I was so tired and so sick I couldn't even get off the ship at the next stop. We arrived in Athens, concluding the trip, and boarded our flight home to Little Rock. I was sure after a day or so I'd be back to full speed, but when I wasn't I decided to take another pregnancy test just to be certain—and sure enough this one had two faint little lines on it. I was pregnant.

I couldn't wait to tell Bryan but wanted to do it in a fun way, so I made a little bright yellow sign that said, "Big Brother . . . Coming Soon" and tied it around our Cavalier King Charles Winston's collar and sent him into Bryan's home office. I waited several minutes and nothing happened. Bryan was focused on his work and didn't notice Winston. So I yelled for Bryan and asked him to take Winston out. He asked if I could do it. I was getting frustrated. I said, "My hands are full. Take a break and take him out!" I heard him sigh in frustration (this was not going how I wanted) and then heard his desk chair push back. I braced myself in anticipation and he came running around the corner with Winston in his arms and the biggest smile in the world on his face. "Finally!" he said.

We were thrilled. Bryan asked me a million questions, most of which I couldn't answer. At our first appointment we found out I was already nine weeks pregnant. We also heard the beating of a little heart. We had tears of joy in our eyes as we listened to Dr. Sellers confirm we had a baby on the way. We got in the car and immediately started calling our families. Soon after, we found out we were having a girl. She would be the first granddaughter on my side of the family and the first grandchild on Bryan's side. She would definitely be spoiled.

During the pregnancy I had trouble sleeping. For Christmas, Bryan bought me one of those gigantic body pillows that are supposed to help pregnant women sleep. I hated the pillow. It didn't work and I still couldn't sleep. I asked Bryan to talk to me at night in order to get my mind off all the things we needed to do, hoping it would help. He was running out of things to ramble on about (which I didn't think was possible) and I asked if he could read to me instead. Bryan had never read the book *Gone with the Wind,* and I couldn't believe I was about to have a child with someone who had never read one of the greatest American novels of all time, so it was a perfect fit. He could read the thousand-plus-page book out loud to me every night and I could get some sleep. It worked! And more importantly, we finally settled on a name for our daughter we both liked. After a week or so of reading *Gone with the Wind* we named our daughter Scarlett. Scarlett O'Hara was not always the best role model, but she was tough, independent, and nobody got in her way. We wanted our daughter to have some (though certainly not all!) of her qualities.

We were growing more in love with Scarlett every day. I was busy buying outfits and monogramming everything I could get my hands on while Bryan was putting together cribs, babyproofing the house, and learning to install the car seat, something that I have still refused to learn how to do. We went to a child birthing class, which to this day still seems so odd to me. We were having our baby in the hospital where we would be surrounded by doctors and nurses, who knew exactly what to do through the labor and delivery process. Yet for some reason the entire class didn't teach us much of anything about what to do with the baby once we got her home!

Thankfully, my sister-in-law Lauren had just given birth to my nephew Chandler so she answered a lot of my questions. After our car wreck in the Ozark Mountains, Lauren and I should not have been alive, much less bringing new life into the world. Nearly losing my life and later creating and caring for a new one was something that weighed on me. I was glad I had experienced both that fear and joy with Lauren. She and my mom coached me for months, but when the big day came I still didn't feel prepared. I was definitely ready to not be pregnant anymore, but I wasn't so sure I was ready to care for a newborn.

Scarlett was already five days late and we went in for our final checkup. Dr. Sellers asked if we wanted to schedule a time for induction the following day. It was May 7 and the plan was to check into the hospital the evening of the eighth and we could expect Scarlett to make her appearance sometime on the ninth. Mother's Day was on the thirteenth that year and since both of our moms would be in town for the birth of our first child, I figured I would get them Mother's Day gifts before we checked into the hospital. I was so proud of myself for planning ahead and getting what I considered a very thoughtful gift—engraved frames that read "We love you!—May 9, 2012" for Scarlett's newborn picture. Before going to the hospital we took our moms to dinner and gave them the engraved frames. They loved them and were so excited to meet their granddaughter.

We checked in and settled into our hospital room. I had several first outfits to choose from and laid them all out, along with my matching robe and gown for postdelivery. I'd also read that the husbands don't have it great during delivery, so I brought Bryan some of his favorite snacks. Dr. Sellers was the doctor on call so he came by to check on me and start the induction. He told me to expect some discomfort, and instructed me not to eat anything for the next twenty-four hours. The next morning the nurses told me nothing had changed. We had made no progress. I began to question whether naming our daughter after the stubborn Scarlett O'Hara was such a great idea after all. Dr. Sellers tried again to induce and put me on Pitocin. I waited, and as I waited I came to the conclusion that any woman who tells you she enjoys pregnancy and childbirth is lying to you. I was starving, sleep deprived, and totally over it, but kept on. I had agreed to an epidural, but refused any more powerful drugs that might make me forget holding Scarlett for the first time. For a day that was supposed to be one of the greatest joys of my life, I was miserable. May 9 came and went— Scarlett still had not made her appearance and with her birthdate now wrong on the picture frames, I'd have to get the grandmothers new Mother's Day gifts! I went to sleep for the first and only time in my life hoping Scarlett would wake me up in the middle of the night. Again, nothing.

The following day Dr. Sellers came to check in on me before heading to the clinic and asked me to be patient. I was doing the best I could. Around lunchtime the nurse stopped by and asked if anybody was hungry. I said, "Yes, ma'am. I have not eaten anything but ice chips for thirty-six hours!" She replied, "Oh, honey, I'm so sorry. You still can't eat, but maybe your husband would like something?" Bryan ordered a cheeseburger and fries, and I lost it. When the food arrived, I said, "If you take one bite of that burger in front of me, Scarlett will be raised by a single mother because I will kill you!" Dr. Sellers came in again and I wasn't having his typical sunny positive attitude. He asked how I was doing and I fell apart. I said, "You're out of time. Get this baby out!" Dr. Sellers calmly told me that he wanted to try one more thing and said if it didn't work, we would have no other choice but to do the C-section. I agreed to his one last step, but had I known what it was I would have said no. The next few hours were too awful to describe in words, a test in patience and perseverance I wouldn't wish on my worst enemy. Having no other choice, I did it. About an hour later, things started happening—fast. The nurse called Dr. Sellers and three hours later, at 6:03 p.m., a seven-pound-three-ounce perfect miracle entered the world. I couldn't believe our baby was finally here. The nurse placed Scarlett in my arms and I held her tightly and looked at Bryan. We knew our lives were forever changed.

The nurses gave Scarlett a bath and took all her measurements and brought her back over to me to feed her. They put her in a little white hospital shirt and a pink, blue, and white striped cap. Then we opened the floodgates—our parents and my brother David and Lauren were in the waiting room and Bryan went out to tell them the good news and invite them in. They were enamored with Scarlett, too. We didn't know it that day, but this was just the beginning of a difficult journey for our little family.

A couple days later Dr. Sellers said it was time for us to take Scarlett home. It was the Saturday before Mother's Day and there was a baby dedication at our church. Because we had expected Scarlett to show up a week or two sooner, we had signed up to participate. My nephew Chandler would also be dedicated that day and we thought it would be really special to do it all on the same day and have a little party after. We had already sent invitations so I didn't want to miss it. Also, my dad was doing a Mother's Day special on his Fox News television show *Huckabee* that aired on Saturday and Sunday evenings. He wanted to have my mom, grandmother, Lauren, Scarlett, and me on together for a segment honoring mothers. After five long days and sleepless nights at the hospital, I showered, got ready, and went straight to the church, where we used the pastor's office to tape the segment. It was only fitting that Scarlett made her first appearance on Fox News before she even made it home from the hospital!

Our first night at home with Scarlett was a bit overwhelming. All of the nurses who had helped us and guided us through the first hours of her life were gone and we were now left to care for her on our own. Thankfully my mom stayed with us the first week and my mother-in-law, Julia, was scheduled for the following week. We put Scarlett in her crib and she fell asleep pretty fast. We thought we were doing well until about 1:00 a.m., when Scarlett woke up with a vengeance. Bryan changed her and I fed her, but she just kept screaming. I couldn't get her to stop. My mom came in and sat with me for hours that night, telling me nothing was wrong with Scarlett, she was just adjusting.

This would be the first of many times I needed her to reassure me I was doing okay as a mom and not to worry. My mom can be a great cheerleader. As a kid when I played sports she came to every single game to cheer me on—loudly. It was embarrassing at the time, but looking back as an adult it's one of my favorite memories of her. Janet Huckabee is a strong southern woman. She almost died of spinal cancer when she was twenty, just after she and my dad had gotten married. The doctors told her she might not live, and if she did live, she'd never walk again, and if she did walk again, she'd definitely never have kids. Not only did my mom live, and walk again, but she went on to run a marathon; serve on the international board of Habitat for Humanity, building houses all over the world; and have three kids and six grandkids.

Like many moms I struggled in the weeks following Scarlett's birth. I loved Scarlett deeply and cherished our time together but

I didn't immediately connect with her. I was having difficulty being "happy" as a new mom. I spent much of the day, especially the evenings, crying over the smallest things. I knew I was supposed to be joyful about being a mom, but I felt so isolated. I was always alone somewhere nursing, up at night while the rest of the world slept, and then sleeping during the day when others were out and about. Bryan was great and did all he could to help. He got up every night and changed Scarlett and gave her to me to feed. He watched her during the day so I could sleep, but I felt disconnected and upset that Bryan bonded with Scarlett from the second he held her and I didn't.

One of Bryan's friends, a beautiful girl he'd grown up with in Kansas City, hanged herself in her bedroom while her newborn baby girl slept in the nursery down the hall. Bryan and I attended her funeral in Kansas City together not long after we first started dating. In 2019, the Cleveland Clinic estimated that "as many as 50 to 75 percent of new mothers experience the 'baby blues' after delivery. Up to 15 percent of these women will develop a more severe and longer-lasting depression, called postpartum depression, after delivery." My friends with kids had warned me about postpartum depression and told me if I ever experienced it to talk to them about it. I tried to open up, but hated the idea of admitting I was failing as a new mom and instead tried to hide my sadness. I felt even more guilty knowing how hard some of my friends were struggling to get pregnant and have children but couldn't. I knew this was supposed to be a blissful time in my life and seeing all the happy, successful moms around me made it even harder.

Women can be our own worst enemies. I've often said that social media, while a great tool, can also be one of the most negative forces in our society. We remove personal relationships from our lives and replace them with screens that only highlight the greatest hits of everyone else's lives. It's difficult enough to be a good spouse, parent, child, friend, or coworker without constantly feeling you aren't living up to the world's idea of success. Being a new mom is tough, and spending your time nursing—isolated and lonely—looking at image after image of "perfect" moms on social media can drive even the best mom crazy. Most moms aren't posting pictures of their kids having a meltdown in the grocery store. So instead we post the cutest pictures we can coax out of our kids, pressure ourselves to throw them Pinterest-worthy birthday parties, and post articles about how wonderful it is to be a mom.

The good news is it actually is wonderful to be a mom, but that doesn't mean it isn't hard. About six weeks after Scarlett was born, I was holding her in her little nursery in the middle of the night and she looked up at me and gave me what I am sure to this day was the biggest, happiest smile I've seen from her. In that moment it happened. I knew I would do anything to protect her, love her, and show her the amazing world God created for her. I felt a warmth and peace cover me and I knew things were going to get better. I later had two perfect and adorable baby boys—Huck and George—and experienced postpartum depression again with Huck, but this time I was more prepared and able to talk about it with my family and friends, which made all the difference. Being a mom is not easy, but the best things in life aren't easy, and there is nothing in my life that brings me more joy than my three wild, crazy, beautiful kids.

I kept working after having kids. After John Boozman's successful campaign for US Senate, I was a senior advisor to Tom Cotton in 2014 when he defeated incumbent Democratic US senator Mark Pryor in Arkansas. I also consulted for companies and nonprofits, including the ONE campaign, founded by U2's Bono to take action to end extreme poverty and preventable disease, particularly in Africa. In 2015, my dad decided to run for president again. This time around we knew what running for president looked like, which made the decision much harder. The expectations were higher and the stakes were, too. My parents for the first time in their lives were comfortable. My dad had the highest-rated weekend show on Fox News and a beautiful home on the beach in Florida with room for the grandkids. Life was good. Throwing himself into another campaign for president would put it all at risk. But my dad felt called to run and so again we dove in with everything we had. I signed on as the campaign manager and was actually pregnant with my third child due just a month after he announced. My dad kicked off his campaign in May 2015, and less than a month later we welcomed George Huggins Sanders into the world, making us a family of five. I took off only two weeks for maternity leave and sent a few epic 2:00 a.m. emails under the influence of pain medication in the hospital to the campaign staff with some of my "great ideas." Bryan was also devoting nearly all of his time to the campaign and so George came to work with us every day. He quickly became the star of the office, especially the finance team, where the five women in charge of raising money passed him around the room between scheduling fund-raisers and making donor calls. George was loved by the staff and we even featured him in a web ad for the campaign.

But we quickly realized that 2016 wasn't going to be anything like 2008. From the moment Donald Trump entered the race, he dominated it and established himself as the Republican front-runner. It was impossible for candidates like my dad with fewer resources to break through and get attention from the media, the lifeblood of a presidential campaign. After nine months of grueling work, my dad ended his campaign on the night of the Iowa caucus. We'd come up short—way short. I felt like I had failed my dad and the team. It was devastating. After three kids and my dad's two presidential campaigns, I was exhausted and having trouble finding motivation, but Bryan encouraged me not to give up. He said I should go work for Donald Trump, who was still battling it out with Senator

Ted Cruz (TX) and Senator Marco Rubio (FL) for the nomination. A few days after my dad exited the race, Mr. Trump's campaign manager Corey Lewandowski reached out and invited my dad and me to meet with Mr. Trump at a campaign stop in Georgia.

We flew from Little Rock to Atlanta to meet with Mr. Trump. We waited at the private airport terminal for a while—they were running late. Finally Trump Air, a huge 757, landed, and we boarded the plane. It was as nice and elegant as any plane my dad or I had ever flown on. Corey Lewandowski, Hope Hicks, Dan Scavino, Keith Schiller, Michael Glassner, and George Gigicos—the original Team Trump—were on board. My dad and I sat down at a four-top table and Mr. Trump walked in to join us. We talked and shared stories about how crazy the campaign had been. Mr. Trump, always hospitable, offered us both Cokes but we declined. I remember being taken aback by his larger-than-life personality and charm. Trump made a hard sell to get my dad to come to his event that day in Georgia to endorse him ahead of the "SEC primary." My dad wanted to, but Fox News, who he'd just re-signed with, had asked him to stay neutral to maintain his impartiality as an on-air commentator. So my dad told Trump he couldn't endorse him but the next best thing he could offer him was me: "If Sarah joins your campaign, it will send a clear message," he said. Mr. Trump turned to Corey and told him to get me on the team. On the way home to Arkansas with my dad, he said I should do it: "Only Trump can win the nomination and beat Hillary." I'd spent the better part of a decade working to get a Republican elected president and this was my chance. It was going to be Trump or Hillary—help save the country or let it go to hell. It was one of the easiest decisions I've ever made. A few days later the Trump for President campaign announced me as a senior advisor.

I was hired to focus on outreach to women and Christians, but a few weeks into my new role I got a call from campaign headquarters, asking me to go on TV to represent Mr. Trump as a surrogate. My first interview for the campaign was on CNN. I had managed and consulted for a lot of campaigns, but my background wasn't really press or communications. Still, the campaign wanted a female surrogate on TV who could speak to women and Christians and I fit the bill. My first appearance must not have been a disaster, because the next day the campaign called me back and asked me to do it again tomorrow. And so I did. And my role on the Trump campaign quickly changed. From that moment forward, Mr. Trump only wanted me to go on TV.

I did hundreds of media appearances making the case for Mr. Trump during the campaign, and was one of the first Trump surrogates to go on air after the *Access Hollywood* controversy. It was a low point in the campaign, and Republican leaders were abandoning Trump en masse. When asked on MSNBC at the debate if the president is a good role model for my kids, I said that as a person of faith, I believe there can only be one perfect role model—Jesus.

Like every other human being on the planet, I had no illusion that Mr. Trump was a perfect person—far from it—but in a race against Hillary Clinton, Donald Trump was clearly the better choice. Even when the polls showed him down and the media and political establishment—including many Republican leaders—counted him out, I believed Trump would win. I believed his message was resonating in states like Michigan and Pennsylvania that hadn't gone Republican in a long time. I also believed—having grown up in the Clintons' shadow in Arkansas—that a Hillary Clinton presidency would be a disaster America might never recover from. On November 8, 2016, Donald J. Trump was elected the 45th President of the United States of America, the biggest political upset in the history of our country. Standing in New York City on election night watching President-elect Trump give his acceptance speech was one of the proudest moments of my professional life. I had spent the better part of a decade working to elect a Republican president, and now we finally had one willing to stand up and fight for the forgotten men and women of America.

During the campaign and even right up to the moment Trump won, I never expected to leave Arkansas and go work in the administration. Arkansas was home, and Bryan and I had no interest in moving our family to Washington. But after investing so much of our lives and careers trying to get a Republican elected president, I realized it was going to be hard to say no and walk away if the right opportunity in the administration presented itself.

Two weeks before the inauguration I got a call from incoming White House Press Secretary Sean Spicer. Spicer had worked at the RNC during the campaign and he and I had worked well together. He asked me if I'd be interested in joining the White House communications office. I said no, but told Spicer he should instead hire me in the press office as his principal deputy. I either made a good case or he was desperate to fill the role because he immediately agreed and said, "F—— it. Let's do this." The next day President-elect Trump called me to officially offer me the job and I said yes. I accepted the job on Monday evening and within seventy-two hours we had signed a two-year lease to rent a house in Arlington, Virginia, we had never seen before, and were under contract to sell our house in Little Rock. Our amazing friends Megan Turner, Ashley Caldwell, Cathy Lanier, and Katy Faulk helped us pack everything we owned onto two moving trucks, and Megan, one of my most loyal and trusted friends since college, threw a going-away party for us at her home in our neighborhood. It was an emotional night, and it was really hard to say good-bye to family, friends, and the state and hometown I loved, even if only for a temporary move to Washington. But with the inauguration fast approaching and duty calling, it was time to hit the road.

4

Press Sec

Bryan and I drove a thousand miles across the country to Washington, DC, arriving just a few days before the president's inauguration. When we pulled up at our house in Arlington alongside the two moving trucks it was the first time we'd ever seen it—or the neighborhood, for that matter—in person. We had spent our entire marriage in Little Rock, and our three kids had never lived anywhere else. It would be nearly a year before we'd return home to visit family and friends in Arkansas.

The first couple of days in Washington we unpacked boxes and met the kids' teachers at their new school. We put our marriage through the first of many tests assembling a bed we purchased from IKEA—and survived that challenge only because we swore an oath never to do it again. We were hardly functional when Inauguration Day—my first official day at the White House—arrived. Bryan and I stood out in the freezing cold and proudly cheered when the president said, "Today we are not merely transferring power from one administration to another, or from one party to another—but we are transferring power from Washington, DC, and giving it back to you, the American People."

As soon as the president was sworn in and took the oath of office, we made our way through the mass of people to the Trump transition office. Here Bryan and I separated. He went back to the house to continue getting our family settled in, and we agreed to meet later that night to attend the Inaugural Ball together.

I arrived at the transition office and waited in the lobby to be cleared in. As I waited, I introduced myself to new coworkers and hugged old friends from the campaign. We were euphoric. The impossible was unfolding in front of us, and we weren't just witnessing it—we were participating in the dawn of a new era for our great country.

I was finally directed into an office where a group was waiting to be transported to the White House—part of the second wave of Trump administration officials to go in. The five of us loaded into an unmarked white van and the three-minute drive felt like an hour. There was so much anticipation and none of us had any idea what to expect. I was sitting in the van next to my friend from the campaign and new Deputy Communications Director Jessica Ditto. We had bonded over our love of the South, dads who had both been pastors, and an appreciation for good bourbon. Also in the van were three staffers from the White House staff secretary's office—Derek Lyons, May Davis, and Nick Butterfield. Jessica and I had no idea what the office of the staff secretary did, other than that they handled a lot of paper and had all graduated from Harvard!

We pulled up to the West Wing entrance. The van stopped and we stepped out. We didn't know where to go or what to do. Finally someone came out and escorted us into the Roosevelt Room, where we were paired with a member of the White House Military

Communications Office and assigned phones, emails, computers, badges, and other essential items for our new roles. After a few hours we were shown to our offices. Jessica and I went to Upper Press, where we had offices next to each other and discovered we were just a stone's throw from the Oval Office down the hall. It was surreal.

Everything was a mess, almost like a business that had been shut down and abandoned, which is basically what happens during a transition. An entire government moves out one morning and by the afternoon a new one moves in.

Sean Spicer showed up shortly after and invited us into his office to get acquainted and start figuring out some of the basic responsibilities for the press and communications teams. We ended up staying there so late I had to call Bryan and ask him to bring my dress and meet me at our friend's hotel room so I could get ready there. Bryan brought the wrong dress—more beach wedding than Inaugural Ball gown—but I had no other option so I put it on, borrowed makeup from my friend, had her help me with my hair, and off we went. Traffic was awful, and by the time we arrived at the Inaugural Ball the president was leaving and people were starting to clear out. We had all but missed it, but found some of my new colleagues in the VIP room still celebrating and joined in. We'd made it to the White House, but that night as we raised glasses, I had no idea that the fight of our lives was only just beginning.

I had to be at the office early the next morning for my first full day of work. As part of my orientation I was given a parking pass. They said my parking area was on West Executive Avenue but didn't tell me where exactly. As I pulled my GMC Yukon through the 17th Street White House entrance, I went through multiple checkpoints and Secret Service agents just kept sending me through each gate. I couldn't believe how close I was getting to the West Wing. It hadn't really hit me yet that as the principal deputy White House press secretary I was considered a high-level official at the White House.

I was surprised to find an open parking space right at the entrance to the West Wing. I didn't want to overdo it and take the spot closest to the door so naturally I took the spot second closest. But as I unpacked boxes and moved into my office, I received a call from the Secret Service notifying me to move my car because the vice president was en route to the White House and I was in his space. A great start to my first full day on the job!

My poor parking choice turned out not to be the only bad decision made that day. We woke up the morning after the inauguration expecting to see positive headlines, but as would become usual, that wasn't the case. Instead the press delivered a barrage of negative stories—the crowd was too small, the address was too controversial. The president wasn't happy. He wanted Spicer to do his first press briefing and set the record straight. We started pulling information from as many reliable sources as possible. We called the National Park Service to get their numbers for estimated attendance on the Mall and cross-referenced it with the Secret Service's numbers for how many people had gone through the metal detectors. We pulled Metro numbers, TV ratings, and made sure we had good photos that captured the massive crowd on hand to celebrate the inauguration of our 45th president. Our team did a quick prep session with Spicer, but none of us felt confident rushing into that first briefing. It was a disaster. To his credit, Spicer acknowledged he should have handled it differently, and we all learned from it and got better as a result.

The next day I went into the White House early to prep senior administration officials for the Sunday shows. The main office line in the press office kept ringing. Nobody else was there yet so finally I picked it up and not thinking forgot to answer "White House press office" and instead just said, "Hello." The voice on the other end of the line was familiar. He asked to speak to Spicer. I said he wasn't in yet, and the caller asked, "Sarah, is that you?"

"Yes, sir, Mr. President," I replied, confused as to why the most powerful man in the world was calling the main line of the press office and a bit anxious that I was the one on the other end.

He asked me if I had read a story in one of the papers that morning. Unfortunately, I hadn't yet. He moved on, and asked me about his use of Twitter, and whether or not I agreed with his combative approach. Before I had a chance to reply, he launched into a story about how he was in a secure area for a meeting the day before. He said he had "this beautiful tweet" (by "beautiful tweet," he surely meant "highly controversial tweet") about a Democratic member of Congress, but wasn't able to send it because no electronic communication could go in or out from his secure location. "Divine intervention, Sarah?" the president asked. "I don't know, Mr. President," I said, "but perhaps next time you have a 'beautiful tweet' to fire off maybe you should go spend a little more time there." He laughed and hung up.

To this day I am not sure why I felt comfortable making that joke in my first of hundreds of phone calls with the President of the United States, but I think it put him at ease with me early on.

The West Wing of the White House is grand, but much smaller than you might think. Only a small number of the president's staff actually work there. The vast majority of White House staff have offices in the Eisenhower Executive Office Building across the street from the West Wing. The offices in the West Wing are highly coveted. People are happy to cram into space no larger than a walk-in closet just to be in close proximity to the president. The White House press staff is based in the West Wing and the Upper Press office is in the heart of it all—just down the hall from the Oval Office, across from the Roosevelt Room, where the president and key administration officials often meet, and next to the Cabinet Room, where all cabinet meetings and many of the president's visits with foreign leaders take place. Also in the West Wing is the

Navy Mess—a dining room for senior staff, which has a pickup window to order take-out. I can count on one or two hands the number of opportunities I actually had enough time to sit and have a meal in the Navy Mess dining room during my two and a half years in the White House. Nearly all my meals were from the pickup window and eaten on the run. The Navy Mess is operated by the incredible men and women of the US Navy, who also prepare the meals for the president and first lady. The food is outstanding, and their burger is my favorite in Washington.

Across from the Navy Mess is the Situation Room, home to the most secure communications systems in the White House complex, where matters of war and peace often get decided. The chief of staff's office is also down the hall from the Oval Office, and has a beautiful outdoor patio. The chief of staff and the press secretary's office are the only two staff offices in the West Wing with working wood-burning fireplaces. After I became press secretary, I made sure we got use out of that fireplace for the better part of the year, and we even made s'mores in it once—which I now know is frowned upon by the GSA team that maintains the White House complex. I blamed Hope Hicks—it was all her idea. We had just gotten through a tough week and she decided the team could use a little pick-me-up, so she brought in all of the necessary ingredients and we threw a party in my office and made s'mores. Aside from being a very close confidante of the president, Hope became one of my best friends in Washington. She is absolutely beautiful inside and out, and is a good and loyal person. Hope was one of the first to join the president's campaign and not only survived but proved herself. It was no accident that Hope basically could choose whatever job she wanted inside the White House and ended up with Dan Scavino in an office right next door to the Oval Office. I loved working with Hope and so did the president. Also on the main floor of the West Wing is the national security advisor's office as well as two deputy chiefs of staff and Senior Advisor Jared Kushner's offices. Most of the remaining senior White House staff, including the White House counsel, national economic council director, Senior Advisor Ivanka Trump, Senior Advisor Stephen Miller, and Counselor to the President Kellyanne Conway had offices upstairs in the West Wing.

Less than a month into the job, President Trump fired his national security advisor Mike Flynn for not being more forthcoming with Vice President Mike Pence about his perfectly legal contacts with his Russian counterparts during the transition. Little did we know at the time, Flynn had been set up by the FBI as part of a sinister plot to take down the president and overturn the results of the 2016 election. In the aftermath, I traveled with President Trump to the "Winter White House," Mar-a-Lago, his exclusive and glamorous private club and residence in Palm Beach. On the way there I did my first "gaggle" on Air Force One. Gaggles are question-and-answer sessions that are not as formal as a briefing, but give reporters a chance to ask questions of a senior administration official and oftentimes the president himself. Gaggles have become more common in the Trump administration—the president does a gaggle nearly every time the press is in the Oval Office or he is coming from and going to Marine One on the South Lawn at the White House. Senior staff often gaggle when they finish a television interview in front of the White House. I always stopped and took questions from the media after I did a television interview on the driveway in front of the West Wing. Many in the press didn't like to admit it, but we were regularly accessible to take their questions during my time in the White House.

That first day at Mar-a-Lago, I was headed to meet some colleagues for lunch and when I walked into the lobby, President Trump, Chief of Staff Reince Priebus, and Chief Strategist Steve Bannon were there interviewing General H. R. McMaster for the national security advisor job. The president called me over to join them. As we were wrapping up, the president mentioned he wanted to bring the press in to see that he was interviewing candidates. I was concerned this would create problems and wasn't sure a photo op was a good idea, so I privately shared my concerns with Bannon that a photo op with the president and McMaster—who had not yet been offered the job—was going to lead to questions about whether he was the front-runner. "We're getting killed by the media over this fake Russia BS," I said. "If it's going to be McMaster, let's announce him now and change the news cycle." Bannon said he wasn't sure if the president had made a decision, but either way he didn't like the idea of announcing it now or doing it at Mar-a-Lago.

The president called us into the library, a small private bar area off the main patio, and asked for our input. Bannon, Priebus, and General Keith Kellogg, who was also under consideration for the position, all said they liked General McMaster. The president turned to me and asked me what he should do. I said, "If you're going with McMaster, you should announce it today. Right now it's wall-to-wall negative coverage about Russia. Let's change the narrative and make it a positive story about McMaster." Bannon wasn't pleased that I had suggested this directly to the president, but Reince and Kellogg were on board. The president said, "I like it. I'm good with McMaster." Then he turned to General Kellogg and said, "Keith, I want you involved. I want you to be part of his team. Let's do it. Sarah, go set it up."

I immediately called Spicer, who was at a park with his kids back in Alexandria, Virginia. "The president decided on McMaster for national security advisor, and he's about to announce it."

"When?" Spicer asked.

"Now."

I told him we only had about fifteen minutes. He hung up

and got the team working on a formal press release and prepping for any questions we thought might follow the announcement. I quickly called the White House advance team and asked them to get the lobby at Mar-a-Lago set up for a news conference and to gather the press pool.

The announcement went well and the plan worked. McMaster was a widely respected general and immediately went about assembling a strong team, which included Deputy National Security Advisor Dina Powell, a tough veteran of the George W. Bush administration, State Department, and Wall Street, as well as Sarah Flaherty and Michael Anton to handle NSA communications. Sarah was an active-duty navy helicopter pilot and communications specialist and Michael was a veteran of the George W. Bush administration who had anonymously written the acclaimed *After the Flight 93 Election,* making the case for President Trump during the 2016 election when so many Republican foreign policy experts had opposed him. Dina had already become one of the strongest forces in the building and also one of the more fun people to be around. Both Sarah and Michael were tremendous assets to the NSC and White House communications team, and there's no way we could have done our jobs effectively without them.

From day one after his press briefing about the crowd size at the president's inauguration, Spicer was under intense fire, both from reporters and his detractors inside the West Wing. Spicer and I had become good friends in just a short time in the White House. He worked hard, and as a member of the US Navy and now in the White House he was dedicated to serving our country. But his hot, Irish temper and the way he toyed with the media didn't earn him any friends in the White House press corps. They sensed blood in the water after that first briefing. Many of them hated Spicer and wanted to take him down.

Less than six weeks into the administration, the Associated Press ran a profile on me and the Drudge Report linked to it with the headline "A Star Is Born." It was becoming clear that some senior White House staff not aligned with the Priebus-Spicer RNC faction were pushing for me to take on Spicer's role, which was beginning to create an uncomfortable dynamic in the press office.

The day after my first on camera press briefing from the White House, Bryan and I went to White House Communications Director Mike Dubke and his wife Shannon's Kentucky Derby party at their beautiful home in Alexandria. Mike had become a friend, and his Kentucky Derby party is one of the best on the Washington party circuit. Shannon is from Kentucky and pulls out all the stops to make it a southerner's Derby paradise—mint juleps, roses galore, a line to place bets, fascinators and bright-colored pants on all partygoers, and multiple tables full of southern delicacies. The guests include a who's who of Washington insiders—senior White House staff, media, lobbyists, and political consultants mingling about. We'd been there less than an hour when Reince pulled me into the garage to talk to the president on the phone. It was difficult to hear very well over the course of the nearly hourlong call because the garage was full of caterers preparing food and walking in and out, but the president's message was loud and clear when he said, "Sarah—you're doing all the briefings next week." I had no idea what to say to the president, or how I was going to explain this to Spicer, who was also at the party. Reince and I both tried to talk him back, suggesting that maybe we both do a couple, but he wasn't having it. The president's mind was made up.

About forty-eight hours later President Trump fired FBI Director James Comey. I had no advance warning—and found out about it just a few minutes before Comey and the rest of the world did. The initial reaction to the president's decision was not good. The media was hyperventilating as if the apocalypse was upon us. Not long after the news broke the president called me, Spicer, Dubke,

Hope, and Kellyanne into the back dining room off the Oval Office. This was the place the president spent most of his time working when he wasn't in formal meetings in the Oval. In the back dining room there was a large table with six chairs around it and typically piles of newspapers, magazines, and briefing notes the president read through. Decorating the walls were a famous painting of former presidents with President Trump added in and a UFC championship belt. On the bureau were hundreds of challenge coins given to the president by members of the military, MAGA hats waiting to be signed, a bust of Benjamin Franklin, and a large glass jar of only red and pink Starbursts (the president's favorites), a gift from House Republican Leader Kevin McCarthy. There was a large-screen television on one wall and an intricate gold and wood mirror on the other behind the head of the table where the president sat. A beautiful crystal chandelier personally selected by the president lit the room.

The president was in his chair at the head of the table unhappy with the negative coverage of his firing of Comey. He wanted his team out there telling his side of the story and defending his decision. We told him we would handle it, walked out of the dining room, and called a few other colleagues together, including Alexa Henning, who handled all the booking for the White House staff. We told Alexa to call the shows that were on live now and let them know that White House officials were coming out to Pebble Beach, the driveway of the White House where all of the television cable and broadcast stations have live shots set up. Spicer, Kellyanne, and I divided up the shows that were live and in the hallway outside the Roosevelt Room we quickly discussed our talking points. It was so rushed none of us had time for hair and makeup so I borrowed makeup from another colleague and used the hallway mirror to apply powder, blush, a little mascara, and lip gloss before my live TV appearance in just a few minutes.

I was assigned to do Tucker Carlson's show on Fox News. It was a total free-for-all on the driveway that night. I was the first to finish and when I did and was making my way back to the West Wing entrance I was swarmed by press wanting additional commentary from the White House. I answered a question or two and made my way back inside the building. I knew Spicer and Kellyanne would experience even more of a frenzy around them so I told one of the staffers to meet Spicer on the sidewalk and let him know so he would be prepared when he came around the corner. The sidewalk is bordered by a large row of hedges that block it from the main driveway. Spicer paused behind the hedges to get the update from the staffer and make sure there was nothing new he needed to know before he faced the crowd of anxious reporters. When he eventually stepped around the bushes he asked the press to follow him under the awning so they wouldn't be in the dark. Spicer stood there and took several questions before coming back inside. The pause behind the bushes to get an update from a staffer led some in the press to falsely accuse Spicer of hiding in the bushes and refusing to take their questions. It was an unbelievably unfair attack. Spicer had done no such thing and had in fact taken their questions, but they wanted to make fun of him so they didn't let the truth get in the way of another fake news story.

By morning all of Washington was in total meltdown over the Comey firing and I was scheduled to do only my second on-camera White House press briefing. I was anxious, to put it mildly. I knew this was a big moment for the administration and I had to nail it. We spent the entire morning prepping, but I still couldn't calm my nerves. I told my team I needed a second to clear my head and stepped into my office for a moment of quiet time. On the day of my very first briefing I started a practice that I would carry with me even to this day. I read the daily devotional from the book *Jesus*

Calling by Sarah Young. I opened the book to May 10 and the first sentence grabbed my attention:

> Do not resist or run from the difficulties in your life. They are hand-tailored blessings designed for your benefit and growth. Embrace all the circumstances that I allow in your life. View problems as opportunities to rely more fully on me. When you start to feel stressed, let those feelings alert you to your need for me.

The words calmed me immediately and I knew I was as ready as I would ever be. At the bottom of the devotional page I wrote this prayer: "Thank you God for the challenges in my life and for the reminder to be fully reliant on you. God help me to lean on you in all my answers, to be smart, patient, and honest." As soon as I closed the book, I walked back into the office where the team was gathered and said I was ready.

I went to the podium to brief, and opened by wishing my daughter, Scarlett, a happy birthday. I'm sure Scarlett appreciated it, but it did nothing to lower the temperature in the briefing room, which was standing room only. The briefing room is actually much smaller than it looks on TV. It has only forty-nine chairs but that day the room was jam-packed with reporters standing on top of each other for the first press briefing following Comey's firing. The bright lights had been on for hours and it was hot. I could sense the visceral anger from reporters all around me. As the media fired off dozens of questions about the Comey firing I calmly explained that the president lost confidence in Comey, just like many Republicans and Democrats in Congress had lost confidence in Comey. "Not to sound like a broken record, but since you guys keep asking the same questions, I guess it's only fair that I'll keep giving the same answers. . . . You've had so many Republicans and Democrats repeatedly calling for Director Comey to be gone. . . . If Hillary Clinton had won the election—which thank God she didn't . . . she would have fired Comey immediately and the very Democrats who are criticizing the president today would be dancing in the streets celebrating. It's the purest form of hypocrisy."

I didn't realize it then, but looking back on it now, that was probably the moment I won the president's confidence to take on the role of White House press secretary. The next day a story ran in Axios reporting that the president was considering offering me the job full-time. The Axios story, and so many others like it, were fed by anonymous sources both inside and outside the White House. I didn't always know who leaked which story, but had my suspicions, and in many cases the motivations of the leakers were clear and their identities obvious. I hated the leaks, which hurt the president and his team, and I made clear to my staff that any unauthorized leaks were a fireable offense.

A week later, in May 2017, I joined the president on his first foreign trip, with stops in Saudi Arabia, Israel, and Brussels for a NATO meeting; Rome to visit the Vatican; and Sicily for the G7. The trip was important because it was the president's first trip abroad, and in Saudi Arabia he planned to announce a new strategy for the Middle East focused less on democracy promotion and nation building and more on uniting Arab countries like Saudi Arabia and Egypt in a US-led coalition to isolate and contain Iran, our most dangerous adversary in the region. The president was set to give a major speech and open the new Global Center to Combat Extremism and Terrorism. Leaders from fifty-five Muslim-majority countries attended this meeting in Riyadh. This was the first such gathering and it was a direct result of the leadership of the Trump administration. On the first day of the visit the president also signed an investment deal with the Saudis that promised to bring $110 billion into the United States as well as thousands of new jobs. The Saudi visit was organized by Jared Kushner, a senior advisor to the president who had taken on a growing domestic and foreign policy portfolio, and it was a key early foreign policy win for the administration. Jared was a shrewd negotiator and coalition builder, and without him the Saudi trip and the progress made on it would have never come together.

The president and the first lady were treated like royalty from the moment we landed in Riyadh. There were sword dances, fly-overs, and American flags everywhere. The Ritz-Carlton where we stayed had images of President Trump and King Salman projected across the entire façade of the building. The chandeliers inside the Riyadh Ritz were opulent, including the one that hung over the men-only pool.

While at the Saudi palace, Josh Raffel, who handled press and communications for Jared, Ivanka, and the National Economic Council, and I waited in a holding area while the president had a private meeting. Josh and I hadn't known each other before starting in the White House. He was a liberal, aggressive, foulmouthed Jew from New York City who had spent most of his career working in Hollywood. I was pretty much his total opposite. But despite our differences I had grown to love Josh. He is one of the funniest people I know, intensely loyal, and probably the most talented communications strategist I've ever worked with. Nobody in the White House could work a story better than Josh, and he was always one of the first colleagues I turned to for help on the toughest assignments. Josh and I had been told there would be food in the holding area, and because I had missed breakfast and had been running around for several hours that morning, I needed something to eat. Josh stepped into one of the empty rooms to make a call, and I found a basket with a bag of Lay's potato chips, a Diet Coke, and a milk chocolate Hershey bar. It wasn't a meal or an ideal breakfast, but I figured it would at least keep me going until lunch. I opened the Diet Coke and the chips, and when Josh finished his call he walked back in to rejoin me but stopped dead in his tracks. I was concerned something had gone wrong in the meeting, but that wasn't it. He said, "So . . . turns out we are not in the staff holding room—we're in the president's holding room. The chips you're eating and the Diet Coke you're drinking belong to the president, who will be on his way here to enjoy them any minute." I panicked. I quickly threw away the evidence and scrambled to find the president's military valet to see if he could replace the food and drink I had taken. He was nowhere to be found. I called Keith Schiller, the president's longtime aide, with whom I had become friends during the campaign. I explained what had happened and he said the president was headed my way now and wouldn't care about the chips but would definitely be furious about the Diet Coke. As I began to contemplate my next career move, Keith erupted in laughter and said, "Don't worry, Sarah—the valet always has extra and I'll send him down." Josh and Keith never let me forget that incident and have teased me about stealing the president's snack in Saudi Arabia ever since.

After we returned to the United States, I continued to do more press briefings. Internally, a consensus had emerged from Reince, Bannon, and Spicer to have me take on the role of press secretary, and have Spicer focus his attention full-time on being the communications director, but the president had a different idea.

At a recent press briefing, I had blasted CNN after they forced out three reporters and editors over a fake story they ran linking Anthony Scaramucci to Russia. President Trump noticed Scaramucci on TV taking a victory lap and was impressed. There had been several attempts to bring Anthony into the administration in some capacity, but none had worked out.

In July, I met Bryan and the kids in Maine for our annual summer family vacation, but had to fly back early to return to work.

Rumors were swirling that "the Mooch" was under consideration to be White House communications director. Reince and Spicer were furious. Neither one of them trusted Mooch or believed he was qualified for the job.

The morning I returned from Maine the president called a meeting in the Oval Office, which we were told was to discuss Mooch for the communications director position. Beforehand, Ivanka, whom I had grown to really like over my short time in the administration, asked me to come by her office and said there would be some changes but not to worry about it. Assembled in the Oval Office were Ivanka, Jared, NEC Director and Chief Economic Advisor Gary Cohn, Bannon, Reince, Spicer, me, and Mooch. It wasn't a discussion. President Trump told us that Mooch was the new communications director and that Mooch would report to him directly. The president was rightfully frustrated with all the leaks and the infighting in the White House and hoped Mooch could shake things up. He declared to the group "The leaks have to stop!" and then turned to me and said, "My Sarah has done a great job—thank you for not leaking." This was the moment I first realized that the president must regularly talk to reporters privately off the record and have a pretty clear understanding from those conversations who he could trust not to leak.

Spicer had previously told me that if the president ever hired Mooch he'd be gone, and sure enough, after the meeting in the Oval, Spicer resigned in protest. I was scheduled to do a press briefing in just a few hours, so I pulled Mooch aside and said, "I'm going to be asked who the press secretary is. What should I say?"

"You are."

"Shouldn't we confirm that first with the president?"

"I already did."

I told him I wanted to talk to the president, too. He said, "He's waiting for you whenever you're ready."

So Mooch and I walked back into the Oval. The president said I was ready and he wanted me in the role. He suggested Mooch and I do this first briefing together to announce the changes so that's what we did.

I texted Bryan "I'm the new White House press secretary" as he was hiking with the kids in Acadia National Park. He had bad cell service in the mountains, and before my husband and I even had a chance to talk about it, Mooch and I walked out to the podium in the White House briefing room. I introduced Mooch as the new White House communications director, and then Mooch introduced me as the new White House press secretary. I then opened it up for questions. At the end of the briefing, I was asked about all the chaos in the White House. I responded with the first thing that came to mind as a mom of three young kids: "You should come to my house in the morning. That's chaos. This is nothing." A few days later I actually got a request from a reporter to come to my house in the morning to see all the chaos. I declined, but it illustrated how much my life was about to change.

At our first all communications and press staff meeting, Mooch threatened to fire everyone if the leaks continued. He told the assembled group of forty or so White House aides: "You need to decide right now: Do you want to work in the White House? Or do you want to work outside the White House on Pennsylvania Avenue selling f—— ing postcards to tourists? I'll take this office down to just me and Sarah if I have to!" I was not amused. I couldn't believe Mooch was including me in his threat to our team. I suspected most of the White House leaks were coming from senior administration officials, not low- or midlevel press or communications aides. I had confidence in our team and wanted no part of this madness. Besides, the last thing I wanted was to be left alone with just Mooch!

As Mooch was scaring our staff to death, his phone rang several times. After a few attempts he finally answered and it was his mother. He told her he was in a meeting and asked her if she wanted to talk to Kellyanne. Although they didn't know each other, she wanted to talk to her and so he passed his phone to Kellyanne and went right back to berating the staff and telling a story about how he once caught his cousin stealing from the family ice-cream shop and "fired his a—." It was clear he was serious. The president had given him a task of finding the leakers and he was going to make an example out of someone.

There was a guy on the press team whom several people had identified as a leaker. He was a hard worker and smart. I had seen no evidence to indicate he was a leaker, but Mooch was convinced otherwise. Mooch went outside to do a TV interview, and as is customary, on his walk back he stopped to talk to the press. During his gaggle he announced this staffer was going to be fired and others would follow if they kept leaking. I was appalled and confronted Mooch as soon as he came back inside. He agreed he should have probably talked to the young man first before he announced his firing on national television. So we went to Deputy Chief of Staff Joe Hagin to take the necessary steps to have the conversation with the staffer. After all, this was the White House and there was protocol that needed to be followed. I soon learned that Mooch's paperwork hadn't been completed yet so he didn't even have the authority to fire anyone. I was told that the White House counsel's office would handle it, but I didn't like counsel's office firing someone on my team so I told them I would do it. I didn't agree with Mooch's decision, but the decision had already been made. The least I could do was give the poor guy the courtesy of a conversation on why he was being let go and thank him for his service to the president. So we sat down in the office and I let him know that that day would be his last. It was a rude awakening to the new responsibilities that had fallen to me.

A few days later the president flew to speak at the Boy Scouts

Jamboree in West Virginia, and Mooch came along for the ride. While we were in the staff vans en route to the Jamboree, Mooch announced, "I'm proud to report I crossed a major item off my bucket list today." I assumed he would say something like "riding on Air Force One," but instead Mooch said he'd just "taken a huge sh—— in the West Wing." The rest of us in the van sat there speechless as Mooch proudly told us he'd immediately called his son afterward to share the big news.

As we stood in the hot sun listening to the president address the Boy Scouts, Mooch told me, "My wife just had a baby, and I'm here instead of there." I could sense the pain in his voice and my heart hurt for him and his family. Given all his erratic behavior, I knew there had to be something going on, and for that moment he put the tough-guy act aside and I could tell how much he loved his family and regretted not being with them.

A few days later Mooch forgot to go off the record talking to *New Yorker* reporter Ryan Lizza and Lizza released the interview in full. Among other things, Mooch warned Lizza he was going to "eliminate everyone on the comms team" if Lizza didn't tell him who leaked the guest list for a dinner at the White House. "I'm asking you as an American patriot, this is a major catastrophe . . . give me a sense for who leaked it!" He then blasted Reince Priebus as "a f——ing paranoid schizophrenic" and leveled a disgustingly foul insult against Steve Bannon.

It was insane. I had the terrible misfortune of having already scheduled an interview on Fox News for that evening, which meant I was the first White House official to go on the record to answer for Mooch's tirade. The best I was able to come up with was, "We should be focused on who has a job in America, not who has a job in the White House." I'll admit it wasn't a great defense, but in my own defense, there really wasn't one!

In the middle of the night, Senator John McCain voted to kill the Obamacare repeal. It was the final nail in the coffin of the Obamacare repeal effort, and the first major legislative defeat for the Trump administration. The president and Republicans across the country were furious. Republicans in Congress had spent years fighting to repeal Obamacare and finally had a chance but couldn't get it done. Only six months into the Trump presidency, Chief of Staff Reince Priebus was fired on Air Force One, and four-star Marine General and Secretary of Homeland Security John Kelly was announced as his replacement.

On General Kelly's first day as chief of staff we were set to have a cabinet meeting. This would be my first time to attend a cabinet meeting and so I arrived a few minutes early and quickly found my seat along the back wall next to other senior White House staff. As I sat there waiting on the meeting to begin I noticed General Kelly come in and motion toward me. I pointed at myself as if to ask, "Are you talking to me?" A bit exasperated, he nodded yes. I cautiously walked toward General Kelly and he told me his first order of business as the chief of staff was to fire Mooch. Mooch had only been on the job for ten days, but it had felt like an eternity. General Kelly told me that for now I would be managing both the press and comms teams until we found a new communications director. He said, "You got it?" I said, "Yes, sir," and returned to my seat. Once again things were happening so fast I didn't have much time to process it all. After the meeting and a few hours later Mooch walked into my office and said, "I'm out. Kelly fired me. All I need to know is this . . . have you laughed harder at any point during your time in the White House than you have over the last ten days?"

"Probably not."

"Good, then my job is done here." We hugged good-bye and Mooch walked out of my office and out of the building.

5

No-Man's-Land

Every day as White House press secretary was a bit different but some things never changed. Most days I got up at 5:30 a.m. to emails, texts, and missed calls from reporters and morning show producers. I would respond to as many inquiries as I could before getting out of bed, and then rush to the shower before my three kids came running in needing clothes, breakfast, and lunches packed for the day.

Usually by 6:30 a.m. the president was tweeting and making news, which could completely alter our day.

I kissed my kids and husband good-bye and by 7:15 a.m. I was out the door in the car and on the phone returning calls from the president, senior administration officials, or reporters, and checking in with staff on any breaking news we needed to be ready for that morning. I would arrive in my office in the West Wing by 7:45 a.m., where I had a pot of coffee and the senior White House press and communications staff there to do a quick rundown of the news of the day, the message we planned to drive, and what stories or events we needed to monitor. This was a tight-knit group. The original group consisted of Hope Hicks, Josh Raffel, Michael Anton, Raj Shah, Hogan Gidley, Jessica Ditto, Lindsay Walters, Adam Kennedy, and Ory Rinat, and as roles changed and staff was added, others included Mercedes Schlapp, Bill Shine, Judd Deere, Stephen Groves, Julia Hahn, and Alexa Henning. This meeting was half-work, half-play. We said things we couldn't say to anyone else and joked about responses we wished we could say publicly. In this short window we did life together and became friends. Then we got serious and focused on the onslaught that was coming at us.

After this group met we added the rest of the press and communications staff to the meeting to go over a more general overview of what was needed for the day and walked through the daily schedule. It was only 8:30 a.m. and I was already on my second cup of coffee with three hours of work behind me. After I wrapped the press and communications meetings, I headed to the White House senior staff meeting in the Roosevelt Room where a few senior members of our team and I weighed in on the news of the day, our messaging recommendations, and made requests from senior administration officials for information or to do media appearances. We also got information we needed regarding the president's schedule and other major events, as well as detailed answers we needed for the many stories reporters were working on.

Around the time the White House senior staff meeting finished, I would often get a call from the president if I hadn't already. He would give me a list of things he wanted me to handle—some related to my job, and many not. He'd always want to know "how things are playing" in the media. It also gave me a chance to ask him for guidance on some of the incoming I was getting that morning and his latest thinking on an issue or news development. If there was something big driving the day and he hadn't called me yet, this was usually the time I called him to check in and get an update so I could do my job and accurately speak on his behalf.

After the senior White House staff meeting or call with the president, I had a little time to respond to email, return calls, and often do quick meetings with reporters who were constantly waiting outside my office throughout the day looking for updates on stories. By 10:30 a.m. the president's private meetings and calls from the White House residence had finished and policy and internal staff meetings in the West Wing with the president were starting. Over the next couple of hours, I spent my time in and out of these meetings. Around noon our team would gather in my office to begin briefing prep. During our early morning meeting we discussed key topics we thought would be important that day and divided up who would be responsible for making sure we had the most up-to-date and accurate information on any given topic. Oftentimes, this meant bringing in a subject matter expert to give me a quick briefing and allow me to ask questions. For instance, if we knew that a new jobs report was about to hit, I would connect with National Economic Council Director Larry Kudlow. Kudlow, always the happy warrior, was one of my favorite people in the White House, and brought a smile to my face every time I saw him. He was somebody everyone in the building loved to be around. The day Larry had a heart attack it felt like the spirit of our team had been crushed, and I made it my personal mission to get him to quit smoking. I'm still fighting that battle!

Although constantly at odds with the press, the president still appreciated their power, and knew that it was impossible for me to do my job effectively if I wasn't in the room. It was the only way I could understand the president's thinking, know his position on a range of issues and policy debates, and clearly articulate his message on a day-to-day basis to the country and to the world. As a result, I spent more time with and talking to the president over the course of my two years as press secretary than any senior White House official other than Ivanka Trump, Jared Kushner, and Dan Scavino. I realized quickly that while updates from senior administration officials were critical for me to do my job, the president had the final word and in the end his word was the only one that mattered to effectively speak on his behalf.

During the White House press briefings nothing was off-limits—so prepping could sometimes be an impossible task. I had a great team who did an excellent job tracking the news and identifying the most likely topics. Raj Shah and Adam Kennedy could see blind spots I couldn't, and were masterful at finding information and data points to support the administration's message. I would have been lost without their preparation and guidance, but occasionally we missed something and I either had to go with my gut instinct or just get back to the reporter following the briefing with an answer. The most effective briefing prep for me was a murder board—where my team hammered me with one difficult question after another. Briefing prep was stressful but it was also one of the best parts of our day. It helped inform our team of where we were on a wide range of issues and also created a team atmosphere because we had to look at most every briefing as us against them, which brought us closer together. A lot of reporters were coming to the briefing hoping for a big gotcha moment that would go viral, or to ask something that made the president or the administration look bad. It was our job to do the opposite—get accurate information out and deliver the president's message directly to the American people, not the 150 or so reporters, photographers, and videographers in the room.

I would read through the script that I would deliver at the top of the briefing. At the beginning of my tenure it was written by communications aide Cliff Sims, an excellent writer and fellow southerner who shared my desire to use the topper to tell a story. We collaborated to find good stories that would illustrate how the president's policies were working and lifting Americans up. Some days we used the topper to make announcements about the president's or first lady's schedule or initiatives that were important to the administration. We saw this as five minutes to talk about whatever we wanted and drive the narrative.

One of my favorite things to do was to find letters to the president from kids who dreamed of coming to the White House. A boy named Frank had a lawn-mowing business and sent a letter offering to mow the lawn at the White House. He wrote:

> Dear Mr. President:
>
> It would be my honor to mow the White House lawn some weekend for you. Even though I'm only ten, I would like to show the nation what young people like me are ready for. I admire your business background and have started my own business. I have been mowing my neighbors' lawn for some time. Please see the attached flier. Here's a list of what I have and you are free to pick whatever you want: power mower, push mower, and weed whacker. I can bring extra fuel for the power mower and charged batteries for the weed whacker. I will do this at no charge.
> Sincerely,
> Frank

I read his letter from the podium and invited Frank to come and do just that. We coordinated with the National Park Service, which maintains the White House grounds, and Frank and his dad came to the White House and Frank mowed the lawn in the Rose Garden. As he was mowing, the president walked out of the Oval Office and high-fived Frank and thanked him for his letter and hard work. The pictures and video of Frank and the president went viral and it was really fun to watch it come together. Afterward, Frank told a reporter that "so far it's pretty much the best day of my life." It was moments like this that made my job so fulfilling, reminding us all how special it was to do what we do and who we got to do it for.

After Cliff left the White House, Judd Deere, one of my deputies, a fellow Arkansan, and one of the best hires I've ever made, took over writing the introduction for the briefings. The briefings were often intense, but I loved doing them. It was a crazy adrenaline rush to walk out under the bright lights into a room full of some of the most aggressive reporters in the world and have them fire questions at me, knowing one mistake could hurt the president and his team, not to mention cost me my job and career. I did more than one hundred televised briefings as White House press secretary, and many more gaggles with reporters in the White House driveway, on Air Force One, and on foreign trips. Going head-to-head with the media to stand up for the president and make the case for his policies was one of my favorite parts of the job. After the briefing wrapped, I often went into the Oval or the president's private dining room to check in and get his feedback. He'd usually watch the briefings live or record and watch them later, but knowing that my boss—along with hundreds of reporters and millions of Americans—was tuned in to every word I said only added to the pressure to not mess it up! Often the rest of the afternoon was spent with the president in the Oval Office or his study off the Oval participating in his afternoon calls and meetings. The president is one of the most fun people to be around I've ever known. He has a huge personality and a laugh-out-loud sense of humor. I loved hearing his stories and watching him engage with members of Congress, CEOs, and foreign leaders, and spending this time with him was how I really got to know him and understand what he wanted and how best to do my job.

My evenings were often filled with more meetings and calls with reporters looking to get the last information they could before they filed stories for the day. At 6:00 p.m. our full press and communications team gathered again to talk about anything that needed to be closed out for the day and what was on deck for tomorrow. I'd then tie up any loose ends before I'd head to an event or home to try and catch my kids briefly before they went to bed. Many people think the only time the press secretary interacts with the press is during the briefing, but in reality that's the least of it. I spent much of the day and night responding to their many questions and working stories, which is one of the most underappreciated but important parts of the job. There are hundreds of reporters around the world who had my direct cell or email or could simply knock on the door of my office in the West Wing, so the notion that we weren't accessible to the press is absurd.

When I arrived home, I would read books to my kids, tuck them in, and kiss them goodnight. Afterward, I would eat a quick and often microwaved dinner while talking to my husband about my day. Then I would sit down on our couch and return more calls and emails until I went to bed around midnight, only to get up and do it all again the next day. It was exhausting, but exhilarating. I was always tired, but I ran on adrenaline and wouldn't have traded my job for any in the world. I was honored the president chose me and worked tirelessly to move the president's agenda and our country forward.

In the raging battle between the president and the media, I often felt like I was on the front lines in no-man's-land. In one of my first briefings in my new role, I noted that I was the first mom to ever hold the job of White House press secretary, and said to my daughter, Scarlett, "Don't listen to the critics. Fulfill your potential, because in America you still can." It was the summer of 2017, and the president had only been in office for about six months, but the message I'd delivered for Scarlett was one I'd need to take to heart again and again under relentless attacks in the years ahead. Nothing was off-limits to the angriest Trump haters: my character, my weight and appearance, even my fitness to be a mother. MSNBC host Nicolle Wallace said I was "vile," "not even human," and should be choked. In response to her hateful vitriol and incitement of violence against me, MSNBC did nothing.

The attacks from the media—particularly from liberal anchors and commentators on MSNBC and CNN—quickly intensified as I established myself as the spokesperson for President Trump. In response to one particular attack from a well-known media figure, my friend and colleague Josh Raffel sent an email defending me:

> Subject: A personal note
>
> We've always had great back-and-forths so I feel comfortable sending this note. . . .
>
> Sarah is one of the classiest, smartest, wittiest, most generous, toughest people you would meet. Not to mention she is fun as hell. And I say that as a liberal New York Jew who never met a religious woman from the South.
>
> And I think if you spent a day watching her behind the scenes, you would feel the same way and would not send a tweet like you sent. . . .
>
> Would just ask you to consider that next time you consider attacking her like that.
>
> Not sure how much credibility I have, but very few people I'd put it behind and Sarah is at the top of that list.

It's an honor to work for her and if you spent any time with her, you would feel the same way.

Thanks for reading.

—Josh

The media often reported about infighting in the White House—and yes, there was unfortunately too much of that—but what those reporters often missed was the close relationships many of us established battling together in the trenches. When I was home sick with strep throat and high fever Ivanka had matzo ball soup sent over from her favorite deli. When I'd had a rough day, Hope and Josh had pizza delivered so I didn't have to make dinner for my family. On my birthday, my deputies Hogan Gidley and Lindsay Walters and my assistant Janet Montesi planned a surprise party with dozens of White House staff and friends. Hogan kept cough drops in his pocket for me for before and after every briefing and interview, once Ubered across town to pick up my dog Winston while I was traveling with the president, and despite being the neat freak he is, let my kids destroy his office every time they came by the White House. In fact, it was there my youngest son, George, learned his favorite phrase, "not cool, man!" from Hogan after George smeared syrup from his pancakes all over Hogan's desk. When I wanted to leave the office early to make it to my daughter's school performance or a parent-teacher conference, Raj Shah, my principal deputy, Hogan, Lindsay, Judd, and the rest of the press team covered for me and did an outstanding job so I didn't have to worry about not being there. It's been said that "if you want a friend in Washington, get a dog," but from my experience in the Trump White House nothing could have been further from the truth. I had real friends in the White House who quickly became like family to me.

As we departed on the president's first big trip to Asia later that fall, the *Los Angeles Times* ran a column by their Pulitzer Prize–columnist David Horsey referring to me as a "chunky soccer mom," the first time a mainstream media outlet explicitly insulted my appearance. En route to Japan, nobody on Air Force One said anything about it. My husband hadn't said a word. I suspect nobody wanted to bring more attention to it and offend me. We arrived in Tokyo for the state dinner hosted by Japanese prime minister Abe. Earlier in the day, we had bilateral meetings between the United States and Japanese delegations and I was part of the US delegation. As we walked into the meeting the president pulled me aside, looked me straight in the eye, and said, "Sarah—you're tough, you're beautiful, and you're good at your job. That's why they attack you. Never let those f——ers get you down!" He then slapped me on the shoulder and said, "Okay? Now, let's get back to work."

It was exactly what I needed to hear. The president could be a very kind and generous man. It was a side of him I regularly witnessed but unfortunately very few Americans got to see. Again and again, as a woman and a working mom, President Trump not only empowered me—he defended me and reaffirmed me when the feminists and liberals were tearing me down with cruel and dehumanizing personal attacks.

For Thanksgiving, I went with Bryan and the kids to his family farm in Kansas. As I did every Thanksgiving, I made my bourbon chocolate pecan pie. I'll admit, this was a perfect-looking pie, and I was pretty proud of it so I posted a picture of it on social media. The next morning I woke up and noticed that April Ryan, a White House correspondent and CNN political analyst, had accused me on Twitter of lying about making the pie. (In previous briefings, April Ryan had asked me—among other ridiculous questions—whether President Trump believed "slavery is wrong.")

I replied to her tweet: "Don't worry April because I'm nice I'll bake one for you next week #realpie #fakenews ;-)" to which April said she still won't eat the pie and still didn't believe I made it.

Fox & Friends ran a segment on the #PieGate controversy and interviewed loyal Trump supporters Diamond and Silk, who said, "Only thing April can cook is fake news," and that they wouldn't eat April's cooking anyway because "It be nasty!" My dad weighed in, suggesting Special Counsel Bob Mueller would now have to investigate #PieGate. The controversy spilled into the following week, getting extensive coverage on MSNBC and ABC's *The View*.

Our team at the White House had been invited to the Christmas potluck lunch hosted by the White House correspondents in their offices behind the press briefing room and in the basement below the West Wing. Martha Kumar, an avid researcher who knows everything there is to know about the history of the press and presidency, is the main organizer and always brings a large ham as the entrée. There was a ton of food and champagne, and this year there would also be my now-famous bourbon chocolate pecan pie. To make sure there was no question as to whether I made it, I chronicled each step of the process on my Twitter feed. I started by laying out all the ingredients on my kitchen table (including pecans from chief of staff to the vice president Nick Ayers's Georgia pecan farm), mixed them in a bowl, assembled and baked the pies, and delivered them the following day to the potluck. #PieGate was over. April still refused to eat the pie, but other reporters seemed to enjoy it, and I got a chance to show that regardless of the false personal attacks, I wasn't going to let it change who I am or the way I treat others with whom I disagree.

At the lunch, Greg Clugston of Standard Radio wrote and read an original poem to the cadence of "The Night Before Christmas" to recap the "highlights" of the year. This was something Greg did every year. Some parts were funny, others not so much, but it was nice for everyone to stop for a moment and enjoy celebrating the holidays together.

'Twas the Night Before Christmas
2017 White House Press Basement Version

BY GREG CLUGSTON

'Twas the night before Christmas and in the White House,
Not a creature was stirring, not even a mouse.
The stockings were hung by the chimney with care,
In hopes corporate tax cuts soon would be there.
POTUS was restless, watching Fox News on cable,
Tweeting as fast as his fingers were able.
Soon he dozed off, dreaming of the past year,
Eleven months in office and plenty to cheer.
Inauguration Day boasted the "largest" ever crowd,
Sean Spicer's debut was angry and loud.
Travel bans were issued, executive orders signed,
Judge Gorsuch was confirmed—a great legal mind.
Trump reversed policies on climate and trade,
And delivered on Jerusalem where others had strayed.
Stocks soared on the Dow, plus a strong S&P,
With low unemployment and a rising GDP.
He blasted "fake news" and media hacks,
Opting instead for "alternative facts."
Trump knocked NFL players for taking a knee,
And shocked a few parents at the Boy Scouts Jamboree.
In Charlottesville we witnessed long-simmering divides,
Trump drew fire citing "fine people on both sides."
With North Korean missiles in the Sea of Japan,
Trump vowed to wipe out "Little Rocket Man."

Soon, in the West Wing, chaos took hold,
And The Donald returned to The Apprentice of old.
He fired Yates and Comey—and Michael Flynn, too,
And the kiss-blowing Mooch—we hardly knew you.
Priebus and Bannon were also let go,
With General Kelly now running the show.
"Liddle" Bob Corker played the role of tormentor,
Calling the White House an "adult day care center,"
Trump tweeted insults to keep the upper hand,
"Cryin' Chuck Schumer" and "lightweight" Gillibrand.
Obamacare revealed a Republican rift,
But the "big beautiful tax cut" is a lovely Christmas gift.
All of a sudden, there arose such a clatter,
POTUS jumped up to see what was the matter.
When, who should appear on the South Lawn below,
But Special Counsel Mueller with his lawyers in tow.
His Russia investigation quickly intensifying,
After adviser Michael Flynn admitted to lying.
POTUS dismissed the probe as simply a stunt,
It's "phony," "a hoax," "a political witch hunt."
Then Trump exclaimed, having reached a conclusion:
"Merry Christmas to all! There was no collusion!"

Later that week I also attended and spoke at the White House Correspondents' Association Christmas party, which was covered in the *Washingtonian*:

> "It's so nice to be among friends," Sarah Huckabee Sanders said Thursday night at a gathering for White House reporters, "which is why we invited so many people from the White House press staff."
>
> Sanders got her turn at the party lectern, and she

brought jokes. "With so many writers in the room and
so many people working on books, we thought the best
way to do that was to walk through the top ten book titles
of the first year of the Trump Administration," Sanders
said. "In true Trump Administration fashion, instead of
ten we actually have 13 because we want to be the biggest
and the best, and frankly we're not that great at math."

Among the faux book titles Sanders suggested: *Off
the Record* by Anthony Scaramucci, the foulmouthed and
short-lived communications director; *An Insiders Guide
to the Hatch Act* by Conway with a foreword by Walter
Shaub, the former director of Office of Government
Ethics who's now one of Twitter's most popular Trump
antagonists; *Please Call on Me* by Brian Karem, a maga-
zine stringer who loudly admonished Sanders in June
after one of her "fake news" riffs; and *Moving Markets*
by Brian Ross, the suspended ABC News correspondent
who incorrectly reported last week that Michael Flynn,
the former national security advisor, was preparing to testify against Trump in the federal investigation into Russian interference in the 2016 election. (Ross's report was
blamed by many on the right wing for causing a brief,
albeit sharp, drop in the Dow Jones Industrial Average.)

Another title I mentioned: *The Joy of Baking* coauthored by April
Ryan and Sarah Sanders.

I closed my remarks and said, "In all seriousness, I think that
often people say I have the worst job in Washington. I think I have
one of the best jobs in Washington. . . ." I really meant it. I loved my
job, and I loved the people I had the privilege to work with every
day, including the president, his family, the White House staff, and
Secret Service. I even loved working with a lot of the White House

correspondents. The White House correspondents are some of the toughest, smartest, most aggressive journalists in the world, and I enjoyed the challenge of going up against them.

There were more than five hundred credentialed members of the press with access to the White House, and only about a dozen staff in the White House Press Office. To say we were outnumbered is an understatement. The journalists covering the White House came at us 24/7 and I had to be regularly available to answer their questions and provide accurate and helpful information, while also making the case for the president and his policies. I doubt many of the White House correspondents voted for President Trump, and often their anti-Trump bias influenced their coverage, but there were journalists covering the White House who were professionals doing their best to get the story right. CNN's Jim Acosta was not one of them.

In the early days of the administration, Jim Acosta was friendly off camera, going so far as to buy a round of drinks for our table at Le Diplomate one night, but the moment the cameras were on, it was the Jim Acosta show—grandstanding to build his profile as the leader of the anti-Trump resistance in the media. It reminded me of a lesson my dad taught me growing up in Arkansas when he was governor: "Just because a reporter is friendly doesn't make him your friend."

Acosta and a few other White House correspondents seemingly determined early on that their best path to a more lucrative TV or book deal was to make a scene at the televised White House press briefings. In previous administrations the White House press briefings were televised in their entirety mainly on C-SPAN. In the Trump administration, the briefings were often carried live on all the major cable TV networks, and clips of the briefing were then rebroadcast again and again throughout the day and the evening on cable and broadcast TV news programs and social media. The media exposure from the briefings was significant and Jim Acosta wasn't going to let the opportunity to *be the story* instead of report on it go to waste. To be fair to his colleagues, most of them couldn't stand him and were embarrassed by his unprofessional behavior.

The relationship between President Trump and CNN wasn't good during the campaign, and got worse in the White House. CNN was desperate to compete with MSNBC for the most vehemently anti-Trump cable TV news viewers, and CNN was losing the ratings war to MSNBC—badly. Many reporters like to pretend that the media is all about reporting the news, when in fact the ultimate objective for any media outlet is to make money. In the TV news business, ratings are king, and CNN's ratings were usually dead last among the major cable TV news networks. CNN's coverage of the president became pretty much wall-to-wall negative, often focused on the latest conspiracy theory about the Trump campaign and Russia. CNN wasted the better part of two years spreading lies and fake news about the president and Russia. "CNN sucks!" became a rallying cry at the president's rallies, at one point so loud it drowned out Jim Acosta's live hit for the network.

One of the worst problems in the media today is the lack of separation between news and opinion. I rarely if ever agree with MSNBC's Rachel Maddow's viewpoint, but she isn't a news anchor, and she doesn't pretend to be one either. She is a commentator, which means she is paid to give her opinion and frankly she's not bad at it. Sean Hannity does the same on the right, and is very good at it, which is why he dominates and has the highest ratings on cable TV news. Maddow and Hannity each have a strong point of view, and that's fine because their shows aren't straight news—they're primarily opinion and commentary. The news should be different. You shouldn't be able to tell what a reporter's point of view is. Their reporting should give the facts, not their opinions, and let you decide. We have lost this in journalism today. One only needs to follow the anti-Trump commentary on many reporters' Twitter feeds to know this is true. Thankfully, not all reporters have fallen into this trap. There are still some excellent reporters and news anchors—and not just on Fox News!—who even after working with them for years I still don't know what their point of view is or which side they're on. But in too many cases in the media the line between news and opinion is blurred and in some cases that line doesn't exist at all. CNN used to be a respected news outlet but is now driven largely by anti-Trump opinion masquerading as news.

In the fall of 2017, CNN announced they'd boycott the first White House Christmas party of the Trump presidency, and I responded: "Christmas comes early! Finally, good news from @CNN." This didn't go over well with the folks at CNN but it didn't bother me at all! In one of my first of many contentious exchanges with Jim Acosta at a White House press briefing, Acosta said, "Journalists make honest mistakes, that doesn't make them fake news," as I patiently waited to let him finish his lecture.

"When journalists make honest mistakes, they should own up to them," I said.

Acosta interrupted me, "We do."

"Sometimes you do. And a lot of times you don't."

Acosta tried again to interrupt me, but I said, "I'm sorry, I'm not finished. There's a very big difference between making honest mistakes, and purposefully misleading the American people."

The exchange immediately went viral, with a meme circulating on social media that featured my face photoshopped over *Xena: Warrior Princess* as "Sarah Warrior Press Secretary." In it, I was standing over Jim Acosta holding a club with a graphic that read "Wielding the fact hammer in a post-truth world."

Not ashamed to make my point for me that CNN was "purposefully misleading the American people," Jim Acosta wrote a purposefully misleading and totally fake story that the president was angry with me because he didn't like one of my briefings. CNN ran it all day on their network, which was then picked up by other media outlets. What had actually happened was the president called me into his private dining room off the Oval Office after that particular briefing to tell me it was one of my best. He then called me in the next day again and said, "This CNN story is total bulls——. You're doing a great job." Ivanka even called CNN to ask for a correction, but CNN refused to do so and kept running the story anyway. It was a classic case of a media outlet taking the lies of one anonymous source "close to the White House" over the on-the-record denials of senior White House officials with actual firsthand knowledge.

It was a problem I dealt with repeatedly. Some reporters were all too willing to write misleading stories based on lies or misrepresentations from anonymous sources so long as it made the president or his team look bad. In some cases, you could easily identify the leakers because the reporters they leaked to often went out of their way to say nice things about them publicly. Some administration officials and "sources close to the White House" leaked to knife their rivals. Others did it to make it appear they were in the room or in proximity to power to feel important. And some leaked to advance a policy agenda that ran contrary to the president's agenda, believing they were smarter than the president but evidently not smart enough to recognize that nobody had elected them to anything! I detested it all. Leaking was a shameful betrayal of the president's trust and never in the best interest of the administration or the country. One of the most frustrating parts of my job as White House press secretary was cleaning up the mess. Even without the leaks, my job was all-consuming 24/7, but I sacrificed way too many nights I'd planned to be home to tuck my kids in bed or enjoy dinner with my husband to instead spend hours working to correct a story based on false or misleading leaks from administration officials or "sources close to the White House." At one point the leaking got so out of control I'd had enough and lost it at a senior White House staff meeting in the Roosevelt Room of the West Wing. I erupted at my colleagues, and told them they were hurting the president and to cut it out. I was so angry and frustrated by a team I genuinely loved and cared about. No one said anything as I finished my impassioned plea, got up, and stormed out of the room.

As we neared the end of 2017, the Senate was set to vote on the president's tax cut—the biggest in American history. The legislation would cut income tax rates for families and businesses and double the child tax credit, and also repeal the Obamacare individual mandate and make America more energy independent. Democrats were unified in opposition to the president's tax cut and determined to stop it, but across the administration this fight had become a great unifier. We had a common goal to work toward and we all knew that if we could get it done, it would be a historic, legacy-defining victory for the president and unleash America's economy.

As we closed in on the vote, our press and comms team worked closely with key administration officials and Republican leaders to aggressively make the case for the tax cut and hold Republicans in line. This would be a key test of whether the president could get his agenda through Congress after the failure to repeal Obamacare. It was a must-win. President Trump and Vice President Pence campaigned hard across the country for the tax cut, and I repeatedly made the case for it in White House press briefings and media interviews. As our momentum increased, so did the personal attacks against the president and me from liberals in the media. Criticism of me professionally is fair game and to be expected, but the personal attacks reeked of hypocrisy. Mika Brzezinski, the author of several books on empowering women and combating sexism, said on her MSNBC show *Morning Joe* that I was unfit to be a mother. On

Fox News's Laura Ingraham's show I responded: "I think it's sad that they're attacking a lot of us while claiming to champion women's causes and women's issues," and later added, "the president's historic tax cuts plus doubling of the child tax credit will do infinitely more to empower working moms than liberals' personal attacks on women they disagree with ever will."

Just a few days before Christmas the Senate passed the president's tax cuts with unanimous Republican support, and the president signed it into law. We celebrated at the White House, and American businesses celebrated by handing out Christmas bonuses to millions of their employees. We had finished the president's first year strong, and despite some setbacks, it was clear the president had a lot of major achievements to be proud of:

- ✦ a booming economy;
- ✦ millions of new jobs & trillions in new wealth;
- ✦ lower taxes on families & businesses;
- ✦ repeal of the Obamacare individual mandate;
- ✦ greater energy independence;
- ✦ confirmation of Neil Gorsuch to the Supreme Court;
- ✦ ISIS on the run and their caliphate in ruins.

The press never gave the president much credit for these achievements—90 percent of the media coverage in the first year of the Trump presidency was negative. The American people ended 2017 much better off under President Trump than his predecessor, but you certainly wouldn't know it from the media coverage.

The annual White House Correspondents' Dinner, also known as "Nerd Prom," has long been one of the most high-profile social events of the year in Washington. There were dozens of parties all over town hosted by media outlets large and small leading up to the dinner, and brunches the following day. The dinner itself included major reporters, news anchors, professional athletes, Hollywood stars, and too many politicians to count. In years past the president and first lady often attended the dinner as well. It was a must-attend event for the political and media elite. The men traded in their sports coats for tuxedos and the women were adorned with floor-length gowns, blowouts, and designer clutches. Held in the Washington Hilton Hotel, the purpose of the dinner was to raise money for the organization, present awards to journalists for their work that year, and give scholarships to journalism students.

In 2017 the president not only declined to attend the dinner, but decided none of the administration would attend either. The year 2018 was different. While the president still declined an invitation to attend and speak, he encouraged administration officials to attend on his behalf. Since the president wasn't going I was asked to sit at the head table onstage as the official representative of the White House.

Even though the president wasn't attending the dinner he graciously agreed to invite the journalism students being honored to the White House for a tour and to meet with him and the vice president. The president loved hosting people in the White House. He was proud of its history and the grandness of the building and grounds and enjoyed showing it off to people who otherwise might never get to see it. I personally worked with the board to make sure all the students were invited to attend.

In response to the announcement that I'd attend instead of the president, Michelle Wolf, the comedian invited to be the main speaker at the dinner, said, "So happy Sarah Sanders was finally invited to prom!" Later I talked to Margaret Talev, a reporter for Bloomberg who served as president of the White House Correspondents' Association, and said, "I appreciate the invite and want to come to the dinner. In fact I canceled on my annual girls' trip with my best friends from college in order to make it. But if your featured speaker Michelle Wolf is just going to trash me and my colleagues while I'm up there onstage in front of thousands of people in the room and millions of people watching live on TV I'll have to respectfully decline and go spend the weekend with my friends instead." That year my friends were traveling to Asheville, North Carolina. Given all the stress and craziness of our new life in Washington, I had really been looking forward to a relaxing stress-free weekend with them and hated that I'd be missing it. Margaret said she understood and to let her talk to Michelle. Not long after, Margaret called me and said she had spoken to Michelle's manager who reassured her it was not something I needed to worry about and that Michelle even planned to say some nice things about me. Despite Margaret's reassurances, I had no illusions Michelle was going to be nice. Still, I had made a commitment to the president and the White House Correspondents' Association to attend and represent the administration and I decided to honor that commitment.

Bryan and I met up with several of my other colleagues at the White House to get ready and go to the dinner together. I was wearing a bright-blue floor-length Chiara Boni dress and my hair was pulled up in a low bun. Bryan looked handsome in his custom-tailored tuxedo and I thought we had cleaned up pretty well! We arrived early and made our way down the red carpet, where we stopped for photos and even a couple of on-air interviews, including with CNN. We went by a few predinner receptions to say hi to friends and right before the dinner started Bryan and I separated so he could take his seat at a table at the front of the room with the Bloomberg team. Margaret had invited him as their guest.

I arrived backstage for a reception for the "VIP participants" who'd all be onstage together just before the dinner was set to start. I hugged several members of the White House Correspondents' Association and thanked them for having me. We all enjoyed a glass of wine together and took a couple of group photos as we waited on the other dinner participants to take their seats. Michelle Wolf came in the room just before we went onstage and I introduced myself to her. She was a bit cold. Her arrival to the small reception immediately changed the mood of the room. I wasn't sure if other people felt it or not, but she was the outsider in this group, not me. I worked with these reporters every day. I knew if they were married, had kids, and where they were from. I knew when one of their parents had passed away, about a road trip across the country one of their kids had recently taken, and that one of them loved pottery and another loved flying airplanes. These were not strangers to me. They were people I knew well and for the most part actually had a good working relationship with and respected. But Michelle's presence in the room took that comfort away.

We all got in line in order of where we would sit at the table onstage and waited for our cue to walk out. We entered the room to polite applause and found our seats. I was in the seat second closest to the podium at stage left and Olivier Knox, a reporter for Sirius Radio and the incoming WHCA president, was on my right. Jonathan Karl from ABC News, who was next in line to be WHCA president after Olivier, sat on my left. I knew both of them and we chatted easily as we waited for the program to begin. The servers weren't quick to refill the wineglasses and Olivier assured us that would not be the case next year when he was president!

Part of the program was to honor the journalists selected by the WHCA for their work that year and the students. As each journalist's name was called out and they made their way to the stage the room would stand and applaud them. There was a video from outgoing Speaker Paul Ryan where he made a joke about his LinkedIn page and smoking pot, a few reporters made remarks about "Me Too," but the real focus of the dinner program was the keynote speaker—Michelle Wolf.

I sat quietly onstage as Michelle Wolf only a few feet away from me repeatedly mocked my appearance and attacked my integrity. It wasn't funny—it was cruel. She went on to make awful comments about the president, the vice president, and several other White House officials. As I sat listening to her hateful comments, I debated walking out or perhaps even throwing my wineglass at her. But ultimately I stayed in my seat and held my head high.

Even though Bryan was seated with Margaret's colleagues from Bloomberg at the center table directly in front of the stage, I couldn't see his face or his reaction. Few people in the room were laughing, and most appeared to be in shock. I found out later that Margaret was nearly in tears when she approached Bryan after the event, at a total loss for words. To their credit, many of the White House correspondents were appalled. The White House Correspondents' Association should not have invited Michelle Wolf to speak at the dinner and they recognized just how damaging it was to the media's credibility to have given Michelle a major platform to maliciously attack me and other women in the White House, just moments after other reporters onstage had lectured us about women's empowerment in the "Me Too" era.

The easy thing to do would have been to walk off the stage, or go home after the dinner, but Bryan and I agreed it would be better to send a message that I was not going to be bullied or intimidated. I wouldn't let her nastiness get to me or define me. We went with several of our friends to the after-party hosted by NBC and stayed until last call. Many reporters, including CNN's Don Lemon and his partner, were gracious and apologetic that night. It had been an epic fail for the White House Correspondents' Association. I didn't want it to be, but it was, and everyone knew it.

The next morning Axios's Mike Allen summarized the evening in his newsletter read by Washington's political and media elite:

The White House Correspondents' Dinner ended with a barrage of vulgar anti-Trump jokes by comedian Michelle Wolf, who attacked the appearance of White House Press Secretary Sarah Sanders, who was sitting with her at the head table. . . .

Why it matters: If the dinner can only attract liberal presidents and liberal comedians, the conclusion is inevitable.

How things went off the rails:

The Gridiron Club, which hosts another major dinner for Washington reporters, has a rule for its roasters: "Singe, don't burn."

And one guest told me a good rule of thumb for comedy is not to attack how people look or who they are.

Wolf—an alumnus of *The Daily Show* who has a Netflix talk show coming May 27—didn't follow either of those . . .

New York Times' Maggie Haberman: "That @PressSec sat and absorbed intense criticism of her physical appearance, her job performance, and so forth, instead of walking out, on national television, was impressive."

Trump held a counterprogramming rally in Washington Township, Michigan, where he said:

You may have heard I was invited to another event tonight, the White House Correspondents' Dinner. But I'd much rather be at Washington, Michigan, than in Washington, DC, right now—that I can tell you. [*Cheers*]

The bottom line: Watch for big debate whether to end the dinner as we know it, and whether some news organizations announce they will no longer attend.

The fallout after the correspondents' dinner was intense. The clip of me staring at Wolf as she trashed me played over and over on TV for days. I felt like everywhere I turned, it was on. I did my first interview after the dinner on *Fox & Friends* and said, "That evening says a whole lot more about her than it does about me. I am very proud of the fact that I work in this administration for this president, and we're going to keep pushing forward."

I am well aware that I am not perfect—far from it. I made mistakes in the White House, but I learned from those mistakes and got better. I was committed to my job, loyal to the president, and determined to serve the country I love. Being the White House press secretary for President Trump was a tough job. In the darkest moments I questioned how much more our family could endure and at what cost. But knowing that I had the president's trust, a loyal team fighting with me, a family who loved me, and a faith that defined me and gave me purpose made the worst days manageable. Through it all, I learned to put my trust more completely in God, who even in the midst of tremendous adversity is always in control. And if God is willing to forgive me, again and again, unconditionally, for my mistakes—surely I can extend that same grace to others. I was not going to be consumed with anger or bitterness at my critics and I sure as hell was not going to be a victim. I'd have to trust in God and keep fighting.

6

Fire and Fury

In the spring of 2018, US and North Korean officials negotiated a potential summit between President Trump and North Korean dictator Kim Jong-un. A summit between the American and North Korean leaders would be a historic first—and unthinkable to many who feared the two countries were on the verge of war.

After President Trump defeated Hillary Clinton in 2016, President Obama warned him that North Korea was the most dangerous threat to the United States and encouraged him to make it a top foreign policy priority. The Trump administration settled on a policy of "maximum pressure," and in his first year in office President Trump achieved a major diplomatic victory when the UN Security Council voted 15–0 for aggressive new sanctions against North Korea.

It was August 2017—a slow, hot, and humid month in Washington. I had only been White House press secretary a few weeks.

Congress was on recess and the West Wing was under renovation. I traveled with the president to his private club and residence in Bedminster, New Jersey. Set in the serene countryside, Bedminster was a beautifully kept and elegant club, with a friendly membership who mostly kept to themselves. For those who have only experienced New Jersey from the turnpike, you certainly wouldn't recognize you were in the same state. The rooms were housed in all-white buildings, including the president's villa, surrounded by the oversized pool, where kids splashed around. Near the residences was a covered poolside café where you could order the "Melania wrap," "Ivanka salad," or the president's favorite: hot cast-iron skillet chocolate chip cookie covered with ice cream. On more than one occasion, when a group of us were seated at one of the outdoor tables at the café, a waiter surprised us with hot cast-iron skillet ice-cream cookies sent over by the president. He was always hosting and entertaining at Bedminster, and loved to be out and about mingling with members of the club and their families. Sometimes he even invited the traveling press pool to come and dine there. The entire pool and residence area was surrounded by the stunning golf course, set to host a major—the Men's PGA Championship—in 2022. In back of the residences was a parking lot with a food truck for staff and Secret Service as well as a playground and basketball court. Up the hill from the pool and residences was the main clubhouse—a beautiful Georgian-style mansion that was previously the home of John DeLorean, maker of the DeLorean sports car featured in *Back to the Future*. Jared and Ivanka had their wedding there.

Unfortunately we didn't get much of a break that August. North Korea threatened retaliation for the new UN sanctions and at Bedminster, the president said, "North Korea best not make any more threats to the United States. They will be met with fire and fury like the world has never seen."

The chances of military conflict with North Korea were escalating and many feared an outbreak of war. Upon our return to Washington, North Korea conducted another nuclear test. I attended an emergency principals small group meeting on North Korea in the White House Situation Room. The White House Situation Room was not just one room, but several. There were multiple meeting rooms and a main control center where members of the military and the National Security Council gathered and received intelligence, monitored crises around the world, and provided support to White House staff on a number of national security matters. The Situation Room staff also compiled and handled the dissemination of the Morning Book, an intelligence report given to the president, vice president, White House chief of staff, and national security advisor. They also put together morning and evening summaries, hand-delivered to a few senior officials around the building, myself included. Reading the morning and evening summaries from the Situation Room staff was a sobering way to start and end the day. The primary meeting room for the president in the Situation Room was the John F. Kennedy Conference Room. It had a large table in the middle of the room that seated fourteen in large black leather chairs, with rows of smaller leather chairs on each side of the room lined against the wall for additional staff to participate in meetings. Seats were designated by protocol order. Whoever chaired the meeting always sat at the head of the table. Any time the president was present that was his seat. A Presidential Seal hung on the wall behind the president's seat and clocks set to different times in key locations around the world adorned the other wall. There was a large screen in front of the table used for secure video conferencing and to present briefing materials to the group. There were no windows in the Situation Room, and phones and computers were strictly prohibited.

At the table in the Situation Room sat Chief of Staff John Kelly, Secretary of State Rex Tillerson, Secretary of Defense Jim Mattis,

CIA Director Mike Pompeo, National Security Advisor H. R. Mc-Master, Chairman of the Joint Chiefs Joseph Dunford, Secretary of the Treasury Steven Mnuchin, UN Ambassador Nikki Haley, and me. The president was given the threat assessment and options to respond from his national security team. We discussed how strong the administration's statement should be, who it should come from, and whether it should be issued in writing or on camera. I hadn't said much since the meeting started, but the president suddenly turned to me and asked me what he should do. I said I liked the idea of delivering a simple, clear message on camera from the White House because it would present a unified front from the administration and command more media attention than a written or on-camera statement from State or DOD. The president agreed and we spent the last part of the meeting finalizing the statement that would be delivered outside the West Wing by General Mattis, with General Dunford standing beside him. Having two distinguished military leaders issue the statement would project strength and confidence to the world and especially North Korea.

We wanted the leadership of North Korea to understand clearly that America wasn't going to be bullied. They were threatening the strongest military on the face of the earth, and if they started a war against the United States it would end in their deaths. General Mattis delivered the statement, which included a line I wrote: "Because we are not looking to the total annihilation of a country, namely North Korea. But as I said, we have many options to do so." Afterward General Mattis turned to me and said, "You're tough. The only job in the administration I'd want less than mine is yours."

Days later we headed to the United Nations. It was the president's first trip back to New York since his inauguration and his first time to speak at the UN. The president ratcheted up his maximum pressure campaign against North Korea: "Rocket man is on a suicide mission for himself and his regime. . . . If the righteous many do not confront the wicked few, then evil will triumph."

North Korea also dominated the agenda on the president's first trip to Asia, which lasted twelve days and marked the longest foreign trip ever taken by an American president. At the South Korea State Dinner hosted by President Moon Jae-in at the Blue House, we were served grilled sole from Geoje Island, the hometown of President Moon, with brown bean sauce consommé and pine mushroom rice in a stone pot, accompanied by grilled Korean beef ribs, seasoned with a special sauce made with a 360-year-old soy sauce, a delicacy in South Korea. I was enjoying my dinner when a member of the Secret Service tapped me on the shoulder and asked me to step out. I was escorted to "the Beast," the presidential limousine. Along with Air Force One, the Beast was one of the cooler perks that comes with the job of being president.

I was joined in the Beast by Dan Scavino, Deputy Chief of Staff Joe Hagin, and Head of the Presidential Protection Detail Tony Ornato. Joe Hagin had served nearly all eight years in the Bush administration as the deputy chief of staff and had come back to the White House to help President Trump. It would be nearly impossible to find someone who knew as much about White House and presidential operations as Joe. His job was to oversee every movement the president made, as well as his family and staff, and to keep all of us safe and on schedule. Joe also oversaw all White House administrative staff and personnel. It was a huge job and one he did exceptionally well. Joe was a quiet guy who didn't like the attention but was one of the smartest hires the president made early on in the administration.

I didn't expect good news when I was asked to step out of the state dinner with President Moon and into the Beast that night, but having Scavino, Hagin, and Tony there helped ease my nerves.

Hagin and Tony walked Scavino and me through our plan to travel to the DMZ early the next morning. We discussed how I would brief the press and what information I was allowed to share with them. I was given very strict instructions to not verbally give the location away or send anything electronically out of fear it would be picked up by foreign surveillance. We walked through what the stop would look like. I asked a few questions and then got out of the Beast and walked back in and took my seat at the dinner as if I had not just been briefed about our secret trip to one of the most dangerous and heavily militarized areas in the world in only a few hours.

The next morning the media pool report stated: "Your pool was summoned earlier than originally scheduled Wednesday and briefed by Press Secretary Sarah Huckabee Sanders about the president's surprise trip to the Demilitarized Zone. 'This is where we're going,' Ms. Sanders said, holding up a piece of notepaper on which the letters 'DMZ' were scrawled. She said that was the way she had been instructed to alert us to our destination. . . ."

I boarded a Chinook helicopter along with Stephen Miller, Secret Service, and members of the US Army. It was much colder than I had anticipated and I immediately regretted not packing a heavy coat. Wearing only a thin dress, I was freezing. Thankfully US Army Chief Warrant Officer Bobby Zizelman was one of the pilots on my helicopter and after he noticed me shivering he handed me his camouflage army jacket. I thanked him, wrapped myself in it, and moved closer to Secret Service agent Colin Johnson, who was seated next to me.

Colin was one of the biggest guys I'd ever met, with an even bigger heart. His fellow agents referred to him as "the Eclipse" because he stood six-foot-seven and weighed about three hundred pounds. I don't think an ounce of that three hundred pounds was body fat—Colin was absolutely ripped, and looked like an action hero straight out of Hollywood central casting. He was assigned to General John Kelly's detail and was a dedicated Secret Service agent for twenty years and a former marine. Colin's kindness was infectious, to meet him was to love him. Colin shielded me from the bitter cold near the DMZ that day. Another time he shielded me, Hope Hicks, and Dina Powell from being pelted with chunks of ice and snow as Marine One landed. He turned his back to flying debris to absorb the beating for all of us. Tragically, Colin was diagnosed with pancreatic cancer and died in September 2018, six weeks after our trip to Asia, leaving behind his wife, Fanny, and two beautiful little boys, Maximo and Magnus. I, along with many of my colleagues from the White House, as well as former staff from the Obama and Bush administrations, attended his funeral. There wasn't a dry eye in the room. Colin was loved by all. Former White House chief of staff to President George W. Bush Josh Bolten, like Colin an avid motorcyclist, led a group of bikers down Pennsylvania Avenue in front of the White House as a tribute to Colin following his funeral.

The media pool report from near the DMZ continued: "a half-dozen camouflage-clad guys in tactical gear were seated at the back of your press pool's bird, closest to the open back door. Wheels up at 7:43 a.m. The skyscrapers and dense neighborhoods of Seoul were barely visible through thick fog as we lifted. . . ."

As we approached the DMZ, a bad weather call forced us to turn back. We had been less than five minutes from the landing zone in the DMZ. Upon our return to Yongsan, I got into the Beast along with General Kelly to discuss the situation with the president. Our very unhappy commander in chief waited for more than an hour hoping the fog would clear so we could try again. I briefed the press while still wearing Officer Zizelman's army jacket, and during our informal gaggle on the military base the press photographers snapped several shots of me in the jacket. Back in the United States, liberals erupted in fury that I was wearing a military jacket, again demonstrating there may be nothing—not even a simple act of kindness from an army officer—that won't trigger outrage from liberals against the Trump administration. A year later on a different trip to Japan with the president I boarded another army Chinook helicopter. As I sat down in my seat, I noticed one of the flight operators waving at me. I waved back, but he kept trying to get my attention. He wasn't too far away from me, but it was too loud on the helicopter to hear anything. Finally he held up his army jacket and pointed to the name on the left side: "Zizelman."

The fog at Yongsan hadn't cleared, but had actually gotten worse. We canceled the trip to the DMZ so the president could make it back in time for his address to the South Korean national assembly. In the packed hall, the president delivered a warning to North Korea: "Today, I hope I speak not only for our countries, but for all civilized nations, when I say to the North: Do not underestimate us, and do not try us. We will defend our common security, our shared prosperity, and our sacred liberty." The national assembly roared with applause and gave President Trump a standing ovation.

The next day we departed South Korea for China. On Air Force One, General Kelly told me a story about a trip he had made years earlier to the Forbidden City. I told him I'd never been, but hoped to go if we ended up with any downtime. He told me I should be in the delegation to the Forbidden City with the president and offered me his spot. Since becoming chief of staff, General Kelly had brought order and discipline to the White House at a time when we desperately needed it. He implemented processes and got rid of some of the bad actors on staff. His tough military approach served the president and administration well in his early days as chief, but his unwillingness to compromise and pick his battles later became a problem. He never could wrap his head around the president's family at the White House and the direct line they had to the president. It frustrated him and didn't fit his chain-of-command leadership style. Having grown up in a political family, I warned Kelly that in a fight between family and staff, family always wins. Kelly loved his country and served it admirably in the military for many decades. When General Kelly spoke about his son Robert who was killed in action in Afghanistan it brought tears to my eyes and a thankfulness to my heart. His family had made the ultimate sacrifice, but continued to serve. When controversy hit the White House over a call the president made to a military family to offer condolences on behalf of the country, it was Kelly who came to me and said he wanted to take the podium in the White House press briefing room. Kelly was not only a general who had sent men and women into battle who never came home but also a Gold Star father. He gave an emotional account about learning about the death of his son, who took his last breath surrounded by the "best men on Earth." Kelly explained in graphic detail the process by which a family member is notified and the body is returned to the family. It was heart-wrenching.

We touched down at Beijing's airport and were greeted by a Chinese military entourage alongside a crowd of kids wildly jumping up and down waving American and Chinese flags. General Kelly manifested me to be part of the US delegation at the last minute in his place and we drove straight from the airport to the Forbidden City, which normally had thousands of people in it but was closed for our visit. Our delegation included the president, the first lady, Secretary of State Tillerson, National Security Advisor McMaster, US Trade Representative Robert Lighthizer, Ambassador to China and former governor of Iowa Terry Branstad, Jared Kushner, and me. We had the entire place to ourselves. The Forbidden City, spanning 180 acres, is a majestic site including nearly a thousand historic buildings in the heart of Beijing. Its Imperial Palace was formerly the home to emperors and their families for more than five centuries. You could spend many days there and not see it all.

We did part of the tour via golf cart to cover more ground. I was seated next to Ambassador Lighthizer, and this was the first time we really got to know each other. He was wearing a sweater and a blazer and was nice enough to loan me his jacket. This gesture was one that I often thought of when the president described Lighthizer as a killer. I soon got a chance to witness for myself what the president was talking about. The mild-mannered Midwesterner who offered me his jacket was a brilliant, no-nonsense negotiator unafraid to take on the Chinese or anybody else. Robert became a friend. I loved working alongside him and learning the art of a ruthless negotiator. It was no wonder he and the president got along so well!

This was the first time an American president had received a private tour of the Forbidden City, and President Xi put on quite the show. We toured areas normally closed to the public, had tea in the Hall of Three Rare Treasures, and were ushered into an ancient two-thousand-year-old theater where we sat on blankets to watch an opera. Afterward, President Trump and the first lady had a private dinner with President Xi and his wife in the Forbidden City—another first for an American president—while the rest of our delegation met with our counterparts in the Chinese delegation to discuss North Korea and trade.

While China clearly wanted to impress the president—our amazing visit to the Forbidden City was followed the next day by a spectacular show featuring hundreds of performers doing stunts and acrobatics in unison to the music of Michael Jackson—it didn't deter the president from going after what he came for. President Trump was firm and resolute on both trade and North Korea in his discussions with Xi. The president hit on the major trade imbalance with China, but careful not to offend his hosts, put some of the blame on past US administrations for letting China take advantage of the United States. He called on China and Xi in particular to do more on North Korea. I took it all in knowing that America's competition with China for global leadership would be a defining struggle of the twenty-first century.

Upon our return from Asia, North Korea again fired an intercontinental ballistic missile, its first since September. The president called a meeting at the White House with Senate Majority Leader Mitch McConnell and Speaker of the House Paul Ryan (their Democratic counterparts Senator Chuck Schumer and Representative Nancy Pelosi refused to attend). General Mattis said North Korea was now nearing a capability to carry out a nuclear strike anywhere in the United States.

On my first day back in the White House for the New Year, I did a press briefing, and Ivanka invited my family to join hers at the Monster Jam coming to the Verizon Arena in Washington. The president told Hope and me in the Oval he wanted the classic Guns N' Roses song "November Rain" added to his rally playlist. He told us it was the "greatest music video of all time," and made us watch it to prove his point even though neither of us had disagreed. At home after work, while I was watching the season premiere of *The Bachelor*, I was alerted to a tweet from the president: "North Korean leader Kim Jong-un just stated that the 'Nuclear Button is on his desk at all times.' Will someone from his depleted and food starved regime please inform him that I too have a Nuclear Button, but it is a much bigger & more powerful one than his, and my Button works!"

The president used his first State of the Union address to again hammer North Korea. He told the story of Mr. Ji Seong-ho:

> In 1996, Seong-ho was a starving boy in North Korea. One day, he tried to steal coal from a railroad car to barter for a few scraps of food. In the process, he passed out on the train tracks, exhausted from hunger. He woke

up as a train ran over his limbs. He then endured multiple amputations without anything to dull the pain. His
brother and sister gave what little food they had to help
him recover and ate dirt themselves—permanently stunt-
ing their own growth. Later, he was tortured by North
Korean authorities after returning from a brief visit to
China. His tormentors wanted to know if he had met any
Christians. He had—and he resolved to be free.

Seong-ho traveled thousands of miles on crutches
across China and Southeast Asia to freedom. Most of his
family followed. His father was caught trying to escape,
and was tortured to death.

Today he lives in Seoul, where he rescues other defec-
tors, and broadcasts into North Korea what the regime
fears the most—the truth.

Today he has a new leg, but Seong-ho, I understand
you still keep those crutches as a reminder of how far you
have come. Your great sacrifice is an inspiration to us all.

Seong-ho's story is a testament to the yearning of
every human soul to live in freedom.

Seong-ho raised his crutch high in the air as everyone in the House
Chamber for the State of the Union burst into applause. As I stood
in the House Chamber, I felt chills go down my spine. It was the
most powerful moment of the night.

The following morning, I departed for the Winter Olympics in
South Korea as a member of the official American delegation led
by Ivanka Trump. I had dreamed of going to the Olympics since I
was a kid. I love America and I love sports—so really what could be
better? When Ivanka invited me to be part of the US delegation, at
first I thought she must be kidding, but she told me it was already
done and I had been cleared to go. I couldn't have been more

excited. I knew this trip was more than just the Olympics—the escalating conflict with North Korea would play a major role in the trip. The team from the White House included Ivanka, her chief of staff, Julie Radford, a fellow mom to three young kids and close confidante; senior advisor to General McMaster and the NSC staff Sarah Flaherty; and NSC Korean specialist Allison Hooker. The incoming chairman of the Senate Foreign Relations Committee Jim Risch (R-ID) also joined our delegation. We spent weeks prepping for the trip—mapping out logistics, attending security briefings, developing a communications plan, and going through a variety of scenarios that could play out.

On our way over to South Korea we spent the first couple hours visiting, but shortly into our flight while Julie, Sarah, and I chatted, Ivanka peeled off to study her briefing book. She took her responsibility as the leader of the delegation seriously and knew she had a big job to do. This wasn't just a trip to support our athletes, it was also a trip to reaffirm our commitment to our ally South Korea and to stand strong against North Korea.

Vice President Mike Pence had led the US delegation for the opening ceremony and there had been a mixed response to his trip. The vice president planned to meet briefly with the North Korean delegation, led by Kim Jong-un's younger sister, but the North Koreans canceled just hours before they were scheduled to sit down. The vice president was attacked for not standing for the joint Korea Olympic team but his critics missed the point. The vice president's trip had been planned to send one message: The United States would maintain its maximum pressure campaign and not allow North Korea to use the Olympics as a propaganda show—and he executed it well.

As our delegation landed in South Korea, the administration announced the toughest sanctions ever against North Korea. We knew our job had just gotten more difficult. From the moment we stepped off the plane Ivanka was a superstar in South Korea. There were dozens of cameras waiting at the airport exit to catch a glimpse of her. Sadly for the rest of our delegation, it was hard to look presentable next to Ivanka.

Our first stop was all business. Ivanka, and the other members of the delegation, including Senator Risch; General Vincent Brooks, the commander of United States Forces Korea; Mark Knapper, the Chargé d'Affaires for South Korea; and I had a small private dinner at the Blue House with President Moon, his wife, and Kang Kyung-wha, the South Korean foreign minister. Ivanka carried a letter from her father to deliver to President Moon. I had gotten to know Ivanka pretty well over the last year of working in the administration, but this was one of the first times we spent an extended amount of time together in this type of setting. I was used to being in the room when her father was the principal. She of course weighed in and contributed in those meetings, but tonight was different because she was the principal and expected to carry the water not just for her father, but for the country. Her hard work paid off. She was engaging and knew personal details about our dinner hosts that kept the conversation moving and interesting. She managed to find common interests to discuss, even getting the South Korean first lady to open up and throw her head back in laughter at one point. It was impressive. We took official photos in front of the Blue House with the South Korean president and first lady, said our good-byes, and concluded our first day.

The next day we watched Team USA men compete in snowboarding, bobsledding, and curling. The South Korean first lady as well as Olympic gold medalist Angela Ruggiero joined our group, and as we cheered on Team USA there were photographers all around us. The British tabloid the *Daily Mail* captured several shots and did a photo montage and story about our trip, but mainly just attacked me. The headline read: "Out in the Cold in Pyeongchang?

Sarah Huckabee Sanders Cuts a Downbeat Figure at the Snow-boarding Final as She's Snubbed by South Korea at 'Slipper-Gate' Dinner." The headline was as absurd as the story itself. I didn't care for the *Daily Mail*'s false account of being "snubbed" at the dinner because I had on a regular pair of slippers instead of the gold embroidered ones Ivanka wore, but I was most insulted by their ridiculous claim that I had been distracted at the snowboarding final rifling through a bag of chips, when in fact I was opening a pair of hand warmers that the South Korean first lady had given me to endure the freezing cold! If I ever need to humble myself a bit, all I have to do is visualize that *Daily Mail* image from Pyeongchang of Ivanka looking like a supermodel in her one-piece snowsuit while I appear to be wrestling with a bag of Doritos next to her.

The *Daily Mail* story notwithstanding, we had a blast cheering on our Olympians. I never thought I could get so excited about curling, but the atmosphere was electric and the crowd, including our delegation, went crazy when Team USA defeated Sweden 10–7 to win the gold.

Our time at the games closed hanging out and taking photos with the internationally acclaimed K-pop group EXO, who had performed at the ceremonies. Ivanka knew that Sarah Flaherty's stepdaughter loved K-pop and arranged for her to meet the group. It was quite the contrast: one minute we had been discussing how to engage with one of the world's most evil regimes and the next we were snapping pics with a Korean boy band.

Just hours before the closing ceremony began, South Korean president Moon met with North Korean general Kim Yong-chol. Moon had announced following their meeting that the North Koreans were open to talks with the United States. This announcement came just three days after President Trump issued the largest sanctions ever against North Korea. Near the conclusion of the Winter Olympics from South Korea I announced:

President Donald J. Trump's Administration is committed to achieving the complete, verifiable, and irreversible denuclearization of the Korean Peninsula. The United States, our Olympic Host the Republic of Korea, and the international community broadly agree that denuclearization must be the result of any dialogue with North Korea. The maximum pressure campaign must continue until North Korea denuclearizes.

Weeks later I was in a meeting with the vice president's communications team and Natalie Strom from the press office ran into the room and said, "The president is walking into the briefing room." I quickly made my way down the hall to find the president standing at the briefing room door telling reporters there will be a major announcement tonight on North Korea. He left them hanging and then turned and said, "Follow me." We walked along the iconic colonnade by the Rose Garden where he told me about his meeting with the South Korean delegation. He had not been scheduled to attend, but when he heard the meeting was taking place he interrupted it to ask for an update from the South Korean delegation and his national security team. The South Korean national security advisor told President Trump that North Korea was open to direct talks with him on denuclearization and they'd be willing to suspend nuclear and missile tests. The president agreed on the spot and said he'd like for the South Korean delegation to announce it from the White House right away. The president left the meeting and went directly into the press briefing room to let reporters know an announcement was coming.

President Trump asked me to introduce the South Korean delegation from the briefing room but I recommended having South Korean national security advisor Chung Eui-yong do it from the "sticks" in the driveway outside the West Wing, which is where guests visiting the White House usually addressed the media. After talking further with the president, I then briefed the US and South Korean teams on the plan and at 7:00 p.m. EDT South Korean national security advisor Chung Eui-yong walked out of the West Wing to make the announcement.

The next week the president fired Secretary of State Rex Tillerson while Tillerson was in Africa. The president called me into the Oval Office and told me he planned to appoint CIA director Mike Pompeo as secretary of state and elevate CIA deputy director Gina Haspel to lead the CIA. I was one of the few people in the White House who knew about the president's decision and had to quickly develop a plan to announce it. For months the president had asked what he should do about Tillerson, and I had strongly agreed with him that Pompeo was a good fit for the job. The president loved to tease me about Pompeo being my "favorite," and I was thrilled with his decision to make him our nation's top diplomat. CIA director Pompeo had a good relationship with the president, senior administration officials, and members of Congress. He had a wealth of knowledge from his time in the military, Congress, and as director of the CIA, and immediately built a team atmosphere and sense of cooperation that had been missing from the State Department. Pompeo brought a swagger to the job, and most importantly, the president trusted him.

Gina Haspel, a thirty-year veteran of the CIA, was also a strong pick to lead our nation's top spy agency. Gina faced a tough Senate confirmation battle and the White House counsel's office, led by Don McGahn, worried she couldn't get through confirmation because of operational work she'd done at the agency. At one difficult point in the process, Gina told Pompeo she planned to withdraw as the president's nominee because she didn't want the focus on the controversy to hurt the reputation of the CIA. Marc Short,

the White House legislative affairs director, and I had read everything in her file and firmly disagreed with McGahn's assessment.
We were on the phone with Pompeo and explained why it was a
bad idea for her to withdraw. There was nothing in her file we
couldn't vigorously defend. He said we should make that case to
Gina directly, and to meet him at CIA headquarters immediately. I canceled my date with my husband to a cocktail party at
Deputy White House Chief of Staff Chris Liddell's house at the
moment our babysitter was walking in the door. "I'm not going to
be able to come," I said. "I can't answer any questions or tell you why.
I won't be at the office and I won't have my phone. I'm really sorry."

Marc, his deputy Mary Elizabeth, and I rushed to CIA headquarters at Langley, and the three of us along with Pompeo urged
Haspel not to quit. After making our case, she finally agreed to
sleep on it. The next day Gina called me and said she had changed
her mind. She had decided to stay in and fight, and was ultimately
confirmed by the Senate to be the first woman ever to lead the CIA.

One of Pompeo's first missions for the president as his top diplomat was to secretly fly to North Korea over Easter to meet with
Kim Jong-un. The goal was to set the stage for a first-ever summit
between the leaders of the United States and North Korea. After
Pompeo returned to the United States, news of the secret mission
leaked. The president called me into the Oval, and when I came
in Pompeo was there. He held three photographs of him with Kim
Jong-un. He handed them to me. We talked about their meeting,
and I couldn't stop asking questions. The president asked me what
I thought, and how people were reacting to the leak of Pompeo's
meeting with Kim Jong-un. I told him that so far it was playing well
and further demonstrated that the maximum pressure campaign
was working. The president told me to release the pictures and
confirm Pompeo's meeting on the record with the media. Pompeo
teased me not to lose the photos because those were the only ones

he had and there wasn't a digital file. I personally walked the photos to the Lower Press office and worked with staff to get them scanned and watched as they were distributed far and wide and started appearing on news programs across the country throughout the day.

Following Pompeo's meeting with Kim Jong-un, North Korea announced suspension of all nuclear and long-range missile testing ahead of the upcoming summit, and just a few weeks later, I received a secure call that I had been waiting on all day. It was from my colleague State Department spokesperson Heather Nauert, traveling with Pompeo, who told me their plane had cleared North Korean airspace with three American hostages safely on board and that Secretary Pompeo was calling President Trump now to brief him.

The secretary called me immediately after he hung up with the president to relay their conversation: "Just wanted you to know in case the president tweets it." I laughed and replied, "Too late." During our call the president had already tweeted: "I am pleased to inform you that Secretary of State Mike Pompeo is in the air and on his way back from North Korea with the 3 wonderful gentlemen that everyone is looking so forward to meeting. They seem to be in good health. Also, good meeting with Kim Jong-un. Date & Place set . . . Secretary Pompeo and his 'guests' will be landing at Andrews Air Force Base at 2:00 a.m. in the morning. I will be there to greet them. Very exciting!"

Pompeo told me the three male hostages had walked onto the plane by themselves and the doctors said they were in good condition. He joked, "I'm so tired they'll probably be able to walk off the plane better than I can."

I hung up and issued the official White House statement: "President Trump appreciates leader Kim Jong-un's action to release these American citizens, and views this as a positive gesture of goodwill. The three Americans appear to be in good condition and were all able to walk on the plane without assistance. All Americans look forward to welcoming them home and to seeing them reunited with their loved ones."

I went home and slept for a couple of hours before going back to the White House at 1:00 a.m. to ride on Marine One with the president, first lady, and National Security Advisor John Bolton to Andrews. There were more than 250 credentialed press waiting when we landed. The president, first lady, Bolton, and I went into the VIP visitor's center and waited on Secretary Pompeo to come off the plane and brief the president. The meeting had gone well, he said. "Believe it or not, Kim Jong-un said he wants to come to Miami," said Pompeo. "He loves the NBA and is a big fan of the Heat." We quickly wrapped up and Secretary Pompeo said he'd give the president a deeper dive the next day. The president and first lady went on board the plane, met privately with the three liberated hostages and the doctors, and then they escorted the men off the plane and addressed the press. It was emotional to watch these three men who had been held captive just days before walking down the stairs of the plane into freedom on American soil and being greeted by the President of the United States. This was the most significant gesture of goodwill from the North Koreans up to this point. So much had changed since the president's threats of "fire and fury." The visual of the first freed American hostage throwing his hands up with peace signs as he stepped off the plane flanked by the president and the first lady demonstrated that President Trump's maximum pressure campaign and unconventional approach to diplomacy was delivering results. The group took the last step off the plane and walked toward the media where they made brief remarks. The president said, "These are probably the best ratings anybody's had at 3 a.m.," concluding the joyous occasion in a way only he can.

I returned on Marine One with the president to the White

House and rushed to Duck's Donuts where I picked up glazed donuts with sprinkles, Scarlett's favorite, for her sixth birthday. I hung a birthday banner and finished tying balloons to her chair just minutes before she walked downstairs. We celebrated and then dropped the kids off at school. Exhausted and sleep deprived, I returned to the office to start another day.

On June 10, 2018, we departed on Air Force One en route to Singapore for the much-anticipated summit between President Trump and Kim Jong-un. Over the Pacific, we played spades and tried to lighten the mood. We joked about possible tweets the president could fire off to set the stage for the meeting. The president suggested "getting ready to land in Singapore. This is Chairman Kim's only chance—he will either live or die!" but we all knew that given the high-stakes nuclear diplomacy, this summit was anything but a joke.

When Air Force One touched down at Paya Lebar Air Base at 8:21 p.m. local time, Chairman Kim was already in Singapore, where he fit in a visit to a casino and nightclub. Kim was staying at the St. Regis and most of our delegation was at the Shangri-La Hotel—less than a mile away. The summit had already been carefully orchestrated and negotiated for months, but when President Trump realized that Kim was already there and we were going to have a mostly empty day he said we should move it up. I told the president if we did so, the summit would be broadcast in the middle of the night in America and few would see it. The president agreed to stick to the original plan. We all breathed a sigh of relief.

As was customary when hosted by another country, we had a bilateral meeting with Singapore's prime minister prior to the summit. I was part of the US delegation for that meeting. We covered a lot of ground in a short amount of time—the opioid problem in the United States and why Singapore didn't have much of a drug problem, religious persecution, China's growing power, trade, and of course North Korea. Prime minister Lee Hsien Loong had just met with Kim so the president was interested in his take. The prime minister said that Chairman Kim had been "chatty" and "wanted to make a deal." He explained that he had recently been to North Korea and Kim was sensitive to the perception that international sanctions had weakened his regime. Prime Minister Lee had stayed in the same room in the same hotel as Secretary Pompeo during his secret mission to North Korea. Secretary Pompeo said when he was there, the hotel was empty. Lee said, "It was clean, well maintained, but very little traffic. At night it was the dimmest big city I had ever seen." The meeting was interrupted by a large group who came in singing "Happy Birthday" to President Trump. They were very excited, but it was clear the president wasn't in any mood to celebrate. He was ready to get on with the summit. We concluded the meeting and returned to the US Embassy.

That night Pompeo, Kelly, Bolton, his deputy Mira Ricardel, NSC Director for Asia Matthew Pottinger, and I gathered in the president's hotel suite to walk through the day and do one final prep meeting. Mira screened the video the president planned to show Kim in the one-on-one meeting following the leaders' initial handshake. The video was highly produced and showcased the economic prosperity North Korea could achieve if they made a deal to denuclearize in exchange for the lifting of sanctions. We knew that Kim loved Western culture, including movies and basketball. He was also very interested in developing and modernizing the North Korean economy. The president liked the video and agreed it was worth a shot to show it to Kim. We sat discussing the movements of the next day, and as we were wrapping up the president asked me how things were going. I told him the coverage around the summit was mostly positive, but lots of people still doubted anything would come of it. As we talked, former NBA star and *Apprentice* contestant Dennis Rodman came on screen on a TV that was playing in the background. We stopped to watch. Rodman was complimentary of both the president and Kim and said that if anyone could make a deal, it was Donald Trump. It was bizarre to watch Rodman offer insights on such a serious topic, but he was one of the few people in the world who had a relationship with both Kim and President Trump. The president turned to me and said, "Call Rodman and thank him."

We left the president's suite and I announced the official schedule for the next day: 9:05 a.m. handshake between the two leaders, followed by a one-on-one bilat, then an expanded bilat and lunch. At 8:00 p.m. President Trump would hold a press conference. When I got back to my room, I called Rodman. I was told he was traveling but they'd pass along a message. I didn't have much of an expectation that I would hear back from him.

I woke up early the next morning to my phone ringing. I answered and sure enough it was Dennis Rodman on the other end of the line. I remember being careful with my words because I wasn't sure how much of our exchange he might repeat later. I offered the president's thanks for all he'd done and his kind words regarding the summit. He was friendly but not super talkative. Rodman said to pass on his thanks to the president and that he looked forward to shaking the president's hand after the summit. I told him the president would like to see him once we were all back home in America. My call with Rodman was brief, and good thing I was careful with my words because I found out later he had a TV crew from VICE News in the room filming him and the phone on speaker during our conversation.

Later that day Rodman went on CNN live from Singapore wearing a red MAGA hat and said he'd just talked to the president's "secretary." He was emotional, and said, "Obama didn't give me the time of day . . . but that didn't deter me. I kept going back, going back, going back . . . I showed my loyalty to this country and I said, 'the door will open.'" Rodman started crying, tears streaming down his face: "When I said those things, when I said those d—— things I got death threats . . . and I couldn't even go home! But I kept my head up high, brother, I knew things were gonna change! I just knew it! I was the only one, no one would hear me. But I took all those bullets and I'm still standing and today is a great day for everybody . . . everybody! I'm here to see it and I'm so happy."

We left our hotel and arrived at the Capella Hotel on Sentosa Island. No one else was at the resort except those who were part of the summit. I went with Dan Scavino to the president's hold room where we met up with Secret Service lead Tony Ornato and President Trump. We had a few minutes and everyone was a bit on edge as we waited. I told the president the shot was going to look amazing. Joe Hagin had done a great job putting it all together. The president asked if he had any missed calls to return. His personal aide Jordan Kareem listed off a few, including those of members of the House and Senate, but the one that piqued the president's interest was from world-renowned golfer Jack Nicklaus. I suspect the president was looking for someone to talk to about something lighter than North Korea and nuclear armageddon so he asked for the phone and called Jack. They spoke and laughed for a few minutes like old friends do. We motioned to the president it was time. He told Jack he had to go, and said, "I'm about to do something big. Turn on your TV. You won't believe it, and you don't want to miss it." The president hung up, stood up, and gave us a look like "Can you believe this!?" I couldn't. Considering many Korean experts and pundits feared a war with millions dead just a short time ago, it was quite a turn of events for the president and Kim to be the first leaders of the United States and North Korea to meet. The president was ready, and we wished him luck.

Both leaders were in place a couple minutes early and at 9:03 a.m.

they both stepped onto bright red carpets and walked along an outdoor corridor, meeting in an open space against a backdrop of alternating US and North Korean flags. Every network carried it live, and millions in America and around the world tuned in to witness the leaders' handshake and embrace. "Fire and fury" had been replaced by de-escalation and diplomacy. Kim later said it was like something out of a "science-fiction movie." The two walked together, chatting briefly using interpreters, and then stepped into a doorway out of sight of the press to start their one-on-one meeting. After their meeting—during which the president showed Kim the video offering a glimpse of North Korea's untapped potential on a preloaded iPad—they walked down the corridor again to shouted questions from the press.

The pair went to the expanded bilat and then we moved to the working lunch where I joined the delegation. Our group included the president, Pompeo, Bolton, Kelly, Pottinger, Ambassador Kim, and me. The North Korean delegation included Chairman Kim and General Kim Yong-chol, who I had seen at the Olympics and who was suspected of being involved in the assassination—ordered by Kim Jong-un—of his own half-brother at Kuala Lumpur International Airport in Malaysia in 2017. Kim's sister, one of his most feared enforcers, was there as well, among other senior regime officials. Hoping to lighten the mood as we walked in, I joked to Pompeo that "I may be the only person at this table who hasn't killed someone." He looked around and said, "Yep, you're the only one." It was a bit unsettling.

The president, always the gracious host, told the photographers to make him and Kim look "nice and handsome and thin." The lunch consisted of a nine-course menu that included prawn cocktail, green mango kerabu salad with honey lime dressing, fresh octopus, soy-braised codfish, and braised short ribs.

As the lunch was starting the president offered Kim a breath mint. "Tic Tac?" Kim, confused, and probably concerned it was an attempt to poison him, wasn't sure how to respond. The president dramatically blew into the air to reassure Kim it was just a breath mint and took a few from the box and popped them into his mouth. Kim reluctantly accepted the Tic Tac from President Trump and ate it. I was seated to President Trump's left with only General Kelly between us, and just diagonal from Kim. I spent a good bit of the lunch taking notes, exhilarated by what I was witnessing. The president was masterful at moving the conversation along and covering the key issues while mixing in topics of interest to Kim. Both sports enthusiasts, they discussed golf, women's soccer, Kim's favorite NBA basketball player, the late Kobe Bryant, and their mutual acquaintance Dennis Rodman, before continuing on to more pressing matters like the better future North Korea could achieve for its people if Kim agreed to denuclearize.

At one point during the lunch as Kim finished speaking and the translator was conveying his message to the president, I looked up to notice Kim staring at me. We made direct eye contact and Kim nodded and appeared to wink at me. I was stunned. I quickly looked down and continued taking notes and for the rest of the meeting only looked up from my notes in the direction of the US delegation. I tried to get General Kelly's attention but he was focused on the conversation. All I could think was *What just happened? Surely Kim Jong-un did not just mark me!?*

When the lunch ended, our delegation moved to President Trump's suite at the hotel. There was a general agreement on the signing statement between the two leaders but a few minor details were still being finalized at the staff level. The team went downstairs and left the president to have a few minutes of downtime prior to the signing ceremony. There was a small room attached to the signing room where most of the members of our delegation waited.

Hagin and his deputy Patrick Clifton were arguing with their North Korean counterparts when we came in the room. Pompeo, Kelly, Bolton, Pottinger, and I sat down. Bolton was angry and wanted no part in the signing statement. He didn't trust the North Koreans and considered talks to be counterproductive. Nobody else on our team trusted the North Koreans either, but assuming the toughest-ever sanctions on North Korea remained in place, talks were better than risking an all-out war.

There was debate on who would sit first and who, if anyone, would speak. We had a thirteen-member press pool and the North Koreans only had seven. We had been fighting all day to have all thirteen members of the American press pool included and the North Koreans refused to accommodate us because they wanted everything to be even. Hannah Salem, head of press advance for the White House for the trip, never let up, and eventually we just pushed all the American press into the room. Hagin and Clifton finally got agreement on the signing process and both translators agreed to the copy. We were ready.

Just minutes before the president and Kim walked in, a North Korean official came out with white gloves to inspect the pen Kim would be using to sign the agreement to make sure it wasn't weaponized to assassinate him. President Trump and Chairman Kim walked in, sat down, and signed the comprehensive agreement. The president was in a good mood and ready to take a victory lap at his press conference. He did one quick stand-up interview with Voice of America's Greta Van Susteren and back-to-back sit-down interviews with ABC's George Stephanopoulos and Fox News's Sean Hannity. They went well, and the president walked into his press conference to the largest gathering of media he'd faced.

Ahead of the president's remarks we played the video the president had screened for Kim. It had the feel of an action movie trailer showing what North Korea could look like in the future if it denucle-arizes, opens up to foreign investment, and modernizes its economy with the refrain "What if?" The narrator intoned, "Only the very few will make decisions or take actions that renew their homeland and change the course of history. . . . Two men. Two leaders. One destiny. A story about a special moment in time when a man is presented with one chance that may never be repeated. What will he choose?"

The president opened the press conference with hundreds of reporters by saying:

> It's my honor today to address the people of the world, following this very historic summit with Chairman Kim Jong-un of North Korea. . . .
>
> I stand before you as an emissary of the American people to deliver a message of hope and vision, and a message of peace. . . . I want to thank Chairman Kim for taking the first bold step toward a bright new future for his people. Our unprecedented meeting—the first between an American president and a leader of North Korea—proves that real change is indeed possible. . . .
>
> Nearly seventy years ago—think of that; seventy years ago—an extremely bloody conflict ravaged the Korean Peninsula. Countless people died in the conflict, includ-ing tens of thousands of brave Americans. Yet, while the armistice was agreed to, the war never ended. To this day, never ended. But now we can all have hope that it will soon end. . . .
>
> The past does not have to define the future. Yester-day's conflict does not have to be tomorrow's war. And as history has proven over and over again, adversaries can indeed become friends. We can honor the sacrifice

of our forefathers by replacing the horrors of battle with the blessings of peace.

I stood along the wall of the crowded room and watched President Trump. I knew it would take a miracle for Kim to ever give up his nuclear weapons. After all, few countries with nuclear weapons had ever voluntarily relinquished them. But the president had already succeeded in liberating American hostages from North Korea, persuaded the regime to freeze its nuclear and long-range missile tests, and had started the process of building a relationship with Kim to de-escalate tensions and lower the risk of a devastating war that could result in the deaths of millions of innocent people. It was a big risk for the president to meet with Kim, but I was proud of the president for taking it.

After the president answered questions from the press for about a half hour he turned to me and asked in front of the entire room, "Should we keep going for a little while, Sarah? I don't know . . . it's up to the legendary Sarah Huckabee Sanders . . . should we keep going, Sarah? Okay . . . go? I don't care . . . you know it just means we'll get home a little later in the evening."

As the president walked off the stage a few of us were there to greet and congratulate him. He grabbed a Diet Coke from the military valet, took a long sip, slapped me on my shoulder, and said, "You know what, Sarah, you did pretty good today, ride back with me." That meant a lot to me. He had just finished one of the most important days of his presidency and was in a good mood and wanted me to share the moment with him.

I climbed into the Beast and sat next to the president and across from General Kelly. Tony Ornato was in his usual place in the front passenger seat. As we sat there recalling the events of the day en route to the airport in Singapore, the president asked me what I thought of Kim. "I was surprised by his sense of humor, but am a bit concerned that he may have marked me," I said. I explained that during lunch, I had looked up from my notes to find Kim staring at me. "We made eye contact and he nodded and winked at me."

The president and General Kelly exploded with laughter.

"Kim winked at you?" the president asked.

"Yes!"

"Are you telling me Kim Jong-un hit on you!?!?"

"No, sir, that's not what I said."

"Kim Jong-un hit on you! He did! He f—— hit on you!"

"Sir, please stop," I said.

The president turned to General Kelly and asked: "General?"

"He definitely hit on you," Kelly said.

"Well, Sarah, that settles it," said the president. "You're going to North Korea and taking one for the team! Your husband and kids will miss you, but you'll be a hero to your country!" Trump and Kelly howled with laughter, as the Beast pulled into the airport and we exited to board Air Force One to return home.

7

Liberal Mob

On a Friday evening in the summer of 2018, I drove myself from the White House to Lexington, Virginia, where Bryan, our kids, and my in-laws were spending the weekend at a farmhouse in the mountains outside of town. It had been an exhausting week and after four hours in the car, I arrived to meet Bryan and the family at a small restaurant in downtown Lexington called The Red Hen. They had just ordered drinks and appetizers. I walked in the front door and said hi and gave hugs to everyone. But shortly after I sat down, a woman at the table next to us approached me and said she was the owner of the restaurant and asked if she could talk to me outside on the patio. I agreed, but had an uneasy feeling as we walked out. It was an empty area and just the two of us were standing there. She again reminded me she was the owner and said, "You're a terrible person. You are not welcome here, and I would like you to leave." I was stunned. I walked away from her and back inside the restaurant. I quietly approached our table, picked up my things, and whispered to my husband that I had been kicked out. I didn't say another word to anyone else. I simply walked out the door and didn't look back. Bryan told his family what had happened, and looked up to see the owner of the restaurant frantically struggling to unlock her phone to video me leaving. It was clear she was hoping to create a viral moment. My father-in-law, Bill, tried to pay the check but The Red Hen refused his money. Bill attended Washington and Lee University in Lexington and named his only daughter, Virginia, because he loved his experience there so much. An attorney from Kansas City, Bill is a loyal husband and father. He is hardworking, funny, and kind, and the way he was made to feel as if his money was somehow unworthy in that establishment was disgraceful.

I got to the car and I was pretty upset. I was already worn out from a tough day at the office and hours on the road, and had really been looking forward to seeing my family, many of whom we only see a few times a year. They asked if we wanted to go to a different restaurant, but at this point I just wanted to go home. Bryan and I drove back to the farmhouse, and kissed our kids goodnight. Scarlett and Huck were cuddled up asleep in each other's arms in the loft. Bryan reassured me it was okay and reminded me to focus on what matters—our faith, our family, and all that we have to be thankful for. I ate a bowl of cereal at the farmhouse and went to bed.

The rest of our group went to dinner across the street at a different restaurant, called the Southern Inn, hoping to put the incident behind them and spend some time together as a family. Unfortunately the owner of The Red Hen wasn't content just to kick us out of her restaurant. She and a group of her friends went over to protest and harass my family at the other restaurant as well. Bryan's dad was appalled. His mom was afraid and worried that it would escalate to violence. Bryan's brother and sister and their significant others—all liberal Democrats—were angry. His brother walked outside and up to the owner of The Red Hen and said, "Sarah and her husband aren't here. Nearly everyone you're harassing right now voted for Hillary Clinton. What you're doing is uncalled for."

The next morning Bryan and I woke up, had coffee, and took the kids out on the farm, set on a hillside in the Shenandoah Valley. Scarlett, Huck, and George gathered eggs from the chicken coop, held newborn piglets, and took turns riding a pony. I had left my phone at the house, and returned to dozens of missed calls, texts, and emails asking me what happened at The Red Hen the night before. Turned out our waiter had posted about the incident on social media and a local Democratic activist rebroadcast it on Twitter, which then caught the attention of the national media. Reporters from around the country were now investigating. Some reporters falsely assumed it had taken place at a different restaurant in Washington, DC, with the same name but no affiliation with The Red Hen in Lexington. I decided that instead of wasting the limited family vacation time I had responding to each media request individually, I'd post one statement on Twitter to set the record straight: "Last night I was told by the owner of Red Hen in Lexington, VA to leave because I work for @POTUS and I politely left. Her actions say far more about her than about me. I always do my best to treat people, including those I disagree with, respectfully and will continue to do so."

Twitter exploded, and The Red Hen controversy quickly became the top news story in America. The lead on Drudge Report was a photo of the front of the restaurant with the headline: "RED HEN CLUCKAAAAAWWWWKS SANDERS." At one point, The Red Hen went from the highest-rated restaurant in Lexington on Yelp to the lowest after thousands of negative reviews poured in from Trump supporters around the country. In an attempt at damage control, The Red Hen owner did an interview with *The Washington Post* and gave a false account of the evening, mentioning nothing about trying to video my family as she kicked us out or following them to a different restaurant and harassing them there. *The Washington Post* never corrected her story, and in the months that followed published not one but two columns on their editorial page by the owner of The Red Hen defending her actions.

At the farm, we decided to stay in rather than venture back into Lexington. We had a beautiful dinner outside on the deck as the sun set over the mountains. The night ended with the family drinking champagne and doing karaoke, and for a few hours we forgot all about The Red Hen and laughed and enjoyed our time together.

On Sunday we loaded up our Yukon for the drive back to Washington, but The Red Hen controversy raged on. Liberal congresswoman Maxine Waters (D-CA) said, "If you see anybody from that (administration) in a restaurant, in a department store, at a gasoline station, you get out and you create a crowd. And you push back on them! And you tell them they're not welcome anymore, anywhere!"

Former White House press secretary for President George W. Bush Ari Fleischer said, "I guess we're heading into an America with Democrat-only restaurants, which will lead to Republican-only restaurants. Do the fools who threw Sarah out, and the people who cheer them on, really want us to be that kind of country?"

Even former president Obama's chief strategist, David Axelrod, no fan of President Trump, said, "Kind of amazed and appalled by the number of folks on Left who applauded the expulsion of @PressSec and her family from a restaurant."

At our senior staff meeting back at the White House, General

Kelly addressed the rising threat level against senior administration officials, and said we should exercise caution in public and when legally permissible carry a firearm in public to defend ourselves. Afterward he pulled me aside and said I needed to meet with Secret Service because they'd determined there had been a credible violent threat made against me.

I was in the Situation Room for a meeting on the border crisis, and the president called me into the Oval Office. "What'd you think of my tweet about The Red Hen? All the attention is kind of cool, isn't it?"

"Actually, sir, it's kind of scary. Threats are being made against me and my family and we don't have any kind of security."

"You don't? You must be kidding."

"No, sir."

The president couldn't believe I didn't have a Secret Service detail. It had never occurred to him that I wouldn't.

I opened the press briefing that day by addressing the controversy:

> Good afternoon. Many by now have heard that I was asked to leave a restaurant this weekend where I attempted to have dinner with my family. My husband and I politely left and went home. I was asked to leave because I work for President Trump.
>
> We are allowed to disagree, but we should be able to do so freely and without fear of harm. And this goes for all people regardless of politics. Some have chosen to push hate and vandalism against the restaurant that I was asked to leave from. A Hollywood actor publicly encouraged people to kidnap my children. And this weekend, a member of Congress called for people to "push back" and make clear to those serving their country in

this administration that they are not welcome anywhere, anytime, for anything.

Healthy debate on ideas and political philosophy is important, but the calls for harassment and push for any Trump supporter to avoid the public is unacceptable.

America is a great country, and our ability to find solutions despite those disagreements is what makes us unique.

I went on *Fox & Friends* and was asked about The Red Hen incident and incivility in politics. "I'm going to continue to do exactly what I tell my kids to do . . . and that's to treat everybody with respect. . . . It's a sad day in America when Democrats' only message is to attack people that support this president and support this country."

In the weeks that followed, hundreds of Bikers for Trump rode through the streets of Lexington in a show of solidarity to protest The Red Hen. The AP, Fox News, and the *New York Post* ran stories about how The Red Hen incident was hurting tourism and the local economy in Lexington. Fox News reported:

> A small town in Virginia is attempting a reputation makeover after a restaurant in the area infamously refused to serve White House Press Secretary Sarah Sanders in June.
>
> The area's regional tourism board is pulling together emergency funds to boost its digital marketing campaign, *The Roanoke Times* reported Sunday. The money is normally saved, however, officials agreed the region is in desperate need of positive coverage after the Sanders controversy. . . .
>
> Following the incident, the tourism board was flooded with thousands of calls and emails—and the complaints

are still coming. The office received a letter Thursday from a Georgia family that wrote to say it would never return because of what happened.

"For a town our size, it was a significant impact," Patty Williams, the director of marketing, told *The Roanoke Times*. . . .

The restaurant closed its doors for nearly two weeks after the controversy broke.

I still couldn't understand why anyone would kick a person out of their restaurant over a political disagreement. The year before, Bryan had been kicked out of his fantasy football league—a league he'd participated in for more than a decade with friends from college—because the commissioner of the league said he couldn't associate with my husband anymore. Not because he worked for President Trump—but because I did.

At my kids' preschool in Arlington, Virginia, a woman approached me as I was walking my three-year-old George to class and holding his hand, and with a look of pure rage in her eyes told me I was an awful human being. Our three-year-olds were in the same class. The woman turned, walked past George and me, and spat onto the windshield of my car.

In the Trump era, many liberals who preached tolerance were guilty of hateful displays of intolerance. Trump Derangement Syndrome (TDS) was spiraling out of control. Bryan and I had many Democratic friends, including some who had worked in the Obama administration. We didn't vote for President Obama or agree with his policies, but it never crossed our minds to be anything but thrilled for our friends who had the opportunity to work in the White House during his administration—to treat them like enemies because of their political affiliation was unconscionable.

I was often told I had a hard job fighting back against President

Trump's critics, but that was never the hardest part of my job. I was proud of the administration's many achievements and defended the president's policies unapologetically. The hardest part of my job was realizing that my kids might not be safe anymore. I was no longer only worried about them falling off the monkey bars or getting sick—I was now afraid that someone might hurt them or take them. I wasn't sleeping. I called their school and talked to their teachers, reminding them that no one who wasn't on the list was allowed to pick them up. I didn't allow my kids to attend most playdates or birthday parties they were invited to and for a while we didn't go out to many places in public.

While Bryan and I attended a party Jared and Ivanka hosted at the Trump International Hotel—one of the few safe places for prominent Trump administration officials in Washington—ABC News broke the story that I would be the first White House press secretary ever to receive Secret Service protection. I woke up the next morning to a line of Secret Service vehicles outside our home and media staked out to cover my departure to the White House with a Secret Service detail for the first time.

As much as some reporters were enraged by the president's name-calling against the media ("a threat to the freedom of the press and democracy itself!"), some of them apparently couldn't care less that their personal attacks against the president and his team incited violent threats against us. I made this point to CNN's Jim Acosta during an intense exchange we had in the White House press briefing room:

> The media has attacked me personally on a number of
> occasions, including your own network; said I should be
> harassed as a life sentence; that I should be choked. . . .
> When I was hosted by the Correspondents' Association,
> of which almost all of you are members, you brought a

comedian up to attack my appearance and called me a
traitor to my own gender. . . . In fact . . . as far as I know,
I'm the first press secretary in the history of the United
States that's required Secret Service protection. . . . The
media continues to ratchet up the verbal assault against
the president and everyone in this administration, and
certainly we have a role to play, but the media has a role
to play for the discourse in this country as well.

After my briefing, Rush Limbaugh weighed in on his radio show:
"Amen! This woman is great. She is fearless!" Rush was a legend
and a hero in the conservative movement, and his support meant
a lot to me. I watched Hannity with the president on Air Force
One later that evening and he pointed at me and said, "You were
amazing today. You were so tough that I'll have to be even harder
on them at my rally tonight . . . it wouldn't be right to let you be
tougher!" He laughed and then said to the group, "My Sarah—
she is beautiful. I love her, the first lady loves her." The staff in the
room on Air Force One applauded.

On my first day with Secret Service detail I was escorted in a
black SUV to the White House. I had grown up in the Governor's
Mansion with my dad's Arkansas State Police security detail and
after a year and a half at the White House I had spent a lot of time
around the men and women of the Secret Service, but this was
something I hadn't really anticipated when I took a job in the
Trump White House. There were roughly a dozen agents who were
part of the detail assigned to me. They rotated time with me, but
someone was with me twenty-four hours a day and someone at my
house twenty-four hours a day as well. It took some getting used to
but I was thankful for their protection. The team assigned to me
could not have been nicer or more gracious. I am pretty sure when
they signed up to be part of the USSS that protecting the press

secretary was not high on their wish list of assignments. My kids thought it was the greatest thing in the world to ride around with the agents and ask them thousands of questions—I often teased them that we were planning a cross-country family road trip. The agents laughed but I am pretty sure they were requesting transfers on the off chance it might happen! I came to be friends with the team that was with me. I joked with them about their inability to find decent music on the radio, and my kids and I baked them cookies as they sat guard outside our home. We tried to make them feel welcome and let them know how much we appreciated their service. Their presence made us feel safe and because they were there we started getting out again. Our family will be forever grateful for the kindness and the protection the agents showed us.

It was not a good feeling to be kicked out of a restaurant in front of my family or to need Secret Service protection because of violent threats made against me, but I was determined not to be angry or bitter about it. One of the most important things about being a Christian is recognizing that God loves us no matter what. Nothing we do can ever change the fact that God loves us unconditionally. Only by recognizing this beautiful truth about God's love for us—to the point of His Son's death on the cross—can we find it within ourselves to love others unconditionally as well. America is divided, and we must look to God and start loving and forgiving each other—*particularly those who don't deserve it*. None of us deserve God's love either but He loves us anyway. I wouldn't have made it long as White House press secretary if I carried the burden of anger and hate in my heart toward those who attacked and persecuted me. My faith liberated me to face the liberal mob with a spirit of love and forgiveness and stay focused on doing my job.

On that first day with Secret Service protection, the agents escorted me to the entrance to the West Wing and I walked to my office. Just when I thought my life couldn't get any crazier, Supreme

Court Justice Anthony Kennedy announced his retirement, setting up one of the administration's biggest fights yet for the future of the Supreme Court.

I sat in the Oval Office as the president called Senate Majority Leader Mitch McConnell. The president told McConnell he was committed to picking a nominee from the list of conservative judges he promised to choose from during the campaign. McConnell said he favored Judge Amul Thapar from his home state of Kentucky, who served on the US Court of Appeals for the Sixth Circuit, but was comfortable with anyone on the president's list.

The next day the president met with Senators Chuck Grassley, Susan Collins, Lisa Murkowski, Joe Manchin, Joe Donnelly, and Heidi Heitkamp to discuss the Supreme Court vacancy, and internally the president and our team agreed on a plan to strike quickly. The president would interview the candidates on his short list over the weekend, decide on the nominee, and announce his pick on the Monday after the Fourth of July weekend. I announced the SCOTUS nomination team, led by White House Counsel Don McGahn; Raj Shah, my principal deputy who was taking a leave from the press team; and Justin Clarke, who had been running intergovernmental affairs and then the office of public liaison. I briefed that afternoon and said the president was considering candidates to fill the vacancy "who have the right intellect, the right temperament, and will uphold the Constitution." The president met with each of the final SCOTUS candidates, including Judge Brett Kavanaugh, Judge Amy Coney Barrett, and Sixth Circuit US Court of Appeals Judge Raymond Kethledge. He was definitely leaning toward Kavanaugh throughout the process, but also liked Judge Barrett on the US Court of Appeals for the Seventh Circuit. The president asked me several times who I liked. I said I liked all three but was partial to Barrett, the young, conservative mother of seven, but added that Kavanaugh might be easier to confirm. I guess you could say I misread that one—but there's no telling what crazy lies Democrats would have manufactured about her!

On Monday, President Trump nominated Brett Kavanaugh to the Supreme Court. He told me his decision, a closely guarded secret, earlier that day ahead of the 9:00 p.m. prime-time announcement. I spent the afternoon working with the nomination team getting prepared with a bio, talking points, and surrogates. I spent an hour on the phone calling through all of the major networks to get them ready to take the announcement live from the White House. As the clock struck 9:00 p.m., I turned to the president, gave him the cue, and said, "It's time," and he walked out and introduced Brett, his wife, and daughters to the nation. The country watched as Brett talked about his family and being his daughter's basketball coach. Because Kavanaugh had worked in a senior position in the Bush administration there were a number of former Bush staffers in the crowd, something you didn't see all that often in the Trump White House. It was standing room only and there was tremendous excitement over the nomination. Brett had impeccable legal credentials, had been vetted several times, was a great husband and father, and a man his friends and coworkers seemed to genuinely like and respect. Most conservatives believed Kavanaugh was a slam dunk.

But from day one, Democrats and the liberal mob were hell-bent on defeating Kavanaugh's nomination at all costs. Sure enough, out of nowhere, the first Kavanaugh accuser, Christine Blasey Ford, went public. To prepare for the Senate confirmation hearings, members of the White House communications and counsel's staff murderboarded Kavanaugh in the Eisenhower Executive Office Building. I played the role of Senator Dianne Feinstein, the top Democrat on the Senate Judiciary Committee, and along with others fired tough questions at Kavanaugh:

"Did you ever attend a party with the accuser?"

"Did you ever black out drinking in high school?"

During the first round of questions Kavanaugh was nervous and sounded too scripted. Our team of questioners was relentless. Deputy Chief of Staff for Communications Bill Shine made him crack first and you saw a glint of real anger in his response. Bill asked when he had lost his virginity and when he first had sex with his wife. It was uncomfortable for everyone in the room, but we knew there was no subject matter too degrading or too humiliating for the Democrats to ask him about. Here was someone who had been praised as a man of high integrity and character, and here we were, many of us only having met him once or twice for a few minutes, interrogating him about the most intimate details of his personal life. We had to do it. It was the only way to get him prepared for the hearings. To throw him off and make him angry, I interrupted his response about the impact of these accusations on his family and said, "With all due respect, Judge, you think you're the victim here? An innocent woman said you sexually assaulted her. Explain to me why you're the victim?" Kavanaugh got angry, teared up, and said, "You ask my daughters about that." By the last half of the prep I felt a little better but still worried how it would all play out and how Brett would withstand the merciless attacks from the Senate Democrats.

I did *Good Morning America* and *Fox & Friends* to make the case for Kavanaugh. Another woman, represented by attorney and soon-to-be-disgraced-felon Michael Avenatti, accused Kavanaugh of drugging and gang-raping her and other women in high school. It was preposterous—a new, desperate low from the liberal mob. Later in the day the gang-rape accuser's ex-boyfriend—a registered Democrat—came forward to say he had to file a restraining order against her. He told Politico: "Right after I broke up with her, she was threatening my family, threatening my wife, and threatening to do harm to my baby at that time. . . . I know a lot about her. . . . She's not credible at all."

I traveled with the president to the UN General Assembly meeting in New York, and in between bilateral meetings with foreign leaders, we waited in a holding room. I talked to Raj, who had sat in for Kavanaugh's first interview with Martha MacCallum of Fox News. The interview had been pretaped, and included Brett's wife, Ashley, as well. Raj walked me through the highlights of the interview to pass along to the president, including a few details that were a bit uncomfortable for me to share with him, like when Kavanaugh had sex for the first time. The president told me to get Kavanaugh on the phone, and said to him, "Brett, I heard the interview went well. Hang in there. I am with you all the way. Keep fighting."

I did *The Today Show* from New York, and when pushed about how I felt personally about the accusations against Kavanaugh as a woman and as a mom, I said, "I'm often asked about being a parent. 'Sarah, you have a daughter.' I also have two sons, and I wouldn't want a false accusation to be what determines the rest of their life."

I flew back on Air Force One to Washington, watching Dr. Ford testify before the Senate with the president, and then joined the president on Marine One to fly to the White House. Kavanaugh categorically denied the allegations and in a powerful moment, he shared that his young daughter suggested their family pray for Dr. Ford. "That's a lot of wisdom from a ten-year-old," Kavanaugh said, on the verge of tears.

After Kavanaugh's opening statement I called the president and said, "Kavanaugh just saved himself."

"Did you cry?" the president asked.

"Yes."

"I knew it," the president said. "You're softer than people think." He laughed.

"Did you cry?" I asked him.

"You know I'm not a crier," he said. "But I'm not going to answer that."

We could sense the tide turning for Kavanaugh, and later in the hearing Senator Lindsey Graham eviscerated the Senate Democrats.

"What you want to do is destroy this guy's life, hold this seat open and hope you win in 2020. . . . When you see Sotomayor and Kagan, tell them that Lindsey said hello because I voted for them. I would never do to them what you've done to this guy. This is the most unethical sham since I've been in politics. And if you really wanted to know the truth, you sure as hell wouldn't have done what you've done to this guy!

"Boy, you all want power. God, I hope you never get it. I hope the American people can see through this sham. That you knew about it and you held it. You had no intention of protecting Dr. Ford; none.

"She's as much of a victim as you are. God, I hate to say it because these have been my friends. But let me tell you, when it comes to this, you're looking for a fair process? You came to the wrong town at the wrong time, my friend.

"Would you say you've been through hell?" Graham asked.

"I've been through hell and then some," Kavanaugh said.

"The one thing I can tell you you should be proud of—Ashley, you should be proud of this—that you raised a daughter who had the good character to pray for Dr. Ford," Graham said.

"To my Republican colleagues, if you vote no, you're legitimizing the most despicable thing I have seen in my time in politics. . . .

"I hope you're on the Supreme Court, that's exactly where you should be."

It was a standout assertion by Graham and one of the biggest moments of the hearing. Graham, who had not always been popular among conservatives or Trump voters, was now celebrated as a hero.

After the hearing, I drafted a statement with the team for the president, and he made a few revisions, then fired it off: "Judge Kavanaugh showed America exactly why I nominated him. His testimony was powerful, honest, and riveting. Democrats' search-and-destroy strategy is disgraceful and this process has been a total sham and effort to delay, obstruct, and resist. The Senate must vote!"

I went on *Fox News Sunday* to make the case for Kavanaugh and did a press briefing from the White House:

"On the night President Trump nominated Judge Brett Kavanaugh, Senator Schumer declared the Democrats would oppose this nomination with everything they had. Before a single document was produced, a single meeting with the senator, or a hearing was ever scheduled, Chuck Schumer and the Senate Democrats telegraphed a strategy to throw the kitchen sink at the Judge with no regard for the process, decency, or standards. They're not opposed to Judge Kavanaugh's judicial views; they're literally trying to undercut the voice of the American people when they elected Donald Trump.

They have questioned his legitimacy, and casually tossed around vicious accusations of perjury—all false and baseless. But now they've sunk lower, as they sprang these 11th-hour accusations and a full-scale assault on Judge Kavanaugh's integrity.

This is a coordinated smear campaign. No evidence, no independent corroboration, just smears. Here are just a few of the examples:

Chuck Schumer said, and I quote, "There's no presumption of innocence or guilt." Chris Coons, who sits on the committee, said

Kavanaugh, and I quote, "now bears the burden of disproving these allegations, rather than Dr. Ford and Ms. Ramirez." Mazie Hirono, who also sits on the Committee, said that Judge Kavanaugh does not deserve the presumption of innocence because of his judicial views.

One thing is clear: Democrats want to block Kavanaugh and hold the seat open until the 2020 election. This is about politics and this is about power—pure and simple. And they've destroyed Judge Kavanaugh's reputation, undermined Dr. Ford's privacy, and tried to upend our traditions of innocence until proven guilty in the process. It's a complete and total disgrace.

We will receive and submit the FBI's supplemental background investigation on his nomination to the Senate. As Leader McConnell said, Judge Kavanaugh deserves a prompt vote and we expect him to get one.

After my briefing, I returned to my office to find Newt Gingrich, Sean Hannity, Bill Shine, Jared Kushner, Director of Presidential Personnel Johnny DeStefano, and Raj Shah all there waiting for me. They applauded as I walked in.

On *Morning Joe,* Mika Brzezinski said I was "rotten to the core" for defending Kavanaugh. White House Communications Director Bill Shine, furious at the nastiness from some of the MSNBC anchors toward women in the Trump administration, called Phil Griffin, president of MSNBC. Shine told Griffin that the White House wasn't going to put anyone from the administration on MSNBC or NBC until further notice, saying, "You're not going to continue harassing women in the White House this way."

"Sarah hit a nerve over here," said Griffin.

"You hit a f—— nerve over here!" Shine yelled and hung up the phone.

I did Fox News's *America's Newsroom* and said, "We stand 100 percent with Brett Kavanaugh. . . . It's time for the Senate to vote."

In the Oval after that appearance, the president told Kelly it was time to give me a raise. Kelly laughed and reminded him that as "assistants to the president" we'd already hit our pay ceiling as senior White House officials.

The next day the president traveled to Mississippi to do a rally for Cindy Hyde-Smith, who was running in a special election for the US Senate. Up until this point the president and Republican leaders had been fairly diplomatic in their statements about the Kavanaugh accusers and the process. But the president had had enough. At his rally the president questioned the credibility of the Ford testimony. He pointed out all the questions she couldn't answer and that there was no one to corroborate her story. The crowd roared with approval. They'd had enough, too. It was a galvanizing moment. Republicans—including many Bush administration officials and former Never Trumpers—rallied behind Kavanaugh and were proud of the president for loyally sticking with him.

Ahead of the vote, Senator McConnell took to the Senate floor and said:

> Nobody is supposed to be guilty until proven innocent in the United States of America. . . . Who among us would not have been outraged by having a lifetime record dragged through the mud with accusations that could not be proven. . . .
>
> So, let's reclaim this moment for what it should be—a chance to elevate a stunningly talented and impressive jurist to an important office for which he is so well-qualified. . . . We have a chance to do good here and to underscore the basic tenent of fairness in our country. So I filed cloture on the nomination yesterday evening. And I will be proud to vote to advance this nomination tomorrow.

Not long after, Senator Susan Collins (R-ME) announced she would be voting to confirm Kavanaugh and Senator Joe Manchin (D-WV) said he'd be doing the same, guaranteeing a majority for confirmation. On October 6, 2018, the Senate voted 50–48 to confirm Justice Kavanaugh to the Supreme Court, cementing a tremendous legacy for the president and a better future for America.

I congratulated Justice Kavanaugh in the East Wing as we did the walkthrough before the official White House reception, but during our conversation I was interrupted by Raj, who told me the president needed to see me in the residence. I walked upstairs and spent the afternoon working with the president on his speech. We were in the Treaty Room. It was dimly lit and had a massive Victorian table serving as the desk, which had previously been used as a cabinet meeting table under President Ulysses S. Grant. Many historic moments, including President William McKinley signing the peace treaty with Spain ending the Spanish–American War, had occurred in the Treaty Room. President Lincoln used the room as a pass-through to get from the Yellow Oval to the Lincoln Bedroom without being seen by anyone, and Eleanor Roosevelt held press conferences for female reporters there. A few aides recommended toning down the rhetoric and said the president should not issue an apology to Justice Kavanaugh for the way he was treated by the Democrats and many liberals in the media, but I agreed with the president and said to leave it in. The president made a joke, and I laughed and hit him with a handful of papers on the arm. Bill Shine said, "You just hit the president . . . you're lucky Secret Service didn't see that." As we finished up, Brett and his family walked into the room. They took photos with the president and visited about the attacks they'd endured.

The president had decided to posthumously award Justice Antonin Scalia with the Medal of Freedom. He wanted to tell his widow, Maureen, his plan that evening. As we waited in the Blue Room of the East Wing, he asked me to walk with him to let her know. The two of us walked over to her and the president said, "I have some news for you." President Trump told her that Justice Scalia, her late husband, would receive the Medal of Freedom. Maureen teared up as I held her hand.

Back in the room before the reception, I visited with attendees as we waited. I talked to Justice Neil Gorsuch and he joked, "Why didn't I get a band at my reception?" I said, "With all due respect, sir, we couldn't find the light switch in the White House bathroom at that point."

Justice Clarence Thomas told me, "You're my favorite, you never back down, but next time you go to The Red Hen let me come with you and I'll set them straight."

Bryan joined me at the reception. In the East Room, the president took the stage at 7:03 p.m. EDT:

> Members of Congress, members of the cabinet, honored guests, and fellow Americans: It is my privilege to address you tonight from the East Room of the White House.
>
> We are gathered together this evening for a truly momentous occasion. I have long been told that the most important decision a president can make is the appointment of a Supreme Court Justice. Well, in just a few moments, we will proudly swear in the newest member of the United States Supreme Court: Justice Brett Kavanaugh. . . .
>
> On behalf of our nation, I want to apologize to Brett and the entire Kavanaugh family for the terrible pain and suffering you have been forced to endure.
>
> Those who step forward to serve our country de-

serve a fair and dignified evaluation, not a campaign
of political and personal destruction based on lies and
deception. What happened to the Kavanaugh family
violates every notion of fairness, decency, and due
process.

In our country, a man or woman must always be presumed innocent unless and until proven guilty. And with
that, I must state that you, sir, under historic scrutiny,
were proven innocent.

Margaret and Liza, your father is a great man. He is
a man of decency, character, kindness, and courage who
has devoted his life to serving his fellow citizens. And
now, from the bench of our nation's highest court, your
father will defend the eternal rights and freedoms of all
Americans.

In the battle for the Supreme Court, the liberal mob had been
defeated. We had prevailed. The mood at the White House was
euphoric. That night our team went to the Trump International
Hotel and celebrated one of the most consequential victories of
the Trump presidency—a more conservative Supreme Court—a
defining legacy that would endure long after our departure from
the White House.

8

Witch Hunt

In the midst of the Kavanaugh confirmation fight, Special Counsel Robert Mueller's team requested to interview me as part of
their investigation into Russian meddling during the 2016 election.

The Mueller investigation represented a dangerous threat to
the Trump presidency and reelection. Mueller had nearly un-
limited power and resources to come after the president and his
team, as well as loyal allies in the media. But a year into his investigation, Mueller had still not turned up any evidence whatsoever of
collusion between the Trump campaign and Russia.

Early in the investigation, the Democrats and the media were
convinced they'd found their smoking gun: a meeting between
Donald Trump Jr. and a Russian woman during the campaign.
Much like his dad, Don Jr. doesn't take hits lying down. He fights
back and does so aggressively. When others would have cowered,
he leaned in. For a time Don Jr. became the face of the fight against

Mueller's team. His hard-charging personality and fearless pushback against his critics made him extremely popular with the president's base and a star in the Republican Party.

While Don Jr. was under attack, I did a press briefing and defended him on behalf of the administration:

> The only thing I see misleading is a year's worth of stories that have been fueling a false narrative about Russia collusion. . . . You guys are focused on a meeting with Don Jr. of no consequence. . . . Bill Clinton was paid half a million dollars to give a speech to a Russian bank, and was personally thanked by Putin for it. Hillary Clinton allowed one-fifth of America's uranium reserve to be sold to a Russian firm whose investors were Clinton Foundation donors, and the Clinton campaign chairman's brother lobbied against sanctions on Russia's largest bank and failed to report it.

The hypocrisy from Democrats and their liberal media allies was shameless. If anyone should have been investigated for ties too close to Russia, it was the Clintons, not President Trump or any member of his family.

Evidence soon emerged that Hillary Clinton's campaign and the DNC paid for the fake Russia dossier used by the Obama administration to illegally spy on a Trump campaign official and then by FBI director Comey to launch the Russia witch hunt against President Trump. I briefed, and slammed the Hillary–DNC–Russia effort to spread disinformation about the president: "We're seeing now that if there was any collusion with Russia it was between the DNC and the Clintons and certainly not our campaign."

During this time, I had been experiencing a lot of trouble with my eyes, which were irritated and watering all the time. The White

House medical team, which is second to none, had done an initial exam one day in the doctor's office in the Eisenhower Executive Office Building next to the West Wing. They wanted to do more substantial tests and a full medical exam and scheduled a day for me to go to Walter Reed. The doctors wanted to rule out some pretty serious issues including a tumor putting pressure on the nerves behind my eyes or even cancer. To say I was stressed was an understatement. I didn't want to make a big deal about it and told only a few people, including Chief of Staff John Kelly, who even in his gruff way was very comforting. Ivanka also came by to see how I was and left an encouraging note on my desk. Bryan went with me to Walter Reed and we spent the entire day getting tests done—an MRI of my brain, blood tests, and dozens of other checks. It was the most comprehensive medical exam I'd ever had. Bryan sat for hours anxiously waiting but never letting on and encouraging me in between each test they ran. By the end of the day they had ruled out some things but were concerned about several large lumps on my thyroid. The doctors did a biopsy on my neck to test for cancer, but said they wouldn't have results for a few days. The biopsy left a huge bruise on my neck, but Katie Price, who did my hair and makeup at the White House before my briefings and interviews, was masterful in concealing it so I didn't have to share my fear that I might have cancer with the world.

After this intense and nerve-racking day at Walter Reed, Bryan and I left the hospital and went out for an early dinner at Salt and Pepper in the Palisades neighborhood of Northwest DC to decompress before returning home to our kids. Shortly after we sat down I looked up to see Robert Mueller and his wife walk in the front door. A soccer team who had just finished their game and the four of us were the only people dining in the restaurant. As if the day hadn't been stressful enough—we were now stuck at a table next to the man in charge of the investigation to take down the president!

After three days of nervous anticipation, I received a call from the White House doctor letting me know I had gotten the all clear on thyroid cancer. The medical team determined there was some nerve damage primarily behind my right eye, and stress and bright lights had made it worse. Not the best news when intense stress and bright lights were a daily part of my job—but I was immensely relieved to be cancer free.

The Mueller investigation continued to roil Washington. It was a major distraction from the president's agenda and deterred many good people from joining the administration. In one of Mueller's first big moves, he indicted Russian nationals for meddling in the 2016 election. Deputy Attorney General Rod Rosenstein—who was responsible for overseeing the investigation after Attorney General Jeff Sessions voluntarily recused himself under pressure from the media—addressed reporters and said the indictment contained no allegation that any American was a knowing participant in Russia's interference or that it altered the outcome of the election. Still, the witch hunt continued.

Meanwhile, unlike the Obama administration, the Trump administration had actually taken a hard line against Russia, which the media hardly ever reported because it didn't fit their Trump-Russia collusion narrative. Since taking office President Trump had imposed crippling sanctions on Russia; closed Russian diplomatic properties in the United States and expelled Russian spies pretending to be diplomats; approved the sale of lethal arms to Ukraine to defend against Russian aggression; persuaded NATO allies to increase their military spending to deter Russia; isolated and sanctioned two of Russia's worst proxies: Iran and Venezuela; made America the number one producer of oil and gas, lowering the cost of energy and hurting the Russian economy; and rebuilt our military so that neither Russia nor any other foreign adversary could challenge the United States.

Furthermore, as tensions escalated between the United States and Russia over human rights abuses in the Syrian civil war, President Trump actually enforced President Obama's "red line." In the White House Situation Room, military options to respond to a Syrian chemical weapons attack on innocent civilians were presented to the president. In the room with the president were Vice President Mike Pence, Secretary of Defense Jim Mattis, Chief of Staff John Kelly, Chairman of the Joint Chiefs General Joe Dunford, me, and a few others. At one point the president turned to me and asked for my thoughts. After I weighed in, he said "Huh. I figured you would have been more ruthless."

President Trump did what Obama refused to do and on April 14, 2018, launched airstrikes against Syrian military targets, demonstrating once again the president's willingness to stand up to Putin and his cronies like Syrian president Bashar al-Assad.

None of this mattered to the Trump haters who had invested everything in the Trump-Russia collusion hoax. Former FBI director James Comey was paid millions to write a book. When he launched his book tour, I held a press briefing to respond on behalf of the administration.

A reporter asked: "The president came out swinging today, calling James Comey a 'liar,' a 'leaker,' a 'slimeball.' Is he worried about what he's saying?"

"Not at all. The American people see right through the blatant lies of a self-admitted leaker," I said. "This is nothing more than a poorly executed PR stunt by Comey to desperately rehabilitate his tattered reputation and enrich his own bank account by peddling a book that belongs on the bargain bin of the fiction section.

"Instead of being remembered as a dedicated servant in the pursuit of justice like so many of his other colleagues at the FBI, Comey will be forever known as a disgraced partisan hack that broke his sacred trust with the President of the United States, the dedicated agents of the FBI, and the American people he vowed to faithfully serve. One of the president's greatest achievements will go down as firing Director James Comey." I called on the next reporter.

"Thanks, Sarah. The Justice Department Inspector General came out with his long-awaited report this afternoon on former FBI deputy director Andrew McCabe, saying that he improperly leaked information about the Clinton Foundation investigation to a reporter, and then lied to James Comey about it and, under oath, to two FBI investigators. Do you have a reaction to that? And does that, in your mind, validate the decision to fire McCabe?"

"I haven't seen the full report, but sounds like two peas in a pod with McCabe and Comey. McCabe was fired in disgrace for misconduct and lying about it. . . ."

"Thank you, Sarah. You said that James Comey was a liar, that he's a leaker, that he made false representations or claims. Other than what the president tweeted this morning about lying under oath to Senator Grassley, what exactly has he said that's false or a lie?"

"Comey claimed reopening the Clinton investigation when he did was based on merit. Now he says it was based because of poll numbers.

"Comey claimed the president told him to stop investigating Flynn, after he previously testified that no one told him to stop investigations.

"He also—even the media has reported that officials have determined that Comey leaked four memos—at least four that we know about—with classified information. I think it's very clear that Comey has a credibility problem."

The other thing is clear, this is one of the few issues in Washington that both Democrats and Republicans agree on. He's been criticized by the legal community for leaking sensitive information, and organizations promoting good government found Comey's leaking grounds for firing.

Multiple Democrats, including some of the biggest leaders in the Democratic Party, have also attacked Comey. Minority Leader Pelosi said Comey was "maybe not in the right job." Senator Schumer said he was "appalled by what Comey did" and "did not have confidence in him any longer." Senator Bernie Sanders said Comey "acted in an outrageous way." Clinton's running mate, Senator Kaine, said Comey is "responsible for the lowest moment in the history of the FBI." Even Congresswoman Maxine Waters said Comey has "no credibility." The FBI should be independent and not led by a political hack. Comey's higher loyalty is pretty clear that it's only to himself. If you can get this group of people and others like Mark Meadows and a number of others to agree on something, I think that you'd have to be right.

"Sarah, what about the dossier, though? Sarah, what about the dossier?"

"The dossier is false opposition research that was funded by the Clinton campaign to attack the president. It was used illegally to justify spying on Americans. And I think that's quite the problem."

"Sarah, what about the content of the president's attacks on Jim Comey, your attacks on Jim Comey? Isn't all of that a bit unbecoming of the presidency of this White House to go after him in such a personal way like that?"

"I think it's unbecoming for the person that is supposed to be the top law enforcement official in the United States, the person that is supposed to protect the people of this country, to lie and leak classified information, certainly to falsify documents . . . if anybody has created this problem, it's Jim Comey and he should be the one held responsible."

After my briefing the president called me into the Oval. He applauded as I walked in, telling the other aides in the room to do the same. He said, "I loved it. You're a f—— killer!" In the ultimate sign of his approval, the president told the valet to bring me a Coke. "When you're on fire like today it's a beautiful thing," he said. Johnny DeStefano, the head of presidential personnel, joked "But, Mr. President, she did say 'thanks, guys' to close it out again." At a briefing a few weeks before, the president had called me into the dining area off the Oval, where he was watching the Masters and going through personnel appointments with Johnny. There was a small pile of Starbursts wrappers on the table and he said, "Great job. You can have all the pink and reds you want, but I think you should quit ending the briefing by saying 'Thanks, guys.' I don't like the word 'guys.' It may even be offensive to some women. Plus some days after they treat you so badly it's way too friendly." Without saying anything to Johnny, the president turned on the TV, played back my recorded briefing using his TIVO, and said, "S—— . . . you're right. Sarah, it was an 11 but now it's only an 8.5," and we all shared a laugh at the president's impossible-to-meet expectations.

During the summer of 2018, I flew with President Trump as a member of the US delegation to Helsinki to meet with Russian president Vladimir Putin. President Trump and President Putin had visited in person briefly a few times the year before—in Vietnam during the president's first trip to Asia, and in Germany for the G20—but this was their first summit. July in Finland was hot, and the sun set at midnight. There was no air-conditioning in our hotel and we sweated as we prepared for the two world leaders to meet face to face.

After their one-on-one meeting, President Trump and President Putin held a joint news conference, during which the president did not publicly challenge President Putin's denial of interfering in the 2016 election. President Trump was blasted by the media and critics on the left and right. It was a missed opportunity to send an unmistakably clear message to Russia and other foreign adversaries not to interfere in our elections, but in the president's view, he had already taken a much harder line against Russia than President Obama, and much like with President Xi in China, President Trump believed it was more productive to be diplomatic than confrontational in face-to-face meetings with foreign leaders.

In many instances President Trump and leaders in the administration had acknowledged and condemned Russian election interference but none of that mattered to liberals. After all, in their minds, President Trump was a "Russian agent" and "traitor to his country," despite no evidence to support these outrageous claims and plenty of evidence to the contrary. Senior Trump administration officials spent an inordinate amount of time and energy working to counter any threat of foreign interference in the 2018 election. Before a White House press briefing with FBI director Christopher Wray, Director of National Intelligence Dan Coats, Secretary of Homeland Security Kirstjen Nielsen, and National Security Advisor John Bolton on the threat posed by Russia in the upcoming election, I ran the prep and murder-boarded all of the nation's senior law enforcement and intelligence officials on questions they'd likely be asked at the briefing. Most of them didn't seem thrilled that I was asking them such pointed questions in an aggressive manner, but I reminded them not to take it personally, that I was asking as if I was a reporter, not a colleague. Unlike the Obama administration, the Trump administration took a serious approach to election security. President Trump, of course, got no credit when the 2018 midterm election concluded without any significant foreign interference—only the blame for President Obama's incompetent mismanagement of the Russian threat during the 2016 election.

As the Mueller investigation was nearing an end, Emmet Flood, the attorney in the White House handling the Russia investigation, came by my office and told me he needed to see me. Emmet was a seasoned pro with experience handling high-stakes investigations in the Clinton and Bush administrations. He had a stoic face but an incredibly funny, dry sense of humor. Emmet and I had grown close working together over the last few months. I trusted him more than anyone else in the building to navigate the Mueller storm threatening us all. Given that I was constantly answering questions about the Mueller investigation and usually the first to know about breaking news surrounding it, we spent a good amount of time working together and briefing the president on the ongoing witch hunt. He regularly tried to water down my fiery statements while I reminded him we had to punch them up or they would never be approved by our boss. Although he was a good friend, I usually wasn't thrilled when he wanted to see me because I knew it wouldn't be good news. As he entered my office he had a look on his face that I knew meant something was up and he wasn't looking forward to our conversation.

He sat me down and told me that Mueller's team wanted to interview me. He said I wasn't required to do it and the decision to do so was mine. The only people in the building who knew about Mueller's request were him and the president. I asked Emmet what the president thought I should do and he said the president wanted me to do it so long as I was comfortable with it. I asked Emmet for his recommendation and he said he thought I should do it as well. Their scope was narrow. They wanted to talk to me about four specific things and they wouldn't be allowed to go into anything outside of those four areas. I told him I wanted to think about it and talk to my husband and the president. He agreed that was a good idea.

I had heard horror stories of innocent people who had done nothing but work for the president and serve their country spending themselves into financial ruin on attorney's fees. I knew we couldn't take that on. We had three kids and were paying a lot on rent and childcare to live in one of America's most expensive cities. A $100,000 legal bill would have been devastating to our family, but I also wanted to do my part, get the truth out, and defend the president. I didn't want to worry Bryan either. I had been assigned Secret Service because of a specific, credible threat to my safety and the last thing we needed was the additional stress of a costly legal fight and to be thrust deeper into this frivolous investigation and become an even bigger target for the media and liberal mob.

Emmet and I went to the back dining room off the Oval and he, the president, and I talked about what I should do. The president made clear it was my decision to make. He didn't pressure me. I told him I was inclined to do it. He said make sure you have a good lawyer and assured me I wouldn't be on the hook for legal expenses. Bryan agreed that it made more sense to be fully transparent than to avoid it and create the perception that I had something to hide. Emmet connected me with a prominent, well-respected Washington attorney named Bill Burck, who represented a few other senior administration officials and knew the Mueller investigation inside and out.

I called Bill but he was out of the country and told me he'd call me back. I anxiously waited two days for him to get back to me and let me know the game plan. He said there were four areas to cover and we would need to do prep sessions to go over any material related to the topics. I had already turned over two notebooks that the investigators were going through. Bill told me they would build a briefing binder for me that included all the emails, statements, and notes on the four topic areas and drop it off at my house. A few days later a courier brought a two-inch-thick, three-ring, binder with sixty-seven tabs to my house, full of hundreds of pages to review. It was the size of a phone book. I tried to familiarize myself with the binder ahead of my in-person session but it was a lot of information to quickly digest.

I made plans with Bill to go to his home and meet with his team on a Sunday afternoon so no one would see me coming and going from his office. I went to church with my family that morning and by late afternoon my binder and I were sitting in his living room at his home in Northwest Washington, DC. We spent hours going over questions and asking why I had made a particular statement; if someone had told me to say it and why; and whether I discussed a particular answer with the president directly. It was exhausting and frustrating trying to recall details of conversations that had taken place months ago that I'd considered insignificant at the time. Some of the conversations I just couldn't remember at all and others I knew exactly how, when, and why I had said what I did. We covered everything we anticipated would come up and Bill and his team felt good about it. He assured me that I was not a subject of the investigation—nor was I a target—I was simply a source on events I had been involved in and I had nothing to worry about.

The morning of my interview I came into the office like normal and went to my morning meetings. I told my assistant and others I was going to be out of pocket most of the day. I loaded into the Secret Service's black SUV and we picked up Bill and his team on the back corner outside their office. We drove to a nondescript gray concrete government building like you'll find on nearly any block in our nation's capital. We went in through the back loading-dock entrance and rode an elevator to the floor where we'd spend the next several hours. We stepped off the elevator and walked down an empty hallway flooded with fluorescent lights to the interview room. The Secret Service agents with me took a seat in a drab lounge area just down the hall where they waited. The interview room was like a psych ward where patients aren't allowed to have sharp objects or contact with the outside world. It had neutral white walls, a couple of tables, and government-issued chairs. There was nothing hanging on the walls and I hadn't seen a ray of natural light since we entered the building. It was an unsettling place. We waited. Eventually Mueller's team walked in and instructed me where to sit. Just before we got started Robert Mueller himself dropped by to say hello and thanked me for interviewing with them. I'd seen hundreds of clips of him on TV and spoken his name thousands of times—and had that one awkward public encounter with him at Salt and Pepper restaurant in the Palisades—but this was the first time we had ever spoken to one another. He was smaller than I expected him to be, standing face-to-face with him. He was pleasant but wasn't sticking around. As he made clear to the world in his disastrous congressional hearing, Mueller was just the "Republican" figurehead of a partisan investigation actually run by a bunch of angry Democratic prosecutors out to destroy the president and everyone associated with him.

We took our seats and the interrogation began. Mueller's team had barely finished introducing themselves before they started firing off questions. They quickly got frustrated at anything I couldn't remember. It was evident the Democratic prosecutors had nothing but contempt for me and considered me no better than a common criminal from the moment they stepped in the room. Despite the fact I wasn't a target nor a subject of their investigation they were arrogant, condescending, and laced every question with doubt. They made me feel guilty despite the fact I had voluntarily come to help them with an investigation I knew was nothing more than political vengeance from Democrats who couldn't accept their defeat to President Trump.

One of the areas Mueller's team was most interested in was the firing of disgraced former FBI director Jim Comey, even though the president has the legal authority to hire or fire anyone he wants—for any reason. When I found out, how I found out, why I said what I said in the interview I did with Fox News's Tucker Carlson after Comey's firing. I remembered much of that night and told them all that I could. They asked questions about the famous statement from Don Jr. about his meeting with a Russian woman during the campaign. I was on Air Force One at the time, but wasn't in the room when the statement was drafted. Still, they wanted to know about my comments in my briefing about Don Jr.'s statement. They wanted to know why I said what I did, who told me to say it, when they told me to say it, and whether or not I knew it to be true. They asked a lot of questions about whether or not the president was serious about firing Mueller and my response to this question during a gaggle aboard Air Force One on June 13, 2017, when I stated that "while the president has the right to, he has no intention to do so." They asked me a hundred different ways if I had spoken to the president directly about this answer and at any other time after it. No matter the question, I gave as much information as possible and answered all of their questions patiently and honestly.

The area where they really drilled down and were relentless was about an answer I gave during a press briefing regarding what we had heard from current and former members of the FBI. I stated in my briefing that along with the president and leaders in Congress, members of the FBI had also lost confidence in Director Comey. I said, "I had heard from countless members of the FBI and they were grateful and thankful for the president's decision." We spent a large amount of our nearly six hours together going over that particular statement, which had nothing to do with their investigation into whether or not there had been collusion between the Trump campaign and the Russians to influence the 2016 election. Mueller's prosecutors hammered me over the word "countless," and I said my use of that particular word was a "slip of the tongue" made in the heat of a contentious briefing, but that I had in fact heard directly or indirectly from a number of current and former FBI agents who supported the president's decision to fire Comey. Later the Mueller team totally misrepresented my statement to them in their official report for no apparent reason other than to vilify me. It was clear the main reason they'd called me in to do an interview had nothing to do with their investigation and everything to do with falsely attacking me in their report as payback for vigorously defending the president and fighting back against their witch hunt.

It was late on a Wednesday evening when we got word that the Mueller team was about to issue their report to the Justice Department. I was already running late for dinner with my family and I texted my husband: "Don't kill me, still at the office . . . Mueller report coming." A few days later, Acting Chief of Staff Mick Mulvaney and Emmet called me from Air Force One as the president was walking across the South Lawn to board Marine One and told me to get on the helicopter now and join the president for his trip to Florida. I called Bryan as I was walking to Marine One and told him not only was I not coming home that night, I was on my way to Florida. Emmet told me Mueller had issued his report to DOJ, and at Mar-a-Lago, I worked with the president, Emmet, and White House Counsel Pat Cipollone to coordinate our response. Attorney General Bill Barr announced that he might issue a summary report by the weekend and we soon learned there would be no more indictments.

On Saturday the president golfed with Kid Rock at his club in Florida. In a great mood, he told me, "It's like Election Day all over again—the pundits on TV don't know what to say!"

I returned to Washington early ahead of the president for the release of Attorney General Barr's summary of the Mueller report. I went out for a quick ice-cream break with my husband and kids and then went to my office to coordinate the administration's response. At 3:27 p.m. I got a call from the president. He was on speaker with Pat and Emmet and Mick and we finalized our statement. In the first public comment from the White House, I said, "The Special Counsel did not find any collusion and did not find any obstruction. AG Barr and DAG Rosenstein further determined there was no obstruction. The findings of the Department of Justice are a total and complete exoneration of the President of the United States." I added: "A great day for America and for President Trump. After two years of wild anti-Trump hysteria, the president and his millions of supporters have been completely vindicated."

A few key decisions saved Trump's presidency from the Mueller threat: the president opting not to fire Mueller, but allowing him to complete his investigation with full cooperation from the White House and campaign staff and no White House interference; hiring Pat Cipollone and Emmet Flood, both of whom were brilliant lawyers who effectively defended the president and aggressively and successfully pushed back on the president doing an interview with Mueller; and replacing Attorney General Sessions with Attorney General Barr, who had the experience and credibility to wrap up the investigation and communicate a summary of the report to the American people.

Upon his arrival back at the White House on Marine One, the president said, "I just want to tell you that America is the greatest place on Earth. The greatest place on Earth. Thank you very much."

The president walked across the South Lawn and into the White House and told Scavino and me to join him in the private residence. We walked in to find the president's legal team there and the room erupted in high-fives, hugging, and celebration. Hope texted me to let me know she was crying tears of joy in Los Angeles that the nightmare was finally over, and I shared her message with the president. He smiled and said, "We've all been through a lot together, but I'm so happy, so proud of the job each of you have done."

For more than two years Democrats and their liberal media allies had slandered President Trump as a traitor to his country for conspiring with Russia. It was all total BS—a malicious lie given wall-to-wall media coverage for two straight years. This should never again happen to an American president. But in that moment in the president's residence of the White House we knew the witch hunt was over. Together we celebrated a triumphant victory over the forces who'd put us through hell for the sin of winning an election.

9

Working Mom

On the eve of the 2018 midterm elections, I traveled with President Trump to three rallies in Ohio, Missouri, and Indiana. To my surprise President Trump called me up onstage in Indiana and asked me to say a few words.

"A lot of people know me in my official capacity and it's one of the greatest honors of my life to serve in your administration and one of the most important jobs I'll ever have," I said. "But the greatest job I'll ever have and the most important title I'll ever have is that of a mom. And that's why I work for the president: because I care about my kids' future and our country's future." That might have sounded like a cliché but for me it was true. I loved my country and the opportunity to serve the president, but as a mom I hated the time I had to spend away from my kids at such a young age—time I could never get back. Other people could be the White

House press secretary. I was the only person who could be mom to my three kids.

Republicans lost the House in the midterm elections, but the president helped deliver a larger majority for Republicans in the Senate, including hard-fought wins against Democratic incumbents in Indiana, Missouri, North Dakota, and Florida. The president also helped Republicans win governorships in key 2020 battleground states like Florida, Georgia, and Ohio. However, losing the House to the Democrats, led by San Francisco liberal Nancy Pelosi, was a major setback, and it exposed Republicans' vulnerabilities in the suburbs, particularly among women.

While many liberal feminists in the media attacked my appearance, character—even my fitness to be a mother—President Trump empowered me not just as a woman but as a working mom. It's one of the things I appreciated most about the president, and I felt an obligation to share that with women across the country. When the president called me on weekends and evenings he frequently would wrap our calls by telling me to get back to taking care of my beautiful children, letting me know he understood I had other priorities and responsibilities. But most importantly, in the office he never treated me any different than any male employee. To me this was far more empowering than anything else he could have done. He included me in key high-level meetings—and not just to check the box and have a woman in the photo op. He frequently called on me to add my opinion to the discussion, which at times could be intimidating, like when he asked me to weigh in on a complex foreign policy issue in a meeting with a foreign leader or a life-or-death national security decision in the Situation Room.

He regularly sought out my advice, complimented me, reaffirmed me, and made me laugh, but he also yelled at me, cursed at me, and pushed me to do better. He never held back and I didn't want him to. I wanted him to treat me the same way he would Mike Pompeo, Jared Kushner, or Dan Scavino, and he did. So many times the idea of women's empowerment is that somehow we should be treated differently, but I just wanted to be treated the same way as my male colleagues. I wanted to earn my place, not have it handed to me because I'm a woman.

The president liked surrounding himself with strong women. He certainly didn't always take our advice but he heard us out. I never felt like I was anything less for being a woman during my time at the White House, but that doesn't mean it was easy. Like a lot of working moms, for me it was a daily battle to strike the right balance between work and family. Almost every working mom I knew struggled with finding that balance. You spent most days feeling like if you were doing your job well you were lacking as a parent and vice versa. When I was at work I'd feel guilty that I was not at every class party, performance, or field trip. During my time at the White House I missed nearly every school drop-off and pickup. That's two and a half years I didn't get to wave good-bye to my kids in the morning before school or give them a hug and a kiss when they came home. Not only did I feel like my kids weren't getting enough of me, I'd question what other moms must think. My kids definitely weren't the ones coming to school with a perfectly composed lunch of organic, homemade items in a bento box complete with a handwritten poem on their napkin. Most days we were lucky to find the time at all to pack a lunch and not forget the drink or snack.

Achieving work-life balance in a fast-paced work environment was daunting, and many days, impossible. If my kids were sick and we were up all night, I'd still have to be "on" at work. If I was dealing with a major story or had gone on a foreign trip with the president, I'd still have to be "on" when I eventually got home. I was constantly looking at my schedule figuring out how to make time for both. On Sundays I'd look at my calendar for the week ahead, and often felt like a failure as a mom before the week even started because I'd see the work obligations I had coming up and knew there'd be no quality time left over for my kids. Or I'd feel like a failure at work because I'd see all the stuff I had to be at for my kids and knew it wouldn't leave enough time for my job. For many working moms the high cost of childcare is a real challenge. At one point before I started at the White House our monthly childcare costs were more than the mortgage on our home. I had friends in the administration who felt like they earned just enough to pay for childcare. And if you could afford it, good luck finding someone who will care for your kids the way you would. It's one of the reasons I was so proud of the Trump administration for leading the fight to double the child tax credit and champion paid family leave. Four years ago Republicans were hardly talking about paid family leave at all, but thanks to the leadership of Ivanka Trump, also a working mom of three, there was now broad bipartisan support for it.

Being a working mom in the White House was tough, but it actually made me a lot better at my job. Some of the best training I got to be the White House press secretary was from being a mom. It taught me how to multitask and prioritize my time. It also taught me about the weight of my words and the importance of being intentional and focused. Most important, it taught me how to answer the same question over and over again and say no. In fact, dealing with some reporters in the briefing room was a lot like dealing with screaming toddlers. Unfortunately the press didn't think that analogy was as funny as I did!

A lesson I learned from my dad was that it's not just about the quantity of time you spend with your kids—it's the quality of time. Growing up in a political family where my dad's time was often not his own I experienced firsthand how much quality one-on-one time mattered. One of my fondest memories of my dad from growing up was our Wednesday morning breakfasts together. It was a set date. It didn't matter if it was a fancy restaurant or McDonald's, on Wednesday morning I felt like the only person in the world who mattered to him and that's what made it special.

I'll never forget my first Take Our Daughters and Sons to Work Day at the White House. I decided to bring my son Huck, who was three at the time. Huck was younger than most of the other kids coming, but it was a risk I was willing to take. How many more opportunities would I get to take one of my kids to work for a day at the White House? I couldn't pass it up. Bryan and I talked about it and he agreed to be on standby in case Huck got to be too much for me to handle.

For President Trump's first Take Our Daughters and Sons to Work Day we decided to not only invite the kids of White House staff, but also the kids of the White House press corps. The White House staff rolled out the red carpet for all the kids—giving them gift bags with hats, coloring books, Secret Service badges, and filling the day with once-in-a-lifetime experiences like seeing the president's limo, the Beast, baking cookies in the White House kitchen with the pastry chef, and closing the day out by meeting the president and vice president for a group picture in the Rose Garden. As White House staff and press kids gathered in the Rose Garden, I briefed the president in the Oval Office about the event. I reminded him that half of the kids' parents are reporters so he may want to be careful with what he said. He naturally ignored my advice! As we talked, the president noticed the rose bushes outside his window violently shaking. I turned and looked up to see a crop of blond hair pop up out of the bushes. "There's a boy in the bushes!" the president exclaimed. The boy with blond hair launched himself out of the bushes and ran to the window, pressing his face up against the glass of the Oval Office. Mortified, I responded, "Yes, sir, that's my son Huck." The president looked at me, shook his head, and said, "Well, Sarah, at least he's handsome."

Moments later, the president walked out of the Oval Office onto the iconic Rose Garden colonnade to say hi and take pictures with the kids and I followed behind him. Out of the corner of my eye, in front of dozens of cameras, I saw Huck running at full speed toward the president. President Trump bent down to greet him, but just as the Secret Service was about to intervene, Huck blew right past the president as if he wasn't even there and dove into my arms. The president turned and gave me a "this kid again" look with a grin. I shrugged back and smiled as I gave my son a big hug. It was an encouraging reminder to all the moms out there: for a three-year-old boy, the most powerful man in the world—the President of the United States—has nothing on his mom! I knew in that moment I hadn't totally messed him up, at least not yet!

At another Take Our Daughters and Sons to Work Day, Vice President Pence joined me at the podium in the briefing room to take questions from dozens of reporters' kids. One of the things I always loved about the vice president was his heart, compassion, and love for the people of our country. He was always the first person to encourage the team, build us up, and take an interest in each of us personally. On more than one occasion he'd engage my kids and make them feel important. The vice president was not only a good Christian man, but a trusted confidant of the president and a calm and stable presence in the White House during tumultuous times.

I came to expect the unexpected when I'd bring my kids to the office. For Christmas at the White House one year, Bryan and I took all three kids. It was perfect. Once again the first lady had done an amazing job. The first lady was not only a gracious and welcoming host but had a spectacular eye for things of beauty and at no time was this more evident than Christmas at the White House. Even though some in the press mocked and attacked her, anyone who spent any real time with her knew what a beautiful spirit she had and she poured all of it into making visitors at the White House feel special and welcomed. Christmas at the White House was magical, each room filled with unique décor and impeccable thought and detail put into every ornament, light, and display. As you entered the East Wing, the first thing you'd see was a Christmas tree that towered over the room adorned with ornaments to honor Gold Star families who had paid the ultimate sacrifice for our country. As you continued into the East Wing, you'd step onto a green carpet with giant all-red Christmas trees made from thousands of small berries lining both sides of the hall. As you left the hall, there were frames on the walls with Christmas cards from previous first families. Just past that you could peek into the China Room where tables were set to display past presidents' china patterns. Across the hall in the White House Library were four Christmas trees that had ornaments with seals representing all our states and territories. As soon as you started to make your way up the stairs you'd begin to hear beautiful music played by the Marine Corps Band, and at the top of the stairs stations were set up for kids to make Christmas crafts. There were all kinds of Christmas treats and a hot chocolate bar, where the parents carefully monitored their kids to make sure they didn't spill all over the floor or themselves. The grand finale was a chance for the families to meet the president and first lady in the Blue Room in front of the eighteen-foot-tall North Carolina–grown Christmas tree and have a photo taken. Like the other attendees I wanted a picture with my kids and the First Family. I had the boys dressed in green dress pants with blazers and bow ties and Scarlett in an ivory dress with gold trim and a Peter Pan collar that looked like a miniature Jackie O dress. I was a proud mom and wanted to capture the moment. Despite the fact the kids had way too much hot chocolate, they were on pretty good behavior for the family photo.

As we finished, the president pulled me aside. The boys ran off and Bryan chased after them, but Scarlett stayed with me. The president was irritated with negative coverage on the Sunday shows. He was particularly offended by that morning's edition of NBC's *Meet the Press,* anchored by a liberal reporter the president often referred to as "that sleepy-eyed son of a b, Chuck Todd." Next to me, Scarlett, listened intently as the president dropped an explosive f-bomb on the media. I interrupted the president and said, "Sir, you can't say that. She's six!" to which the president replied . . . "Oh, sh——!" He then turned to Scarlett, apologized, and said, "Well, sweetheart, it was only a matter of time. Welcome to the real world!" It was a Trump White House Christmas memory I'll never forget— and I pray my daughter was too young to remember!

As much as I wanted to protect my kids, I also wanted them to understand why we were making the sacrifices to serve our country. Politics is a nasty business, but I believed good people have to be involved and stand up for what is right, no matter the cost, because if good people don't get involved, bad things happen. One of the things I admired about the president was he raised good kids and included them in everything he'd done in business and politics. It's been said, "You can't fake good kids." Nobody is perfect, but the president was a good father. I have seen him make world leaders wait so he could take a call from one of his kids. I have watched him step to their defense when attacked and praise them as a proud father when they succeed. He has helped raise kids who are kind, smart, hardworking, and very generous to others. That didn't happen by accident, and it's something I hope people will one day say about me and my kids.

Bryan and I found that even when we couldn't spend as much time as we would like with our kids, being intentional about our time—particularly one-on-one time—made a big difference. However, when you're a parent of multiple preschool-aged kids you had to be careful that being too focused on one doesn't leave the others unsupervised. I have learned this the hard way too many times to count!

One Saturday morning about 9:00 a.m. I was focused on spending time with Scarlett, who was giving me a makeover. After about an hour of getting my hair pulled into ponytail holders and bows and my face covered in makeup and bright blue eye shadow, I went to check my phone and found I had a lot of missed calls, texts, and emails from reporters asking what I was trying to say. I was confused because it was Saturday morning. I was at home with my kids getting a makeover from my daughter. I hadn't been trying to say anything. After a few minutes I found an email that had a tweet embedded in it. The tweet was from my official White House account. It didn't say anything, but it did contain a bunch of stoplight, anchor, plane, and train emojis. In a panic, I yelled, "Huck, get in here!" It had been more than an hour since his tweet had gone out, and I furiously typed out a clarification: "This is what happens when your three year old steals your phone. Thanks Huck! #NeverLeaveYour PhoneUnlocked." It did, however, happen to be Infrastructure Week so at least the boy was on message!

Not to be outdone by his older brother, my son George one evening somehow ordered an $80 Batman toy off our Amazon Echo (why does it automatically select the most expensive Batman? you might ask . . .). Not realizing this was even possible, I posted on social media: "Alexa, we have a problem if my two-year-old can order a Batman toy by yelling 'Batman!' over and over again" into the Echo. To my surprise, Democrats on Twitter were outraged, accusing me of an ethics violation for promoting the overpriced Batman toy, or perhaps even a national security breach for owning an Echo in the first place because surely the Russians must be listening in on all my top-secret conversations with my kids.

In the midst of the uproar, I received an email from the owner of Sure Thing Toys, the purveyor of the $80 Batman toy.

Message from third-party seller:

> Thanks for your order and the inadvertent press! In all seriousness, you can return your Batman figure if you'd like. No hassle! Just arrange for the return through the "Your Account" link on the Amazon homepage. It is a really cool figure though, but probably a bit too detailed and expensive for a two-year-old.
>
> Ryan
> Sure Thing Toys

I replied to Ryan:

> I apologize for the press. I've never been great on the return. Maybe my four-year-old is big enough for it. Who knew a basic post like that could be so controversial, hope it doesn't cause you any problems!

Message from third-party seller:

> It's cool! We'll take all the press we can get. We sell toys and stay out of politics, so I can't imagine it would cause us any problems. People on there are brutal. Such a toxic environment. I don't know how you deal with that! And, for the record, we do have about 400 of those Batman figures left, so a boost in sales would be nice!

Either way, thanks again.

Good luck,

Ryan

Not out of fear of the Russians but out of concern George might bankrupt our family yelling "Batman!" at Alexa, we got rid of our Echo. We still have the giant Batman toy. Sticking with the Batman theme for Halloween at the White House, George and Huck both dressed as the Caped Crusader. We trick-or-treated around offices in the Old Executive Office Building and the West Wing, and the president was nice enough to invite my kids into the Oval Office to say hi. George and Huck, both in full Batman attire, high-fived the president. Some of my favorite pictures from my two and a half years in the Trump administration are from that day.

My kids were too young to fully appreciate how cool it was to get to trick-or-treat at the White House or high-five the president in their Batman costumes in the Oval Office. But it was a relief they were also too young to really understand some of the worst parts of my job. Very early Monday morning on October 2, 2017, I woke up to a call from the Situation Room to let me know about a mass shooting that had taken place in Las Vegas late the night before. I was getting ready to head to the office and Huck, always an early riser, was playing in the living room while I talked to Chief of Staff John Kelly to confirm the president had been fully briefed. I notified the press via the pool and turned off the television so Huck couldn't see the horrific images rolling in from Vegas.

Fifty-eight people were killed and many more injured. I was scheduled to brief that day and would be the first person from the administration to speak to the country. I knew this moment was important. The country was again hurting from a mass shooting and needed a lot more than my words could provide. Cliff Sims and I talked about what my script to open the briefing should include. I

asked him to find stories of concertgoers in Vegas who had coura-
geously risked their lives to help others to highlight the resilience
of the American people. He came back a couple of hours later
while I was doing briefing prep with the rest of the team to do a
read-through. When I started the first read-through of the script
I fell apart. I asked the team to step out of my office for a minute. I sat quietly and cried for the people who had lost mothers,
fathers, sons, and daughters they loved to this senseless act of
violence. I prayed and asked God to comfort the grieving families
and friends and to help me deliver a message of healing and
hope. I then called my team back into my office. No one said
anything. We just hugged. I walked out into the briefing room,
took the podium, and choked up recounting acts of heroism
that saved lives: "What these people did for each other says far
more about who we are as Americans than the cowardly acts of
a killer ever could. The Gospel of John reminds us that there
is no greater love than to lay down one's life for a friend. The
memory of those who displayed the ultimate expression of love
in the midst of an unimaginable act of hate will never fade. Their
examples will serve as an eternal reminder that the American
spirit cannot and will not ever be broken. In the days ahead, we
will grieve as a nation. We will honor the memory of those lost as
a nation, and we will come together, united as one nation, under
God, and indivisible."

After the briefing I went back and sat alone in my office trying
to make sense of it all. I opened up an email from Ari Fleischer,
former White House press secretary for President George W. Bush
and during 9/11. He wrote:

> Sarah, I thought you did a really nice job at the brief-
> ing today.
>
> Every so often, events are so significant that they

take you, at least for a moment, out of the tough and hardened White House life people like us have come to know. Today, you showed your roots, your faith, and your humility.

I was touched by it and I think all those who watched gained an appreciation for who you are and what matters most to you.

I just wanted to say good job.

Best, Ari

I traveled with the president to Las Vegas to meet with the victims' families, survivors, and first responders. Serving as consoler in chief President Trump told reporters, "In the darkest moments, what shines most brightly is the goodness that thrives in the hearts of our American people." A survivor named Thomas Gunderson had been shot in the leg, but when President Trump and the first lady came in to see him he got out of his hospital bed and stood to greet them. The president and first lady pleaded with him to return to his bed but Thomas said, "I will never lie down when the president of this great country comes to shake my hand." As we took off on Air Force One from Las Vegas, I looked down and could see the shattered windows of the Mandalay Bay, from which the shooter had murdered fifty-eight innocent souls, one of the most vivid and visceral images of evil I had ever seen.

The mass shootings that have tragically become all too common in our society made me fear for my kids' safety as they would for any mom. It wasn't lost on me that the more I was in the public eye the more recognizable and more of a target I'd become. There was more interest in the Trump presidency than any other in history. He dominated media coverage and social media interaction 24/7 in a way that no human being ever had before him. The number of senior administration officials who'd become household names was a new phenomenon that none of us who came into the White House had really prepared for. For better or worse, many of us had become celebrities—featured on meme after meme on social media, the target of regular punch lines on late-night television, and caricatured on *Saturday Night Live*. Some of us couldn't go anywhere in the country without being recognized and approached. In my experience, the vast majority of people who approached me in public were positive and encouraging, but around Washington, DC, one of the most liberal cities in America, that wasn't always the case. "You're a terrible person"; "you're not fit to be a mother"; "your kids should be ashamed of you"; "I told my kids to never be like you" were just a few of the pleasantries I encountered from enlightened liberals and feminists who approached me in our nation's capital.

Protecting my kids from a cruel world was difficult. One Sunday afternoon I was driving all three kids to a friend's house to play and George shouted from the backseat, "Mommy, what does it mean to be killed in cold blood?" Huck followed up with, "Yeah, what's a cold-blooded killer?" I was shocked and asked them where they had heard this. George said, "Daddy let us watch you on the news!"

I could always count on my kids for daily doses of reality and humility. One night Scarlett was getting ready for a father/daughter dance. It was one of the first big events like this for her and Bryan. She was so excited. We spent the day picking out the perfect dress and getting her hair and nails done. Scarlett wanted the big reveal moment coming down the stairs. As we were putting on the finishing touches I told her how proud of her I was, what a beautiful girl she was inside and out, and how blessed she was to have such a wonderful daddy. We shared this special moment and I was so thankful and proud to be her mom. A little tear of joy came to my eye. Scarlett noticed and said, "It's okay, Mommy." She reached up, patted my arm, and with a look of empathy and compassion on her face, said, "One day you can be pretty, too." That was not the direction I anticipated our conversation going! I smiled, gave her a kiss, and sent her down the stairs to meet her prince.

No matter how high you fly in this life, kids have a way of bringing you crashing back down to earth. On a quiet Saturday over the kids' Christmas break, Bryan was playing Mousetrap with Scarlett and Huck. I was cleaning up the kitchen from breakfast and all of a sudden water started pouring through the ceiling all over me. I was soaking wet. I yelled for Bryan's help and ran upstairs to find George in the boys' bathroom. He was balancing with one foot on the side of the toilet and one on the side of the bathtub, completely naked. He had a plunger in his hands and a guilty smile on his face as the toilet overflowed everywhere. There was nearly two inches of standing water on the floor of the bathroom. I shouted to Bryan and the other kids to bring towels. I grabbed George and carried him to our shower, and after he was cleaned up, I walked back to the boys' bathroom. Bryan was on his knees soaking up the mess and George, still naked, walked in, patted Bryan on the shoulder, and said, "It's okay, Daddy, . . . my teacher says 'sometimes accidents happen.'" We laughed so hard neither of us could bring ourselves to punish him.

My kids humbled me, but they also made me more appreciative of all God's blessings. On Memorial Day, I accompanied the president to a ceremony at Arlington National Cemetery to honor our fallen heroes. It was technically a holiday so I got permission to bring Huck along with me. Just before we departed, Johnny De-Stefano asked if Huck and I wanted to ride in the front of the motorcade in the Suburban just behind the president's limo from the White House to Arlington. Huck sat in the backseat with one of the military communications staffers, James, who was a friend and also a parent. James was patient and answered all of Huck's questions on the fifteen-minute ride over. James also told Huck that all of the people lining the streets and waving to the motorcade had heard he was coming to work with me that day and that's why they were all there. Huck was thrilled with the size of the crowd there to see him and took great responsibility in making sure he waved to every onlooker we passed!

The event was a somber occasion as we honored the men and women of our Armed Forces who had paid the ultimate price so we could live free in the greatest country in the world. Families of the fallen as well as hundreds of veterans and current members of our Armed Forces were there. A man opening the ceremony delivered an inspiring message that ended with "Hallelujah!" In the silence that followed, Huck loudly yelled back, "Hallelujah!"

I brought Huck with me that day because he had lately expressed interest in joining the military when he grows up. My friend Sarah Flaherty was a helicopter pilot in the US Navy, which Huck thought was pretty cool. In September 2018 I had the honor of conducting Sarah's official promotion from lieutenant commander to commander. Sarah came from a military family, her grandfather having been a major general in the Marines. General Dunford, chairman of the Joint Chiefs of Staff and a four-star marine general, had served under him as a young officer. I officiated the ceremony and administered the oath and, as a thank-you, Sarah gave me the bars from her uniform that I had helped switch out to signify her new rank. Huck loved to look at the bars that I kept in my office and told me he would like to have some like them someday and that when he did, he wanted me to change his, too.

I figured this day would be a good way to show Huck what true sacrifice and bravery really means and for him to meet some real superheroes—not the fake cartoon ones he watched on TV. After the ceremony finished and we were waiting to head back to the White House, General Dunford came by to say hi to Huck. I had gotten to know the general and was always impressed by his bold confidence, but also his kindness. I introduced Huck to him and told Huck he was a real superhero. Huck proudly told him he wanted to be a real superhero, too, and was going to be in the army when he grows up. General Dunford said, "That's not bad, son, but I'm pretty sure you'd rather be a marine." We laughed and Huck told everyone he met after that he was going to be a marine just like his new friend the general.

Being the first mom to ever serve as White House press secretary had its highs and lows. If I didn't have the best partner in the world, I couldn't have done it. Bryan was all the things I wasn't. He was the fun parent who played monster and chased the kids through the house as they squealed in delight. He pushed them higher on the swing than I would dare. He made our boys tough by letting them roughhouse and be boys. And he made our daughter feel special and loved by treating her as she deserved to be treated. He was patient and laid back and he was the rock of our family during a challenging time. Every day when I was too tired to do something he stepped in. When we needed to pretend George's birthday was on a completely different day because I couldn't be home on his actual birthday he just went with it and made it happen. He was and is my perfect partner on this crazy journey. Not only could I not do it without him—I wouldn't want to.

So when an opportunity came along to fulfill his lifelong dream to meet his childhood hero—Kansas City Royals Hall of Famer George Brett—I jumped at the chance. George Brett and his son Jackson were at the White House for a tour. Johnny DeStefano, who like Bryan had grown up a Royals fan in Kansas City, told me he was giving George a tour and asked me if I wanted to meet him. I bolted from my office and went to say hi and asked for a photo I could send to my husband. George said, "I'll do you one better. We are going to dinner tonight. Why don't you join us?" I couldn't believe it and couldn't wait to surprise Bryan. It was actually perfect timing because it was only a few days away from Bryan's birthday and this was better than any gift I could ever give him!

I told Bryan and he was thrilled. I said, "This will only happen under one condition—you are not to ask George Brett about pooping his pants in Las Vegas." The Vegas story was legend to all Kansas City Royals fans. Being married to one, I've heard it retold many times. George Brett was caught on video with a hot mic at spring training talking to a Royals player named Scott Dohmann.

George Brett said, "I sh—— my pants last night. I did . . . I'm good twice a year for that. When was the last time you sh—— your pants?"

SCOTT DOHMANN: "Me?"

GEORGE BRETT: "Yeah. Been awhile?"

SCOTT DOHMANN: "Yeah, it's been a long time."

GEORGE BRETT: "I was in Vegas a couple of years ago. This is an honest to God true story. I'm staying at the Bellagio. I went over to the Mirage for dinner and met some friends of mine over there. Went to Cocomo's, a great little steakhouse. Guy brings out some fresh crab legs. 'These just came in. I have to give them to you guys.' Brings them out. I am eating them. Then we go gamble a little bit. I had a tee time early in the morning. So I said, 'Look, I got to get going.' I'm walking back to the hotel. I get three-fourths of the way out of the lobby . . . I got my butt pinched . . . I can't move. All of sudden . . . BOOM . . . water. I had food poisoning from the crabs! Take off my leather jacket, tie it around my waist, and I'm just standing there and it is just running down my leg. . . . Every time I'm walking something's coming out, it's water. Straight water! Then to tell you how sick I was I am standing outside and I got to get my cell phone. I call the guy, I say, 'Larry, you won't believe this. I'm standing outside . . . I can't move. I got sh—— everywhere. I sh—— all over myself.' And Larry is about a forty-eight waist. So he brings me over a pair of pants and some towels. . . . He finds the closest bathroom. . . . He goes and gets the towel all wet for me, throws it over the stall. I take off all my clothes. Just wipe off. Leave my shoes, my pants, everything right there. The towels right there in the stall, and I am walking barefoot with my shirt and his pants that are forty-eight waist through the lobby at midnight. . . . True story. Who's the pitchers in this game?"

That was the PG-13 version. The actual video (viewer discretion advised) is posted on YouTube, where it has millions of views. Bryan had watched it enough times to repeat some of the better lines from memory, so I didn't think it was necessary or appropriate for him to bring it up the first time he'd ever meet George Brett at dinner. Bryan agreed to my terms, and we joined George Brett, his son Jackson, and a friend of his from Kansas City, along with Johnny and his wife, Sarah, at Bourbon Steak at the Four Seasons in Georgetown. After a couple of drinks, George Brett, a Republican and Trump supporter, started giving me a hard time. He said, "You know, Sarah, you have the toughest job in Washington." I pushed back a bit, and he followed up with: "Actually, you don't just have the toughest job in Washington—you have the worst job in Washington and probably the entire world!" He howled with laughter and I said, "Actually, I have the best job in the world. In fact, if I didn't have this job, we wouldn't be sitting here right now with you." I then really let him have it. I did exactly what I'd repeatedly warned my husband not to do. I said, "George, why don't you tell us about that time you pooped your pants in Vegas?" George Brett, without hesitation, launched into the story in graphic, hysterical detail. The look on Bryan's face was pure joy.

I blamed Jackson. I had been sitting next to Jackson all night and had instantly hit it off with him. He was a young guy with a big personality and while Bryan and Johnny were drooling over George I had been talking to Jackson. I told him I had threatened Bryan's life if he fanboyed too much or asked George to tell the Vegas story, but Jackson had egged me on and told me to do it. That night we all became friends, and to this day, Bryan says it was his best night in Washington. We love George and his family. Every time I am not the perfect wife (pretty rare!) I remind Bryan of this night, hoping it will get me out of the hot seat!

He and I have a great marriage, but we have faced many challenges and we are still a long way off from perfecting parenthood. During our time in Washington we did our best to teach our kids right, from wrong, why it's important to help others, and to love others the way Jesus loves us. Some days we failed miserably and others we had moments to be proud of. Being a working mom these days is not easy. Social media, while a great tool, is also a dangerous place to spend all of your time. It's a permanent highlight reel of our best moments. It's rare to see a mom post a picture of their kid standing naked on a toilet—plunger in hand—flooding her house with dirty toilet water from the second-floor bathroom! No one is a perfect parent and no one has perfect kids, but our kids are a gift from our perfect God. They have been entrusted to us by our Creator and God chose us to be their parents.

On a snow day when all the schools in the Washington area were closed, I went into work. Thankfully Bryan was able to stay home with the kids and they went sledding. They had come in to warm up, and as Bryan was building a fire, three-year-old George said, "Turn on Fox News, Daddy."

"Why, George?"

"Because I like Fox News."

"Really? Why do you like Fox News, George?"

"Because that's where I can see Mommy."

My three-year-old had apparently concluded that if he wanted to see his mom he'd probably be more likely to see me on TV than at home.

That night when I tucked George in he asked me why I didn't wave back to him. I was confused and asked when he had waved at me. He said he had seen me on TV and waved at me, but I never waved back. No matter how many ways I tried to explain to him that when I'm on TV he could see me but I couldn't see him, he never seemed convinced, just hurt.

I loved working for the president and serving my country. It's probably one of the best jobs I'll ever have. But the greatest job and the most important title I'll ever have is that of mom. As I neared two years in the White House—and three years since joining the Trump campaign—I knew I'd soon have to make a decision about how much longer I could do both.

10

Fighting for Us

During the 2016 campaign, President Trump clearly differentiated himself on illegal immigration and trade. The president understood that the Republican Party had lost its way on these issues, and as a result lost its working-class base and the last two presidential elections. Globalization, with its importation of labor and exportation of jobs, wasn't such a good deal for many American workers. In the last two decades, the United States had lost five million manufacturing jobs, and in hard-hit states across the Rust Belt from Pennsylvania to Michigan to Wisconsin the call to "make America great again" deeply resonated.

On trade, the president replaced NAFTA with the USMCA (United States–Mexico–Canada Agreement), which was endorsed by the business community and organized labor, a first for any trade deal. The USMCA, negotiated by the president, vice president, Lighthizer, Mnuchin, Kudlow, and Kushner, was approved with strong bipartisan majorities in Congress. Along with the president, each of these administration officials was instrumental in getting the deal done. It represented a historic victory for the Trump administration and a blueprint for future trade deals that could be both pro–American business and pro–American worker. The president also made progress on trade with China, signing a Phase One deal that included $200 billion in new purchases of US goods and services, as well as better protections for US companies against China stealing their intellectual property and technology. President Trump promised American workers he'd fight for them, and on trade, he delivered. On illegal immigration and border security, however, results varied.

To many Democrats illegal immigration wasn't predominantly a national security issue, an economic issue, or even a humanitarian issue—it was a political issue. These Democrats wanted illegal immigrants to come to America through an open border and give them free healthcare, government benefits, and ultimately citizenship so they'd loyally vote Democrat—and cement a permanent majority for the Democratic Party. Democrats weren't stupid. They knew walls worked and were hell-bent on denying the president his wall.

After the midterms, as our federal government approached another shutdown, the president met with House Speaker Nancy Pelosi and Senate Minority Leader Chuck Schumer. As was typical of many meetings President Trump hosted in the Oval Office, the press were invited into the room to cover it. This infuriated the Democrats, who said it turned the negotiations into a circus, but the president believed it was important for the American people to see. It also gave reporters unprecedented access, despite absurd claims by liberals that the president was somehow a dangerous threat to freedom of the press. I stood just to the president's left, wearing a hunter green dress almost identical to Pelosi's, as he opened the meeting and quickly gave her the floor. She said any government shutdown would be a "Trump shutdown," entirely the president's fault, directly in front of the cameras. To the surprise of everyone in the room, the president vowed to take ownership of a government shutdown. Shortly after he made that declaration he asked the press to leave. I stayed behind for the closed-door meeting. It didn't last long. The Democrats had what they wanted—the president on record, on camera, taking ownership of a shutdown. The Democrats believed they had the president up against a wall and weren't going to give him the funding to build one. We were headed for a shutdown and there was nothing any of us could do to stop it.

On the first day of the shutdown, just a few days before Christmas, Scarlett and I were en route home from the grocery store when I got a call from the White House. On the other end of the line were the president, vice president, Ivanka, Jared, and Mick. They were all in the residence on speaker and the president asked me if he should stay in Washington over the Christmas break or if he should go to Mar-a-Lago. I told him unequivocally that he could not leave Washington to go to Florida during the government shutdown. Everyone else on the line had already given him the same advice, and he had agreed. We discussed a statement to release and after we hung up I sent it out letting the press know the president would remain in Washington and the first lady would return from Mar-a-Lago and join him for Christmas.

Stuck in the White House on Christmas Eve the president unleashed a tweetstorm for the ages, going after his critics on a number of fronts. My family and I were hiking on a trail near our home in North Arlington that led to a ridge overlooking the Potomac River. I spent a good part of our hike looking at my phone to see what would come next. I called the president as soon as we returned home to wish him a Merry Christmas and politely said, "Sir, it's Christmas Eve.

Maybe finish the day with one last tweet that gets everyone more in the Christmas spirit." He laughed and told me to get back to baking Christmas cookies with my kids. I told him I would be happy to do that if my phone quit buzzing from alerts to his tweets!

After our secret trip to Iraq to visit the troops over Christmas, we returned to Washington, and had another meeting in the Situation Room with President Trump, leaders in Congress, and senior administration officials to try and hammer out an agreement to address the border crisis and end the shutdown. Speaker Pelosi interrupted Department of Homeland Security Secretary Nielsen's presentation and snapped at the president: "Mr. President, you need to start dealing with facts."

The president was not one to tolerate being spoken to in that manner, and fired back: "These are the facts. Why don't you listen to the secretary's presentation instead of rudely interrupting her? Okay?"

"I reject your facts and those who work for you on the border," said Pelosi.

"These aren't my facts," Secretary Nielsen said. "These are the facts on the ground coming directly from those on the frontlines. You can attack me but don't you dare attack the men and women who risk their lives every day protecting us!"

The president loved it and piled on. He turned to Pelosi and said, "You're a good Catholic, right? Doesn't the Vatican have a wall?" Senate Majority Leader McConnell tried to intervene, but it was clear the negotiation was going nowhere. Pelosi wanted to prolong the shutdown and deal nothing to the president other than a humiliating defeat.

The following day we were scheduled for a long-planned senior staff retreat and meetings at Camp David. Because it was a retreat we were allowed to bring spouses along so I invited Bryan.

I had been to Camp David a few times but this would be my first overnight. Despite all of the craziness around the shutdown I was excited to be there with my husband.

Camp David, on a hilltop in rural Maryland a few hours' drive from Washington, is one of the most heavily secured facilities in our country. When we arrived at the gate, we had to turn in our phones, as no guests are permitted to have them on the property. After making it through the formidable security perimeter, we were directed to the Hawthorne Cabin. Camp David was rustic but comfortable and peaceful. Each cabin at Camp David had a guest book with all the names of the people who had stayed there. In the Hawthorne Cabin guest book the names of Henry Kissinger and Dick Cheney, along with many Bush and Clinton family members, were inscribed. That evening we enjoyed a relaxing dinner with the Trump White House team, and afterward played pool and socialized around the bar, forgetting for a moment that we were in one of the longest government shutdowns in American history.

The following morning we had breakfast together in the main dining area before breaking off from our spouses for meetings. Bryan had talked to a couple of the other husbands about getting together to go skeet shooting, one of the organized activities offered at Camp David for guests. He called from our cabin phone to the main office to arrange for the group but was told, "I'm sorry, sir, but we don't allow guests to shoot firearms into the air when the president is about to land on Marine One."

When the president arrived for the meetings, he of course threw out the agenda and launched into a story about buying Mar-a-Lago—one of his "greatest all-time deals." Originally built in the 1920s by Marjorie Merriweather Post, heir to the Post Cereal fortune, Mar-a-Lago was donated after her death in 1973 to the federal government to be "the Winter White House," but never used for that purpose. It was returned to the Post Foundation by an Act of Congress, and ultimately purchased for pennies on the dollar in the 1980s by Donald Trump, who, upon winning the presidency returned Mar-a-Lago to the purpose Post had originally intended. It was now his Winter White House, and the president was still a bit agitated he wasn't there this winter due to the shutdown. He said, "The great thing about Camp David is even the fake news knows I'm working when I'm here!"

One of the things we finalized over the weekend at Camp David was for the president to take a trip to the border to make his case for the wall. Prior to the president's border visit we also planned for the president to deliver his first nationally televised Oval Office address to the country on the shutdown and border crisis. I worked with all of the major television networks to nail down a block of prime time for the president to give his address Tuesday night ahead of the border visit. That night I talked to Jared and Stephen Miller to finalize plans for Tuesday as I watched the College Football National Championship game between Alabama and Clemson. We decided a lunch meeting with the president and all of the major television networks as well as some of the smaller ones to preview his speech was a good idea.

The next morning I went to Stephen's second-floor office and worked directly with him, Jared, and Derek Lyons on the address. We spent the next several hours going in and out of the back dining room of the Oval Office, consulting with the president and writing and rewriting. We must have gone back and forth a half-dozen times. The president wanted to open his first Oval Office address to the country with a list of his economic accomplishments. We recommended he keep his remarks focused on the crisis at the border and his solution to it. Still unresolved, we took a break for the media lunch. Because of the shutdown we had to do it in the Roosevelt

Room instead of the State Dining Room, which also meant we had to limit the number of attendees from two to one from each network, and let them decide who to send.

Jared and my principal deputy Hogan Gidley had gone over to the media offices and briefed them ahead of the lunch, and while meeting with CNN, Wolf Blitzer and Jake Tapper (two regulars for the annual network State of the Union lunch) asked why CNN wasn't invited. Jared said, "You were, Chris Cuomo is coming." Blitzer and Tapper were furious that CNN had made the call to send Cuomo instead of either of them.

Later I was in the back dining room with the president, vice president, Mick, Jared, and Shine, and I handed the president the confirmed list of lunch attendees.

"Who the f—— are some of these people?" the president asked.

"It's good to have everyone, including the regional networks which actually have more viewers than CNN," I said.

At the mention of CNN the president noticed something interesting about the list. . . .

"Whoa! Cuomo is coming!?!?"

I told him that was CNN's call, not ours, and Jared retold the story about how Tapper and Blitzer were upset they weren't included in the lunch.

Without hesitation the president said, "Call Tapper . . . get him on the phone right now. . . . Madeleine! Get Jake Tapper on the phone!"

With a mischievous grin on his face, the president said, "Watch this."

"Mr. Tapper," said the White House operator, "the president would like to speak to you. Are you available to take the call? Thank you, I'll put you through . . ."

"Jake! I was just handed the list for the media lunch," said the president. "Why aren't you coming? Cuomo!? I can't believe it!

Why didn't they send you? Do you want to come? Sarah! Can we add Jake?"

"No, sir," I said. "Just one per network."

"So sorry, Jake," the president said. "We'll figure out a way to make it up to you," and he hung up.

That night the president walked down the colonnade to deliver his first Oval Office address. He sat at the *Resolute* desk with pictures of his parents and the American and presidential flags behind him. Only the pool television network and a few senior staff were present in the room. I held my breath as the clock struck 9:00 p.m. and the president began his remarks to the country.

We had won the debate on the opening, and I still have the first page of that draft where we got to strike through it with the words VICTORY written in all red caps at the top of the page.

> Tonight, I am speaking to you because there is a growing humanitarian and security crisis at our southern border. . . . America proudly welcomes millions of lawful immigrants who enrich our society and contribute to our nation. But, all Americans are hurt by uncontrolled illegal migration. It strains public resources and drives down jobs and wages. Among those hardest hit are African Americans and Hispanic Americans. Our southern border is a pipeline for vast quantities of illegal drugs, including meth, heroin, cocaine, and fentanyl. Every week three hundred of our citizens are killed by heroin alone, 90 percent of which floods across from our southern border. More Americans will die from drugs this year than were killed in the entire Vietnam War. . . .
>
> Some have suggested a barrier is immoral. Then why do wealthy politicians build walls, fences, and gates around their homes? They don't build walls because they

hate the people on the outside, but because they love the
people on the inside. . . . This is a choice between right
and wrong, justice and injustice. This is about whether we
fulfill our sacred duty to the American citizens we serve.
When I took the oath of office, I swore to protect our
country. And that is what I will always do, so help me God.

The next day I attended a meeting in the Cabinet Room with
the president and congressional leadership. The president brought
in some candy, and offered to share with Chuck and Nancy. The
candy was from a place in New York that both Schumer and Trump
knew well. They spent the first few minutes reminiscing about life
in New York. There is a bit of friendliness between them, but it
didn't last long once the meeting got under way.

Nancy immediately asked, "Why are you hurting people with
this shutdown?"

"I don't want to hurt anybody," said the president. "I want to
protect our country and our people. We can open up the government today. You say you want border security. If we open the government today, in thirty days will you also fund border security,
including the wall?"

"No," Pelosi said.

The president calmly said, "Okay, then this is a waste of time.
Bye-bye."

The president walked out, and Pelosi lost it. I stayed behind in
the room for a few minutes while the vice president tried to calm
her down. It was no use. The meeting ended and the Democrats
went out to the sticks in the driveway of the West Wing to trash the
president in front of the cameras. Schumer lied and said the president threw a "temper tantrum" and "slammed the table" and the
media ran with it. House Republican Leader Kevin McCarthy went
out right after and refuted the Democrats' account of what hap-

pened. "I know [Schumer] complained when we had the cameras in there but I think we need to bring them back because what he described in the meeting is totally different than what took place."

The next day I flew on Air Force One with the president to McAllen, Texas, in the Rio Grande Valley, one of the most heavily trafficked areas for illegal border crossings. At a US Border Patrol station, the president talked with the brave men and women protecting us along our southern border and with relatives of law enforcement officials killed in the line of duty by illegal immigrants in front of a cache of seized guns, drugs, and money.

CNN's White House correspondent Jim Acosta went down ahead of President Trump to do some "investigative reporting" on the border, and posted a video of himself in front of a section of border wall: "I found some steel slats down on the border," said Acosta. "But I don't see anything resembling a national emergency situation, at least not in the McAllen, Texas, area of the border where Trump will be today." I tweeted back to Acosta: "When I went with President @realDonaldTrump to the border today I never imagined @Acosta would be there doing our job for us and so clearly explaining why WALLS WORK. Thanks Jim!"

As the shutdown dragged on, and much of the federal bureaucracy ground to a halt, there were a few events the president insisted must go on. One such event was the Clemson Tigers National Champion football team's visit to the White House. Frequently when a championship team came to the White House there was a reception or celebration of some kind, but because most of the White House staff who managed these events were furloughed due to the shutdown, the president had to improvise. He came up with the idea to order a bunch of fast food for the players and pay for it himself. The president personally selected the menu, and said to make sure there's enough to feed all the big kids. The amazing team at the Navy Mess worked on the order and the presentation, and made it special by displaying it on White House silver in the dining room. Before the Clemson players arrived, the president came down to inspect it himself. On the tables stacked high were more than $5,000 worth of McDonald's Big Macs, Wendy's spicy chicken sandwiches, Burger King Whoppers, and Domino's pizzas. As the president proudly gazed at the spread he told Nick Luna to carry some of the food upstairs for him and Barron, and then added with a smile, "And be sure to take a few of those Big Macs up there, too, for Melania!" We all knew none of them were for the first lady! Jared, always quick with a good one-liner, said, "He is the only person I know who will buy a thousand burgers so he can have one."

Speaker Pelosi didn't seem too impressed with the president's theatrics, and canceled President Trump's State of the Union address at the Capitol the next day. Pelosi and several Democratic members of Congress had an overseas trip planned in which they would be traveling by government plane—approved and managed through the State Department. In response to her State of the Union cancelation, President Trump personally dictated to us a letter he wanted sent to Pelosi, which read:

> Dear Madame Speaker:
> Due to the shutdown, I am sorry to inform you that your trip to Brussels, Egypt, and Afghanistan has been postponed. We will reschedule this seven-day excursion when the shutdown is over. In light of the 800,000 great American workers not receiving pay, I am sure you would agree that postponing this public relations event is totally appropriate. I also feel that, during this period, it would be better if you were in Washington negotiating with me and joining the strong border security movement to end the shutdown. Obviously, if you would like to make your journey by flying commercial, that would certainly be

      your prerogative. I look forward to seeing you soon and
      even more forward to watching our open and dangerous
      southern border finally receive the attention, funding,
      and security it so desperately deserves.

Pelosi and the rest of her delegation had already boarded buses and were en route to the airport when they received the letter, courtesy of my Twitter account. The Democrats' bus returned to the Capitol and House Republican Leader Kevin McCarthy texted me a picture of Pelosi's luggage cart being wheeled back down the Capitol hallway.

A few days later on a Saturday morning President Trump hosted a naturalization ceremony for five new American citizens. I brought Scarlett along to watch an event that usually takes place in US Citizenship and Immigration Service offices around the country, but this time would be done in the Oval Office. I held Scarlett's hand throughout the ceremony as Secretary Nielsen administered the oath, Vice President Pence handed our new fellow citizens their certificates, and the President of the United States said, "By taking this oath, you have forged a sacred bond with this nation, its traditions, its culture, and its values. This heritage is now yours to protect, promote, and pass down to the next generation and to the next wave of newcomers to our shores." I explained to Scarlett how special it is to be an American. Men and women had fought and died and given everything for our country, and to be an American citizen is a blessing from God. Millions of people all over the world would do just about anything to be an American, a privilege many of us all too often take for granted.

Shortly after the ceremony the president delivered a speech from the White House laying out a compromise with Democrats— temporary protection to young people who had come to the country illegally with their parents—one of the Democrats' top immigration priorities—in exchange for funding to secure the border and re-open the government. It was a major concession from the president. Democrats were getting nearly everything they'd asked for, but as usual they put their politics ahead of the country and rejected the deal because it meant funding the president's wall.

On Sunday afternoon the president called me at home, frustrated by the Democrats' unwillingness to compromise. He was also angry about a former staffer who had betrayed him after leaving the White House. He asked me, "Sarah, would you ever do that?" Before I could respond he answered for me. "I know my Sarah, you would never do that. How do I know? Because you're a Christian and you wouldn't get into heaven if you did." He laughed, and said, "That's why I've always liked religious people!" We talked a bit more and he asked me if I thought the Democrats would ever come around. I said, "No, sir. I doubt it." He agreed and hung up.

It was clear the president was getting nowhere with Congress. The only way he'd be able to build the wall was to declare a national emergency and do it himself. The president was set to give a speech in the Rose Garden and as he was reviewing the final draft of his remarks he said, "I want to say I'm going to declare a national emergency, but White House counsel tells me I need to say I'll 'use authority given to me under the law and Constitution.' I like national emergency better. It's stronger. This is weak. I hate it. But I'm in a good mood so I'll listen to the attorneys this time."

President Trump announced from the Rose Garden he'd support a three-week continuing resolution to reopen government and back pay federal workers to give Congress time to negotiate a bipartisan solution. Following the president's remarks I said, "In twenty-one days President Trump is moving forward building the wall with or without the Democrats. The only outstanding question is whether the Democrats want something or nothing."

With the three-week continuing resolution the president's State of the Union speech was back on, and I spent the day in the Map Room with the president, Miller, Scavino, Derek, Jared, and Ivanka going through it. We worked for more than three and a half hours on the first few pages before the president had to step out for a dinner with Federal Reserve Chair Jerome Powell and Treasury Secretary Mnuchin. As he was getting ready to head upstairs he asked, "You think we are good here then?" Miller said, "Sir, there's a dozen or more pages to go." He told us he would be back in an hour and we could work some more. He came back from dinner in a good mood and we set back to work. Around 8:30 p.m. I grabbed my coat and tried to quietly step out of the room. As I did, the president stopped practicing his speech and asked, "Are you tired? Bored? Heading home for some beauty rest?"

"No, sir, I am on *Hannity* tonight."

"Great!" He immediately started giving me suggestions on what I should say.

The day of the State of the Union most of us went over to the Capitol with the first lady so we could more easily get through security into the House Chamber. I had been so focused on all the details of the day that I missed the memo that the female Democratic members of Congress planned to wear all white in solidarity to protest President Trump. It was a bit awkward when I showed up in a white dress myself!

After the State of the Union, I went with the president to a rally in El Paso, Texas. The atmosphere was electric. I watched President Trump as he walked out onto the stage framed by FINISH THE WALL banners, and the crowd went wild. House and Senate negotiators had just announced a compromise deal to keep government open and fund some border security but the president was noncommittal at the rally: "Just so you know—we're building the wall anyway. . . . Walls work. Walls save lives."

Finally there was momentum to end the shutdown. Prior to the

Senate vote to fund the government, Majority Leader McConnell called the president. Pat Cipollone, Shahira Knight, Mick, Scavino, Kirstjen, and I were in the room when the president answered. He told McConnell: "I don't know, Mitch, some of my people are telling me this legislation ties my hands. If I can't do a national emergency and build the wall, I can't sign this legislation."

"Sure you can," Mitch said. "My lawyers say you can."

The president sensed an opening to lock in the majority leader. "So you'll support the national emergency?"

"If you sign the legislation, yes," Mitch said.

"Great, we have a deal!"

"I'm going to the floor to announce your support now," Mitch said. "Do I have your permission to do so?"

"Yes, get out there, Mitch."

McConnell all but ran to the floor—probably concerned the president might change his mind—and announced President Trump would sign legislation to keep the government open and declare a national emergency, and that he'd support it.

As McConnell addressed the Senate, my phone buzzed with questions from reporters looking for the White House to confirm the senator's statement. I told the president we needed to back him up. The president agreed and I issued a statement that read, "President Trump will sign the government funding bill, and as he has stated before, he will also take other executive action—including a national emergency—to ensure we stop the national security and humanitarian crisis at the border. The president is once again delivering on his promise to build the wall, protect the border, and secure our great country."

As I walked back to my office from the president's dining room there were twenty to thirty reporters lined up in the hall outside my door, and as soon as they saw me they started shouting questions and looking for more details. "How did it all come together?" "Are you ready for a legal challenge?" I said, "We're very prepared, but there shouldn't be. The president's doing his job." I stepped into my office and closed the door, relieved the shutdown was over and the president wasn't backing down from his promise to build the wall.

The next morning Bryan and I went to Scarlett's Presidents' Day performance at Jamestown Elementary School, where the first-graders sang songs about the early presidents. After I got a few pictures with Scarlett and gave her a big hug, I rushed to the White House just before the president walked out to the Rose Garden to address the country and declare a national emergency at the border and reallocate funds to build the wall.

It was a defining moment for his presidency. If there was one promise the president couldn't break, it was his promise to build the wall. For decades Republican and Democratic politicians had said they'd secure the border but had never done it. The problem only got worse, as millions of illegal immigrants and billions of dollars in illegal drugs poured across our southern border. President Trump's supporters believed he was different from other politicians, and would actually do what he said he'd do. By enduring the longest government shutdown in American history over border security—and when all else failed—declaring a national emergency to build the wall, the president clearly demonstrated he'd do whatever it takes.

It often wasn't pretty, and I'm not going to pretend like the president was always politically correct. He wasn't. But that's one of the reasons the American people loved him. He wasn't a scripted robot. He'd tell it like it is, often using colorful and inflammatory language. On occasion his rhetoric went too far. But let's be clear: there's nothing wrong about standing up for the American people. My dad used to say, "Thank God we live in a country people are trying to break into rather than break out of." We are blessed to live in the greatest country in the world, and our people are generous and compassionate. We welcome immigrants who want to come here the right way and contribute to our society, but we are also a nation of laws, and must first and foremost protect American lives and livelihoods.

11

Warrior

On June 3, 2019, I departed Joint Base Andrews–Naval Air Facility on Air Force One with the president as part of the official US delegation on his long-anticipated state visit to the United Kingdom. It was an honor to be included in the delegation and although I'd accompanied the president on every foreign trip since the inauguration and loved them all, I was most excited about this one. A while back I'd asked Joe Hagin, deputy chief of staff for operations for President George W. Bush and President Trump, to recall the greatest trip he'd ever taken in his decade of planning foreign trips for US presidents. Without hesitation, he said the UK state visit he'd done with President Bush. "Don't miss your chance to go with President Trump," he said. Like most American women my age I followed the lives of the royal family and was looking forward to meeting them and getting to experience their world up close. On the trip we'd also go to Normandy to participate in the seventy-fifth anniversary of D-Day, and finish at Doonbeg, the president's golf resort in Ireland. For White House staff, this was the most coveted foreign trip on which to join the president, by far, and I couldn't wait.

Air Force One landed at London Stansted Airport and we went straight to Buckingham Palace for the first official greeting. The delegation arrived at the palace via motorcade while the president, first lady, and US ambassador to the UK and owner of the New York Jets Woody Johnson and his wife arrived on Marine One. As they were landing, the rest of us stood on the second floor of Buckingham Palace in the White Drawing Room, which had twenty-five-foot windows with large golden drapes opened so we could see out. I stepped out onto a balcony just off the room for a better view as the royal family of the United Kingdom—His Royal Highness Prince Charles, Prince of Wales, and Her Royal Highness Camilla, the Duchess of Cornwall—welcomed America's First Family. To no one's surprise the first lady looked stunning. She was wearing a fitted Dolce & Gabbana stark-white dress with midnight blue accents on the waist and collar and an Hervé Pierre custom-designed wide-brimmed hat. The president had on a dark blue suit and a solid light blue tie. The foursome made their way up the stairs where the Queen in her signature styled suit in aquamarine greeted them and received them into Buckingham Palace.

In Buckingham Palace we waited with British Army Major Nana Kofi Twumasi-Ankrah, a Ghanaian-born officer who fought in the Afghanistan War and was the Queen's most trusted assistant. He went by "T.A." for short, had a great sense of humor, and was not only an expert on the palace, but also our guide to royal protocol. He had been with our team when we came for a quick visit to the UK the year before and seeing him was like seeing an old friend. T.A. was the first black person ever appointed as the Queen's equerry and took his job seriously. He knew most of us were ner-vous about breaking protocol and saying or doing something we weren't supposed to. He put us all at ease and made us feel com-fortable and welcome.

The president and first lady had a special greeting with the Queen and the royal family and then we joined together for a formal receiving line. The president introduced the Queen and the first lady introduced Prince Charles to us. We had been told not to reach out to shake the Queen's hand unless she extended her hand first. Thankfully she reached out to take my hand as the president said, "This is Sarah Huckabee Sanders. You have probably seen her before. Everyone knows her."

The Queen nodded and said, "I do. Nice to meet you, Sarah."

The Queen turned to the president and said, "She is tough and does a good job."

The first lady then came with Prince Charles. "It's wonderful to meet you, Sarah," he said. "You are wonderfully talented. I don't know how you do it. I imagine it can be very challenging."

Prince Harry was next. He was charming and gracious, making polite conversation as he made his way down the line. He remarked about how difficult the press could be.

"Hopefully they're nicer to you than the president," I said.

He laughed. "Unfortunately that isn't always the case."

After the receiving line was over the Queen walked the president and first lady through the Grand Hall where royal artifacts from the Queen's collection were on display. The artifacts represented pieces that showed the long and strong bond between our two countries and a few things that would be of particular interest to the presi-dent. There was a historic eighteenth-century map of New York City, old photos of golfers at St. Andrews, the British copy of the Declara-tion of Independence, and a horse statuette that President Trump had given the Queen on his previous visit. Gifts from the president and first lady on this trip were also part of the display.

We then attended a formal lunch where I sat next to Prince Edward, Duke of Kent, best known as the president of the All England Club, which Americans recognize as Wimbledon. Prince Edward presented the trophy to the Wimbledon champion and runner-up every year alongside Princess Kate, Duchess of Cambridge.

We departed Buckingham Palace and went to Westminster Abbey where Prince Andrew, Duke of York, accompanied the first couple. We were all able to tag along on the tour, and Ivanka and I got a few pictures of each other next to the side-by-side tombs of Mary, Queen of Scots, and Queen Elizabeth I, where a plaque read, REMEMBER BEFORE GOD ALL THOSE WHO DIVIDED AT THE REFORMATION BY DIFFERENT CONVICTIONS LAID DOWN THEIR LIVES FOR CHRIST AND CONSCIENCE SAKE.

While everyone was focused on the program, I stepped away to the side of the historic church where dozens of tables had been set with small votive candles, some already lit and some waiting to be lit. I stopped and with the voices from our group echoing off the walls of the church I closed my eyes and said a prayer for my family, as the president and first lady prepared to lay a wreath at the Tomb of the Unknown Soldier.

Afterward I rushed back to my hotel to get ready for the State Dinner that night at Buckingham Palace. I put on a true-red floor-length Chiara Boni La Petite Robe evening gown with Jimmy Choo heels and had my hair pulled back in a low and loose bun. The day had already been spectacular, but that evening was something every girl dreams of. We arrived and I wasn't sure if it was because we were having dinner at Buckingham Palace or all the royals present, but it felt to us in the US delegation like we were royalty for the night. We entered the palace and were immediately directed up the Grand Staircase, which had an elaborate all gold railing and red carpet with full-length portraits of Queen Victoria's family covering the walls, to a holding room. Despite being told not to take too many photos, I called all nineteen of us in the room together and asked T.A. to take a group picture. Among those who joined us were the president's adult children—Ivanka, Don Jr., Eric, and Tiffany. For reasons I still don't understand, a lot of reporters were angry that the president's children attended the state visit with him, despite the fact that many presidents' children traveled and attended events with the president and first lady in previous administrations. President Trump's family had been attacked like never before in our country's history, but to their credit, they didn't let the liberal critics stand in their way of joining their dad for this memorable occasion.

We were moved from the holding room to the Music Room, where most royal christenings take place, including those of Prince Charles and Prince William. It was also home to Queen Victoria's beautiful grand piano that Condoleezza Rice played when she was there with President Bush. Here we were paired with our escort and dinner partners for the evening. My escort into the State Dinner was Prince Michael of Kent, a seventy-six-year-old first cousin of Her Majesty the Queen. I decided after only five minutes of talking to him that I was going to really like him and have fun that night. Prince Michael had a white beard and wore a full service dress accompanied with the traditional sash, and he had military service medals covering the left side of his jacket. He asked if I knew what I was doing and I said, "Not really."

He reassured me in his thick British accent, "Not to worry, just follow my lead and you won't go astray."

Prince Michael then charmingly gave me a piece of advice he said someone once gave him the first time he went to one of these events: "When in doubt, just do as the royals do!"

I gripped his arm tightly and held on as we glided down the red carpeted hallway to the dinner. We were seated at a large horseshoe table big enough to accommodate about 125 people. It was one of the most elegant rooms I had ever seen. Despite its size and grandeur the dinner felt intimate. An orchestra kicked it off by playing both countries' national anthems, followed by toasts from the Queen and President Trump. We had been told that when the Queen puts her fork down it's a signal to everyone that the meal is over and no one should continue eating. We followed suit. As the meal ended, pipers came in from the back of the room and played. The president loved it. He was a big fan of the bagpipes and had a piper play every night at his golf club in Scotland. After dinner we went through another receiving line and thanked the Queen for having us. We then moved into the State Rooms for coffee and petits fours. All of the royal family attended. I had said hello very briefly before the dinner to Prince William and Princess Kate but hadn't really had the chance to talk to them. It was clear everyone wanted to meet them and when I noticed Secretary Mnuchin and Ivanka visiting with them, I slipped into the conversation. Prince William and Princess Kate were both warm and hospitable, and for about ten minutes we traded funny stories about our kids. One of the big topics of the evening among our team was speculating who is taller—Ivanka or Kate? It turned out they were about the same height and standing next to the two of them was a bit intimidating. Kate's hair that night was perfectly done, an intricate braid set low just above her shoulders, and every woman in the room wanted a closer look.

After the dinner we were all chatting and taking our final photos in the palace. I mentioned to Louise Linton, actress and wife of Treasury Secretary Steven Mnuchin, that Americans had earned our notoriety for being too loud and taking too many selfies. She threw her head back and in her thick Scottish accent said, "Well then let's prove them right!" and we took a selfie right there in the hallway. Treasury Secretary Mnuchin had been there since day one for the president and was instrumental on tax cuts and USMCA, and Louise was always the life of the party.

The following day we stopped in at the Churchill War Rooms and had formal meetings, a press conference, and lunch with President Trump and Prime Minister Theresa May at iconic 10 Downing Street. With its unassuming black door and black brick you would have no idea that behind the door it opened up to an expansive space including the Cabinet Room, where we met with May and members of her team. As we concluded the meeting and walked across the street for the news conference, all you could see was press lining both sides and pushing each other to catch a glimpse of the president and prime minister. Prime Minister May's communications director told me the number of press was abnormally large, in part because of President Trump's visit, but also because May was about to resign due to her failure to move Brexit forward.

That evening the United States hosted the reciprocal dinner at the Winfield House, the US ambassador's residence. Earlier in the trip, the Winfield House had been the site of a nasty fight between senior White House officials.

To prepare for every foreign visit we had daily operations meetings and briefings leading up to the trip itself. The UK state visit had lots of moving parts and one area of concern was that there would not be a presidential motorcade to and from most events, because the president would predominantly be traveling on Marine One. The UK security team was allowing one small staff motorcade, and based on their protocol they'd designated it for National Security Advisor John Bolton. In one of the prep briefings Deputy Chief of Staff Dan Walsh asked Bolton's team to be sure to wait on the senior White House staff vehicles traveling to the Winfield House so they could be part of Bolton's motorcade and avoid traffic. Bolton's team acknowledged the request.

As he did on many of our foreign trips, Bolton had a separate agenda and often arrived and departed on a different plane because he didn't want to travel on Air Force One with the president and his team. Bolton apparently felt too important to travel with the rest of us. It was a running joke in the White House.

As we were ready to depart for the Winfield House we loaded into a small black bus. On board were Treasury Secretary Steven Mnuchin, Acting Chief of Staff Mick Mulvaney, Senior Advisor Stephen Miller, Senior Advisor Dan Scavino, Walsh, and me. Based on US protocol, Mnuchin, Mulvaney, and Walsh all outranked Bolton. Mnuchin, one of the highest ranking officials in government, far outranked him.

We waited at the hotel but there was no sign of Bolton or his motorcade. After a while we gave up and headed to the Winfield House to meet the president. While en route, UK police directed us to pull to the side of the road because someone was coming through. As we sat there waiting, we looked over to see who it was and sure enough here came Bolton and his motorcade. We waited and watched as Bolton sped by and left us in the dust. The discussion on the bus quickly moved from casual chitchat to how arrogant and selfish Bolton could be, not just in this moment but on a regular basis.

If anyone on the team should have merited a motorcade it was Mnuchin, but he was a team player. Bolton was a classic case of a senior White House official drunk on power, who had forgotten that nobody elected him to anything. Often Bolton acted like he was the president, pushing an agenda contrary to President Trump's.

When we finally arrived at the Winfield House, Mick Mulvaney, typically laid back and not one to get caught up in titles or seniority, confronted Bolton and unleashed a full Irish explosion on him. He lit into him in a way I hadn't seen him do to anyone before. Mick made clear he was the chief of staff and Bolton's total disregard for his colleagues and common decency was unacceptable and would no longer be tolerated. "Let's face it John," Mick said. "You're a f—— self-righteous, self-centered son of a b——!"

That epithet really didn't have much to do with the motorcade, but was the culmination of months of Bolton thinking he was more important and could play by a different set of rules than the rest of the team. Bolton backed down and stormed off. The rest of us looked on and nodded in approval, proud of Mick for standing up for us. Mick even got a few high fives from officials thrilled someone had put Bolton in his place.

For the reciprocal dinner at the Winfield House, Prince Charles attended as the top representative of the royal family. When we were given our seating assignments for the dinner, I figured my seating assignment must be a mistake. I was seated at the president's table directly next to Prince Charles. I couldn't believe it, but was told the president made the call and insisted that I be at his table next to Prince Charles.

When I was twenty-two years old and my dad was chairman of the National Governors Association, I attended with him the annual Governors' Dinner at the White House. George W. Bush was president and his brother Jeb was governor of Florida. I was seated next to Governor Bush and he taught me a valuable trick. Most formal dinners like this one had a place card with the menu on it. Governor Bush told me one of the best things to do with the card is to pass it around the table and have everyone seated at your table sign it, so you'd always have something to remember the evening by. I thought what better table to do it at than this one with the American president and British royalty! I knew it was a risk as it was totally against protocol, but decided it was worth a shot. I asked one of the table attendants if he had a Sharpie, and he brought one back to me. I passed it around and it eventually landed in the president's hands. He said, "What is this?" I told him it was a way to remember the night and everyone at our table. "Is this your idea, Sarah?" I hesitated, wondering if I was going to be in trouble. "Yes, sir," I said, deciding it was probably for the best not to mention I got the idea from Governor Jeb Bush. He took out his own Sharpie, engraved with his signature in gold, and signed the stack of cards right in the center. After he finished, he handed the stack to Prince Charles. Prince Charles picked them up but without signing set them back down on the table next to me. I was disappointed but wasn't ready to give up yet. "Your Royal Highness," I said. "Would you like to sign first or me?" He looked at me and smiled. He picked up the pen and signed a couple of them, including one that he took and put inside his suit jacket pocket, and then handed one to me. His signature simply said, "Charles." I was told later by members of his staff he never signs anything. I protected that menu card all the way back home, where it now hangs framed in my office next to a picture of me, President Trump, Prime Minister May, and Prince Charles toasting each other that night.

President Trump didn't have to put me at his table for the UK state visit. He could have put anyone more important there, but he didn't. He picked me. He was like that more than he will ever get credit for, and it's one of the things I loved most about the president. He gave me that seat just to make my day.

President Trump was often generous and kind when the cameras were off. Many times I witnessed the president slip a waiter, doorman, or gardener at one of his properties a $100 bill, or several, when he didn't think anyone else was paying attention. It took him months to quit offering tips to the Secret Service agents and military valets assigned to him no matter how many times we explained to him they couldn't legally accept gratuities!

I was once in the Oval Office dining room and the president asked me if I'd ever heard of the Christian group Point of Grace. I was pretty surprised. Not only had I heard of Point of Grace, they were friends of mine. "They have this beautiful song I heard them do on *Fox & Friends* this morning," said the president. "Incredible. Really special. They have a great way about them, Sarah." I told him they attended the same small college I had in Arkansas and performed at my wedding. He smiled. "Of course they did." I found out later that he quietly sent them a $5,000 check because he thought more people should hear their music.

If the president really liked you, he'd go out of his way to demonstrate he cared about you. The night at Winfield House was one of those moments for me. I believe that underneath the tough image he always wanted to project in front of the cameras there was a heart that genuinely cared.

The next day we departed for Ireland, where we were scheduled to spend the next two nights at Doonbeg, the president's golf club. I knew we'd have some downtime there, so I invited my husband to join us for his thirty-sixth birthday. I booked him on a commercial flight and set him up with a tee time to play golf at the president's spectacular course set on cliffs over the Atlantic Ocean.

The first night, the president invited a group including my husband and me to have dinner with him and the first lady at his lodge at Doonbeg. About ten of us sat there with him and listened as he told us stories about the property. He said that during World War II an American pilot had crashed his warplane into the ocean just a few hundred yards off the beach where a little old rock house still stands on the edge of his golf course. An Irish couple was having dinner inside, and when the man at the table noticed the plane crash into the sea, he ran out to the beach, dove into the surf, and swam out to the crash site. He pulled the American pilot out of the wreckage and dragged him safely to shore. The American was badly injured and the Irish couple spent months nursing him back to health. His family back in the United States feared the worst. He had been missing for months, and was presumed dead. But the American pilot fully recovered and returned home, and he came back to Doonbeg every single year until his death more than fifty years later to celebrate Christmas in that little rock house with the Irish family who'd saved him.

After most of our table had finished their fish and chips with mushy peas—the president's recommendation—and a pint or two of Guinness, the president told us to take a few golf carts and go explore the property at sunset. Somebody mentioned the pro shop was already closed, but he said, "Not for you it isn't! Just tell them I said it's okay." He looked over at Bryan and winked at him. "It's a romantic ride!" A group of us raced each other across the course, taking in some of the most beautiful spots along the coast. It was a blast. After dark, we went out to an old Irish pub in the town of Doonbeg and sang and danced as locals played music late into the night.

The next morning a small group of us left Doonbeg early and flew to Normandy for the seventy-fifth anniversary of D-Day. Before the ceremony began, the president was scheduled to do an interview with Fox News's Laura Ingraham. I worked with her team and set it up to do it on-site at Normandy. The backdrop for the interview was row after row of perfectly distanced crosses marking the graves of the brave men who sacrificed their lives to save the free world. We were very tight on time because the event was set to start once the president arrived and there were thousands of people waiting. As the interview wrapped up I was disappointed that the majority of it had centered on the news of the day happening back home instead of the trip. When the interview finished, I stepped in and said, "Laura, could you please ask a few more questions about the event today and its significance?" The president didn't seem pleased. He said, "You have never done that. We have done a lot of interviews, Sarah, and you have never once asked for it to go longer! Are you sure?"

"Yes, sir," I said. "We are at Normandy. This is the seventy-fifth anniversary of D-Day. We need less on Adam Schiff and the Russia witch hunt and more on our fallen heroes."

"Good. Okay, Laura," he said. "Let's go."

Onstage at Normandy, the president addressed world leaders and American veterans who had fought there during WWII:

> We are gathered here on Freedom's Altar. On these shores, on these bluffs, on this day seventy-five years ago, ten thousand men shed their blood. . . .
>
> Their mission is the story of an epic battle and the ferocious, eternal struggle between good and evil. . . . They came from the farms of a vast heartland, the streets of glowing cities, and the forges of mighty industrial towns. Before the war, many had never ventured beyond their own community. Now they had come to offer their lives half a world from home.
>
> This beach, code-named Omaha, was defended by the Nazis with monstrous firepower, thousands and thousands of mines and spikes driven into the sand. . . . The GIs who boarded the landing craft that morning knew that they carried on their shoulders not just the pack of a soldier, but the fate of the world. Colonel George Taylor, whose 16th Infantry Regiment would join in the first wave, was asked: "What would happen if the Germans stopped them? What would happen?" This great American replied: "Why, the 18th Infantry is coming in right behind us. The 26th Infantry will come on too. Then there is the 2nd Infantry Division already afloat. And the 9th Division. And the 2nd Armored. And the 3rd Armored. And all the rest. Maybe the 16th won't make it, but someone will. . . ."
>
> Some who landed here pushed all the way to the

center of Germany. Some threw open the gates of Nazi concentration camps to liberate Jews who had suffered the bottomless horrors of the Holocaust. And some warriors fell on other fields of battle, returning to rest on this soil for eternity . . . 9,388 young Americans rest beneath the white crosses and Stars of David arrayed on these beautiful grounds. . . . From across the Earth, Americans are drawn to this place as though it were a part of our very soul. We come not only because of what they did here. We come because of who they were.

They were young men with their entire lives before them. They were husbands who said good-bye to their young brides and took their duty as their fate. They were fathers who would never meet their infant sons and daughters because they had a job to do. And with God as their witness, they were going to get it done. They came wave after wave, without question, without hesitation, and without complaint.

More powerful than the strength of American arms was the strength of American hearts.

These men ran through the fires of hell moved by a force no weapon could destroy: the fierce patriotism of a free, proud, and sovereign people. They battled not for control and domination, but for liberty, democracy, and self-rule.

They pressed on for love of home and country—the Main Streets, the schoolyards, the churches and neighbors, the families and communities that gave us men such as these.

They were sustained by the confidence that America can do anything because we are a noble nation, with a virtuous people, praying to a righteous God.

The exceptional might came from a truly exceptional spirit. The abundance of courage came from an abundance of faith. The great deeds of an Army came from the great depths of their love.

As they confronted their fate, the Americans and the Allies placed themselves into the palm of God's hand.

The men behind me will tell you that they are just the lucky ones. As one of them recently put it, "All the heroes are buried here." But we know what these men did. We knew how brave they were. They came here and saved freedom, and then, they went home and showed us all what freedom is all about.

It was one of President Trump's finest moments, and I'll never forget it. As we returned home from the UK, Bryan and I talked more about our future. I had served in the administration for two and a half years, and on the president's campaign for a year prior to his inauguration as well. I was torn between my love of serving the president and our country, and my love for my family and need to spend more time with our young children.

A few weeks before our trip to the UK, I'd boarded Marine One at the White House en route to Andrews. The president turned to me and out of nowhere said, "Are you running for governor of Arkansas?"

I was taken aback. We had never had this conversation before. "A lot of people have encouraged me to run, but the election isn't for a few years," I said. "I haven't made a decision yet."

"I think you definitely should," he said. "You'd be great! I'll endorse you right away. You will crush everyone."

I laughed and said, "Sir, are you firing me?"

"I love it when my people do well," he said. "I don't want you to leave but I guess at some point I'm going to have to get used to calling you 'Madam Governor'!"

And as quick as he brought it up, the conversation was over and we were landing at Andrews.

From that moment on, the president referred to me as "Madam Governor" in front of senators, governors, White House staff—even Prince Charles on the UK state visit. Upon our return to the United States, I knew the president and I had to finish the conversation he had started on Marine One.

It was time for our family to return home to Arkansas. Bryan and I had prayed about it and were at peace with our decision, but that didn't make leaving the White House any easier.

I loved working for the president. The previous three and a half years had been the experience of a lifetime. I had traveled to twenty-three countries with the president on Air Force One, met with dozens of world leaders, spoken on behalf of our country on some of our most difficult days, and celebrated some of our greatest victories. I had done more than one hundred press briefings, thousands of interviews with every major outlet in the country, and for better or worse become a household name. I had the trust of the president, the senior White House staff, and my team. I was at the peak of my time in the administration and my career. The chief of staff as well as others had asked me to take on a bigger role, but instead I was choosing to walk away from it all, and for no other reason than to go home to my family. I'd meant what I said before—I loved my job, but I loved my family and being a mom more. Lots of people could be White House press secretary, but only one could be mom to my kids.

I hadn't talked to anyone in the building about my decision. I wanted the first person outside my family to hear I was leaving to be the person who had hired me and given me this opportunity in the first place. I got up earlier than normal, worked out at home, and got my kids ready for school. Bryan and I sat down at our kitchen table with Scarlett, Huck, and George, and I said, "Mommy has some news. I'm going to tell the president today I'm leaving the White House and we're moving home to Arkansas." Our kids erupted in cheers, and at that moment I knew I was doing the right thing. I got in the car and headed to the office. I hadn't been in the car more than a minute or two when my phone rang and the White House operator asked if I was available for a call from the president. He and I talked for a few minutes about a story he had read and wanted my input on. As we were wrapping up I knew this was my moment.

"Sir, can I come over this morning to the residence to talk to you?"

He paused.

"No, you can't. I can hear it in your voice and I don't like it. Not my Sarah. You're going to leave me in the dust."

"Not in the dust, sir. I just want to talk to you."

He said he'd come down to the Oval Office early instead. I asked that it be in private and he said, "Of course. I don't trust any of these a—— holes either."

Not long after, I got a call from Madeleine. "The president would like to see you."

I had made the short walk from my office down the hall to the Oval Office thousands of times, but this one was the hardest. I walked into the back dining room and closed the door behind me. The president was seated in his spot at the head of the table. He looked at me, shook his head, and said, "Lay it on me."

I sat down and burst into tears. To my surprise, the president immediately got up and hurried out of the room. I was left there alone, wondering what on earth he was doing. The president quickly returned with a box of Kleenex in his hand and pulled me in for a hug.

"It's going to be okay," he said.

I explained to him how much I loved my job and how thankful I was to him.

"It's time for me to be a better wife and a better mom, and go home to Arkansas."

"You are going to run for governor, aren't you?"

I laughed.

"I'm not sure yet, but I'm definitely thinking about it and I have been getting more and more encouragement to do it thanks to all your 'Madam Governor' talk."

"You have nothing to worry about," he said. "You'll win and you'll be great. You have to do it. I will come in and endorse you right away. I am going to tweet about it now. You need to get out there early and let people know."

"The election isn't for a few more years, sir. Let's get you re-elected first."

"You need to let people know now. Just trust me, Sarah. After all, am I president or what?"

Mick Mulvaney walked in and I told him the news. He was surprised and said, "Well, that changes things. I was hoping you were going to take on comms, too. I guess I need to come up with plan B." A few minutes later Scavino walked in and I told him. He was supportive but sad I was leaving. We had become close friends as two of the longest-serving aides to the president going back to his campaign. The president said he was ready to tweet something out. I asked him to wait because I needed to tell some more people in the building first.

I walked back to my office and shared the news with the press and communications staff, along with a few senior White House officials, including Walsh, Kudlow, and Ivanka. There were lots of hugs and tears. I was emotionally drained as I walked back to the Oval to check in with the president and Scavino and let him know it was okay to announce it now.

"Are you sure?" he asked. "You could stay. . . ."

"I am sure," I said, and the president hit Send on the tweet.

"After three and a half years, our wonderful Sarah Huckabee Sanders will be leaving the White House at the end of the month and going home to the Great State of Arkansas. . . . She is a very special person with extraordinary talents, who has done an incredible job! I hope she decides to run for governor of Arkansas—she would be fantastic. Sarah, thank you for a job well done!"

We stood there and the president turned on the TV. "Watch this," he said. "I bet we set a new record. Wait for it, wait for it—there it is!" His tweet about me was on Fox News as a breaking news alert. "I think you did it! That was only like twenty seconds from tweet to screen! That's big! You're famous, Sarah!"

"Come with me," said the president. We walked down the colonnade together, with Jared and Ivanka behind us, to the East Room, where hundreds of people were gathered together for an event on criminal justice reform, which had been championed by Jared. Few expected it to get through Congress, but Jared almost singlehandedly made it happen. We went into the green room, where Kim Kardashian, who had partnered with the administration to promote the Second Chance Act, was waiting. The press noticed me and started taking photos of me standing against the back wall. About halfway into his remarks the president invited me to join him, and the crowd gave me a standing ovation as I walked onstage.

"And I thought maybe I'd just take a moment," said the president. "So, at the White House—and been with me now three and a half years, before I won, before the election—is a person, a friend, a woman—a great, great magnificent person, actually—named Sarah Huckabee Sanders. And she's very popular. She's very popular.

"And—and she's done an incredible job. We've been through a lot together, and she's tough but she's good. You know, you also have tough and bad, right? She's tough and she's good. She's great. And she's going to be leaving the service of her country, and she is going to be going—I guess you could say private sector, but I hope she's going to—she comes from a great state, Arkansas. That was a state I won by a lot, so I like it, right? But we love Arkansas, and she's going to be going back to Arkansas with her great family—her husband, who's a fantastic guy, and her family.

"And I don't know, folks, if we can get her to run for the governor of Arkansas, I think she'll do very well. And I'm trying to get her to do that.

"But I just saw her in the room and I really wanted to call her up. She's a special person, a very, very fine woman. She has been so great. She has such heart. She's strong but with great, great heart. And I want to thank you for an outstanding job.

"Say a couple words. . . ."

"Thank you," I said. "Thank you so much. I'll try not to get emotional because I know that crying can make us look weak sometimes, right?"

The crowd laughed.

"This has been the honor of a lifetime, the opportunity of a lifetime. I couldn't be prouder to have had the opportunity to serve my country and particularly to work for this president. He has accomplished so much in these two and a half years, and it's truly been something I will treasure forever. It's one of the greatest jobs I could ever have. I've loved every minute. Even the hard minutes, I have loved it.

"I love the president. I love the team that I've had the opportunity to work for. The president is surrounded by some of the most incredible and most talented people you could ever imagine. And it's truly the most special experience.

"The only one I can think of that might top it just a little bit is the fact that I'm a mom. I have three amazing kids, and I'm going to spend a little more time with them.

"And, in the meantime, I'm going to continue to be one of the most outspoken and loyal supporters of the president and his agenda. And I know he's going to have an incredible six more years and get a whole lot more done, like what we're here to celebrate today.

"And I don't want to take away from that. So I certainly want to get back to the tremendous thing that the people behind me have done.

"And thank you so much, Mr. President. It's truly an honor."

"Thank you, Sarah. Thank you very much. Great. Great person. Great person. Thank you, Sarah. Great.

"She's a warrior. You guys know what warriors are, right? Yeah? You're warriors. Huh? We're all warriors. We have no choice. We have to be warriors in this world. But she is a warrior."

12

Be the Somebodies

For more than two years I had been in President Trump's inner circle in the White House. I didn't just love my job, I loved the president and most of the people I worked with. As White House press secretary I had the opportunity to develop good relationships not only with the president and senior White House staff but also with the president's family, his cabinet, campaign staff, and members of Congress. Walking away from so many friends was one of the hardest parts about leaving, so when more than two hundred people showed up at my going-away party it was a real affirmation. Many departures from the Trump administration weren't so positive, much less given a celebratory send-off. It was meaningful to me that so many of my friends and colleagues had turned out. Ivanka and Jared, along with a few others, including Acting Chief of Staff Mick Mulvaney, Deputy Chief of Staff Chris Liddell and his wife, Renee, and Director of Strategic Communications Mercedes

Schlapp and her husband, Matt, cohosted the party at the Trump Hotel in one of the private rooms. Friends and former colleagues from White House press and comms including Sean Spicer, Bill Shine, Raj Shah, Lindsay Walters, Jessica Ditto, Hogan Gidley, Judd Deere, Julia Hahn, Alyssa Farah, Tony Sayegh, and Stephanie Grisham were there, along with current senior staff Larry Kudlow, Stephen Miller, Pat Cipollone, Marc Short, Derek Lyons, Julie Radford, and Kellyanne Conway, among others. Cabinet secretaries including Rick Perry, Linda McMahon, Wilbur Ross, Sonny Perdue, Alex Azar, Elaine Chao, Ben Carson, and Robert Wilkie also came, as did House Republican Leader Kevin McCarthy and US senator John Boozman, whose first campaign I had managed in Arkansas. Future White House chief of staff Mark Meadows and press secretary Kayleigh McEnany joined us as well, as did Donald Trump Jr. and Kimberly Guilfoyle, who came down from New York. It was an honor and quite the surprise when President Trump walked in, offered a toast, and as usual stole the show.

Just a few days later the president and his team were scheduled to leave for Osaka, Japan, for the G20. I went to the Oval just before the president's departure to say good-bye one last time. The vice president was there, too. I said thank you to the president and gave him a hug. As the president was walking out the door to the South Lawn to board Marine One, he said, "It's not too late. You can still come with us!" But we both knew it was too late. The news had been announced, my replacement chosen, and my kids were too excited to have their mom back to change my mind now. I stood in the door to the Oval as I watched him walk away. The walk back to my office was lonelier than any I had made before. I had been told that when the president leaves the country the West Wing is eerily quiet, but this was the first time I had experienced it myself. I went to my office and looked around, trying to soak it all in just one last time. Thinking about the moments we had fought, laughed, cried, hugged, and cheered together, and hoping I'd never forget any of it.

I hadn't packed up my office yet. I had planned to do some that afternoon and the rest the next day—my last. I enlisted my friend Lindsay Walters, my very type A deputy who had left only a couple months before I did, to come back and help me pack everything from the place I had spent more time over the last two and a half years in than any other, including my home in Arlington. It was a good thing I had Lindsay because without her I am pretty sure some of my stuff would have never made it back to Arkansas. My friends Sarah Flaherty, Jessica Ditto, and Julie Radford came to help as well. Julie and her husband, Wynn, had become close friends during my time in the administration. Later, Bryan arrived to load everything into our GMC Yukon for the drive home.

It was already summer and the kids were out of school but Heather and Michael Giroux, our pastors at the church we attended in Washington, DC, had volunteered to watch them. We had fallen in love with Citizen Heights church and gotten close to Michael and Heather over many long dinners and were very sad to leave them and the church behind. We were glad to know our kids were in good hands as they had four boys of their own and had seen it all. As we finished up, my friends left, and it was just Bryan and me in my empty office. I sat at my desk and followed the tradition of leaving a note behind for my successor, Stephanie Grisham. I tried to sum up on a notecard a job that had changed my life and what I learned that might be helpful to her. In addition to the letter, I left her a copy of *Jesus Calling*, the daily devotional book that had brought me peace and given me confidence to face the challenges of the job every day. I tucked it in the top drawer where Spicer had left a note and a challenge coin for me. I also wrote a note to Hogan, who had been my principal deputy for about a year and was more like family than a colleague. We had first met when we worked for my dad during his reelection campaign for governor back in 2002 and had worked together on many campaigns since, but nothing had made us closer than our time in the White House. I knew it would be very different for him with me gone and I wanted him to know how much I valued his friendship. I had written a similar note to Raj when he left after serving as my first principal deputy. Raj and Hogan had been there to lead the team when I couldn't, tell me things no one else wanted to, or let me yell at them in frustration and still be there when things calmed down. I dropped the note on Hogan's desk, turned off the lights, and took a final look around my office. I closed the door and walked down the same stairs to the West Executive Exit that I had walked in almost exactly two and a half years ago to start this wild adventure. Bryan and I got in the car and rolled the windows down. I waved to the Secret Service agents at the gate, and we drove out. As it closed behind us it felt like more than just a gate closing but the end of one of the most consequential times in our lives.

We didn't know what was next. I didn't have a job lined up or a plan other than returning home to Arkansas with my family. We wasted no time leaving Washington, and were on the road the next morning, never looking back. We had packed only what clothes and other essentials we would need for the next few weeks and to this day our kids haven't been back to Washington. Before going home to Arkansas, we stopped at my parents' house in Florida where we spent a few weeks decompressing in the sunshine before the kids started school. It was quite the transition to go from the center of the political universe in the West Wing to sitting on the beach with my family. I didn't even know how tired my mind and body were until I slowed down. I had been running on pure adrenaline for years, and it was like being hit by a semitruck. I went from every major reporter in the country and people at the highest levels of government, including the leader of the Free World, needing me and calling me every day to ordering school supplies and uniforms and decorating our new home. It was a shock to the system but every time I sat around the dinner table with my family or tucked my kids into bed and was present in the moment with them—not worried about rushing off to deal with the next crisis—I knew I was where I needed to be.

After settling into our new home in Little Rock and getting our kids enrolled in their new school, I signed contracts to be a Fox News contributor and with a speaker's bureau, and was appointed by President Trump to the Fulbright Board, established by the late US senator J. William Fulbright, from my home state of Arkansas. I started doing more campaign events with President Trump and Vice President Pence around the country and for Republican candidates and organizations in Arkansas. I also started writing this book.

That fall I was in Louisiana for an alligator hunt hosted by Jeff Landry, the state's attorney general. After I battled and killed my first-ever alligator, I was sitting around the campfire listening to my friend and fellow Arkansan Tracey Lawrence lead us in singing "Paint Me a Birmingham" when I saw a familiar number pop up on the screen of my phone. I walked to my cabin and answered.

"White House Operator, are you available for a call from the president?"

"Yes, thank you," I said.

"My Sarah! Where are you? What are you doing? Are you governor yet?"

"Not yet, sir. I am actually writing a book. I think you will like it. You have been falsely attacked and misrepresented for too long and it's time for America to know the real story."

"Can't wait. I'm sure it will be great," said the president.

Just a few weeks later the Democrats began their push to impeach President Trump. The Democrats' Russia witch hunt had failed, so they needed to manufacture a new scandal to take down the president. The Trump administration had asked Ukraine to investigate corruption, including why Joe Biden's son was paid millions of dollars to serve on the board of the Ukrainian gas company Burisma despite having no relevant experience to do so. Hunter Biden had been given the board seat and millions in compensation because his dad was the vice president and in charge of Ukraine policy for the Obama administration. And to make matters worse, Vice President Biden had called for the resignation of a Ukrainian prosecutor investigating Burisma, a clear conflict of interest. The US government was spending hundreds of millions of dollars on aid to Ukraine, and President Trump had every right to demand transparency and accountability from the Ukrainian government.

The Democrats and their liberal allies in the media didn't see it that way, but I couldn't believe they would be so stupid to make the same mistake again. The Russia witch hunt had totally backfired on them, and I was convinced the Ukraine witch hunt would as well. At the time I said it would "go down as one of the dumbest and most embarrassing political moves of all time—so bad it should be reported as an in-kind contribution to President Trump's 2020 reelect," and I was right.

As the Democrats marched forward with impeachment, President Trump had an impressive record to be proud of—a stronger economy, historic tax cuts and deregulation, rising wages, fifty-year-low unemployment, better trade deals, energy dominance, a rebuilt military, victory over the ISIS caliphate, the wall going up, and 200-plus federal judges confirmed, including a more conservative Supreme Court. The Democrats had no case against him. They only wanted to impeach President Trump because he was winning.

In the midst of the impeachment fight, I traveled with President Trump to Michigan and Iowa ahead of the Iowa caucus.

At a rally in Des Moines the president said, "We have somebody named Sarah Sanders. Have you ever heard of her?"

The crowd roared.

"That's pretty good!" said President Trump. "Come here, Sarah!"

I walked onstage in front of thousands of cheering Trump supporters in the packed arena.

"How much do we love this president?" The crowd went wild. "This is an incredibly special place," I said. "I actually met my husband here in Des Moines so I love being back in Iowa. . . . We're sorry you have so many crazy liberal Democrats running around here the last year, but the good news is it's not going to matter because at the end of the day, this guy will still be our president!"

When all else failed, Democrats resorted to impeachment because they were afraid they'd lose the 2020 election. But President Trump won and Joe Biden lost the impeachment fight. The president was aided in that fight by a superb team, led by White House Counsel Pat Cipollone, a devout Catholic and father of ten, who masterfully defended the president and cemented his place in the president's inner circle. When the Senate acquitted and vindicated President Trump, his approval rating hit an all-time high in the Gallup poll.

As Democrats harassed President Trump, the president was busy killing the world's most dangerous terrorists. President Trump ordered the successful raid in Syria that killed ISIS leader Abu Bakr al-Baghdadi, and the airstrike in Iraq that killed Iranian general Qasem Soleimani, who had the blood of thousands of American troops on his hands. President Trump was sending a clear message to our adversaries to never mess with America—a force for good against evil in a dangerous world.

The president was riding high as he delivered his State of the Union address on February 4, 2020, a speech that made a compelling case for four more years and that ended with Nancy Pelosi tearing up her copy of it in a fit of rage. One line that didn't get much attention at the time was about the threat of a mysterious, deadly virus from Wuhan, China.

"Protecting Americans' health also means fighting infectious diseases," said the president in the State of the Union. "We are coordinating with the Chinese government and working closely together on the coronavirus outbreak in China. My administration will take all necessary steps to safeguard our citizens from this threat."

The week before, on January 31, President Trump had declared the coronavirus a public health emergency and announced travel restrictions for China. While the president and his team were starting preparations in the event of an outbreak in the United States, many leading Democrats in Washington were too distracted by impeachment to care about the emerging threat.

I talked to President Trump on the phone the day he declared the national emergency. "The American people want you to lead and be strong on this," I said. "Your decision today was a good one. Keep it up."

Despite criticism from Democrats and the media, the president made the right call with the China travel ban. He was also right to declare a national emergency and implement social distancing guidelines—not forever, but until we flattened the curve—which likely prevented the failure of hospitals and saved many American lives.

Bryan and I called my parents, my brother David and sister-in-law Lauren, as well as Bryan's parents, and we all agreed to self-quarantine until the worst of the outbreak had passed so that we could continue to safely be around each other. Once the kids' school closed—and likely to their detriment—we started to home-school them together with David and Lauren's three kids. I quickly developed an even greater appreciation for their amazing, talented, and very patient teachers! And I thought my job in the White House was hard!

A typical morning of homeschool started with a prayer and the Pledge of Allegiance, with two kids assigned each day to hold the American flag. My sister-in-law Lauren and I taught the second-graders, Scarlett and her cousin Chandler. Bryan and my brother David taught the kindergarteners, Huck and his cousin Caroline. The youngest kids—George (four) and his cousin Thatcher (two)—ran wild, disrupting our lessons. For recess, which we had much more of than in regular school, we'd play four square, kickball or basketball, ride bikes, or go swimming. The kids were disappointed not to see their friends, but having their cousins, parents, and grandparents around made up for it. The kids loved having "Papa Mike" lead Sunday school.

Every night at bedtime George prayed that no one in our family would die from the virus. That was tough to hear from a four-year-old, but we leaned on our faith, taking it one day at a time and focusing on the positive. I had gone from the White House to homeschooling, but it was time I needed to reconnect with my family after three and a half years working for the president. At times it was hard not being there in the White House, but I was grateful to God for all He had given us, knowing He had a plan and I could trust Him no matter the circumstances.

My husband and I wanted to help people hurting during the crisis. After talking to my friends Phil Cox and Pete Snyder in Virginia about a nonprofit Pete had launched to help small businesses save jobs in his state, my husband and I founded a similar organization called the Arkansas 30 Day Fund to provide forgivable loans to small businesses impacted by COVID-19. It wasn't a government program. We wrote the first check to get us started and raised charitable donations from other Arkansans to help struggling small businesses bridge the gap until they got relief from the government or demand returned for their product or service. It was quick, easy, and free of red tape. Arkansas State University vetted the applicants. Top business and political leaders came on board to support us. It was a partnership of people who might not agree on anything other than helping others in our community in need, and it worked.

It was an all-volunteer effort, and we couldn't have done it without the help of many of our closest friends. Ashley and Chris Caldwell, Jordan and Noah Rhodes, Janis and Jim Terry, Megan Turner, Jordan Powell, Cathy Lanier, Chip Saltsman, and Karen and Aaron Black—lifelong friends who I had grown up with, battled alongside on campaigns, and who had helped our family pack up and move to Washington to join the Trump administration and then unpack after our move home to Arkansas—set aside their work and family commitments to volunteer their time, money, sweat, and tears to help us save jobs.

Within days of our launch, the Arkansas 30 Day Fund had received hundreds of applications and we started distributing funds to small businesses all across our state. Many of the small businesses we funded were owned by African Americans and by women. One of the first was Belle Starr Antiques & Vintage Market, owned by Beth Price in Fort Smith. In her testimonial video, Beth toured us through her beautiful showroom and spoke passionately about the eighty vendors who sell their products at Belle Starr and rely on her. "Essentially we are creating and supporting eighty small businesses within my business," Beth said. She paused, choking up. "This is my heart. This is my soul. I operate from it and I'm working 100 percent harder for 75 percent less results. So any assistance we can gain . . . we are here and we appreciate it."

I did a Zoom call with Beth a few days later and told her our team had awarded Belle Starr our maximum forgivable loan, which she didn't need to repay. Like so many other small business owners we awarded funds to, Beth broke down and cried. "I'm just so thankful," she said as tears ran down her face. "We have applied for every possible loan that's been out there since all of this started and everything's been shut down, and we haven't received any assistance. So I just can't tell you my absolute gratitude for what you guys are doing and how much it really, really, really is going to help us."

As many Americans came together to help one another during the pandemic, it was disheartening to watch Joe Biden's campaign and many of his liberal allies in the media politicize it. During a Fox News appearance, I said, "It's easy for Joe Biden to launch attacks from his basement bunker. It's much harder to actually lead in a crisis and work tirelessly to save lives and livelihoods as the president is doing."

The next day President Trump called me and said, "I was planning to call you last night after I watched you do an amazing job on *Hannity* but I'm glad I waited until this morning because you were even better on *Fox & Friends*. You need to be on TV more!"

He then moved on to the daily press briefings he'd been doing from the White House and said, "Now I know what you were going through. From the moment you walk in the door you can see it on many of their faces how much they hate you!"

"It's tough," I said. "And don't forget . . . many days you didn't make my job any easier!"

He laughed.

"Continue to lead," I said. "Keep going around the media and taking your message directly to the American people."

"You know, Sarah. If there's one good thing that comes out of this it may be people will forever quit shaking hands."

The president, a notorious germophobe, added, "I mean, sometimes people I don't even know go in for the hug! I know nothing can replace the warm embrace of a hug, but come on!"

He then asked again if I'd run for governor.

"I'll make a decision after we get you reelected," I said. "But if I do run, you know that means you're going to have to come to Arkansas."

"Of course," said the president. "I'll be there for you, and you know what else? You're going to win."

Along with the great economy, the pandemic had derailed the president's reelection strategy. From his basement bunker, Joe Biden used the crisis to attack the president. Joe Biden should have directed his attacks at China, which unleashed the deadly pandemic on the world, but Biden was a friend of China. He said "a rising China is a positive development," his son Hunter cofounded and served on the board of a major investment company there called Bohai Harvest RST, and he initially opposed President Trump's China travel ban that saved American lives.

Biden just didn't get it. China was our adversary, not our friend. Either America would lead the world in the twenty-first century or China would. Under President Trump, it would always be America first. Could the same be said of a President Biden?

A second term for President Trump would be better for all Americans than the Democratic alternative: a weaker military, liberal judges, higher taxes, and bigger government. Until the pandemic hit, our economy had never been stronger. African American and Hispanic unemployment was at an all-time low thanks to President Trump, who had done far more to empower minorities with better jobs, higher wages, and hope for a better future than Joe Biden ever had. President Trump rebuilt our economy before. He could be trusted to do it again.

Even though President Trump was the incumbent, he was still the outsider, disruptor, and change agent against Biden, the ultimate Washington insider and representative of the status quo. Biden was a liberal career politician who has been part of the problem for fifty years. He was for bad trade deals and free healthcare and government benefits for illegal immigrants, none of which helped American workers. And "nice guy" Joe Biden with all his "empathy" and "compassion" supported taxpayer-funded abortion, showing no compassion whatsoever for the weakest and most vulnerable among us—the unborn child.

The Democratic Party had been hijacked by the left, who actually believe they know how to protect our families, choose our healthcare, run our businesses, and spend our money better than we do. Wake up, America—our freedom, prosperity, and way of life are on the line in the 2020 election. And don't think for a moment this campaign is going to be easy. Some of the most powerful forces in the world—the liberal media, Hollywood, academia, big government, and China—are aligned against us. The America we love is under attack, and we must fight for it.

After the 2020 election, the American people will have to put aside some of our differences to face the tremendous challenges before us: a deadly pandemic and its toll on our economy, social unrest, and the dangerous threat of a rising China. We can either be divided and fail or start coming together and prevail. It will not be easy, but we are Americans, and there is nothing we can't do united as one nation under God.

As has been the case for all of human history, we are in the midst of an epic battle between good and evil. America must continue to be a force for good in that battle. As C. S. Lewis once said, "Now is our chance to choose the right side. God is holding back to give us that chance. It won't last forever. We must take it or leave it."

Many years ago an eleven-year-old girl and her family traveled to Israel. Her parents had been going there for decades, but this was the girl's first trip. The family planned to visit the historical and biblical sites that served as a basis for much of their Christian faith. They walked where Jesus walked and performed miracles at the Sea of Galilee, and worshiped at the Garden Tomb where their Savior rose from the dead after giving His life for us. One of the last stops on their trip was to Yad Vashem, which commemorates one of the darkest eras of human history—the Nazi genocide against the Jewish people. The eleven-year-old girl's parents weren't sure if she was ready for it, but they wanted her to understand the importance of standing up against evil, so they decided to bring her. The girl's father would stay with her and if at any point it became too much he would take her out.

Yad Vashem sits on Mount Herzl, often referred to as the Mount of Remembrance. Yad Vashem in Hebrew means "a memorial and a name," and its goal is to memorialize the Holocaust and in particular all the Jewish people who were killed and had no descendants left on earth to carry on their names.

As they walked through Yad Vashem the girl watched videos of Jewish families being marched to their deaths in gas chambers. She saw an exhibit featuring hundreds of pairs of shoes taken off the feet of Jewish children her age or younger and piled high to be burned. She listened as the names of the 1.5 million Jewish children murdered by the Nazis were read off one by one, and was told it takes three months to get through the full list.

The eleven-year-old girl didn't speak as she walked through Yad Vashem. At one point she reached up for her father's hand, gripping it tightly, but she didn't say a word. Her father, never leaving her side, watched his daughter and waited, hoping she understood why her parents wanted her to see this. The father worried they'd made a mistake, that it was all just too much for her at such a young age.

They got to the end and there was a guest book for visitors to sign. The girl reached up and took the pen out of her father's shirt pocket that she knew was always there.

Looking over her shoulder, the father watched as his daughter inscribed her name and address in the book, and then paused at the section for comments. She still hadn't said a word since entering Yad Vashem, but in the book the little girl carefully wrote:

"Why didn't somebody do something?"

Tears welled in the father's eyes, and in that moment he knew that she got it.

"Why didn't somebody do something?"

The little girl understood. All it takes for evil to win is for good people to do nothing.

The reason I know that story is that I was that little girl.

My prayer for America is that like the brave generations before us, we take a stand against evil. Now is our chance to choose the right side. Let us be the somebodies who do something.

Acknowledgments

There have been so many people who have influenced my life and been a part of my story. In this book I tried to put into words thirty-seven years of events and people who made me who I am. Writing this book was therapeutic. At times it felt impossible and overwhelming, but I am proud of the end result. Life isn't much fun if you don't have good people to share it with, and I am eternally grateful for all of the people who have helped me become the daughter, wife, mom, friend, coworker, and Christian I am.

Bryan—you edited and poured your heart and soul into this book. If it's any good at all, it's because of you. You love me even when I make it hard, are the leader of our family, and always make us laugh. You are my best friend and the best decision I've ever made.

Scarlett—you are beautiful inside and out. You are strong, independent, and a great big sister to your brothers. You're a natural leader and nothing will hold you back from fulfilling your God-given potential. I will always love you, even when you become a teenager and I threaten to send you to live with your grandparents!

Huck—you have more enthusiasm and curiosity than anyone I have ever met and I hope you never lose it. You find the good in everything and have a heart so big I know you will change the world for the better. Stay off Twitter, learn to communicate at a normal volume, and keep exploring!

George—you have the sweetest spirit and a brilliant mind like your daddy. You love with everything you have and are destined for great things. You are as messy as our dog Traveler, but because you are so cute and hysterically funny, I'll let it slide. Even when you flood our house (not cool, man!), you bring a smile to my face.

Mom and Dad—you loved me enough to let me be myself and made sure I knew that God loved me unconditionally. Mom, you are one of the toughest people I know and have fought life's hardest battles and won. Dad, you showed us what it means to be a compassionate but strong leader and to never back down from your principles. I pray I can live up to the example each of you set for us.

Bill and Julia—the only thing better than having amazing parents is getting amazing in-laws, too. I couldn't ask for more loving, accepting, encouraging, and generous in-laws. You love me and care for me like one of your own and have always made me feel welcome and a part of the family.

David and John Mark—you made me tough. Without you teasing me our entire childhood I might not have survived my first White House press briefing. John Mark, you are our family's most gifted writer—I hope this book does our family justice. You are the most thoughtful uncle who gives the best gifts, even if they're the ones that make the most noise! David, not only do you make everything fun, you are so giving of yourself and will do anything for anyone. So glad you have always been in my corner.

Lauren and Virginia—I always wanted a sister and now I have

the two best I could ever ask for. You were both worth the wait! Lauren, as one of my best friends you know everything about me and love me anyway. We have laughed and cried our way through life's biggest moments together and I wouldn't want anyone else by my side for any of it. Virginia, you love so passionately. Whether it's your students or your family, you pour everything into the people in your life.

David S.—we may not agree on much, but we disagree without being disagreeable about it. You are so dedicated to your work and even though I don't understand anything about neuroscience my instincts tell me you are going to make big discoveries that help a lot of people.

Chandler, Caroline, and Thatcher—one of the hardest parts about being in Washington for two and a half years was missing you growing up. I am so happy we are home now and I get to see you almost every day! Aunt Silly and your Uncle Bobo are always here for you and if you ever need someone to let you do things your mom won't (like eat ice cream for breakfast!) just come see us!

To my extended family—Aunt Pat (my number one cheerleader who loves and watches every interview!), Uncle Jim, Katie Beth (the most caring person I know), Blake, Aunt Susan (the only one brave enough to boss my mom around), Uncle Mike, Aunt Brenda, Uncle Tal, Aunt Nell, Aunt Patty—we don't have a perfect family and I am glad because that would be boring. I'll take our crazy family full of laughter and love any day!

Leigh and Jordan—after nearly twenty-five years of friendship, you are my oldest and best friends. There isn't much we haven't done together and I am looking forward to many more adventures with you two by my side.

My college crew—Dawson, Mandy, Jodi, Kelly, Megan, Sarah, Hillary, and Mandy A.—it's amazing how close you can get when you go to college in a small town with nothing to do! I love how seamless our friendship is even though we don't get to see each other often enough. Knowing I had this whole crew cheering, defending, and praying for me every single day gave me the confidence to take on anything.

My kitchen cabinet—Chris, Ashley, Chip, Jordan, Jim, Cathy, Katy, and Megan—you tell me all the things I don't want to hear, join me in one crazy project after another, and make everything more fun. You are the loyal friends and team I know I can call on to help when I really need it, no questions asked.

Senator John Boozman—you are a mentor and the nicest person in politics. Washington changes a lot of people but it never changed you. I look forward to many more years of your selfless leadership for Arkansas in our nation's capital.

White House press and comms teams—I couldn't have done the job a single day without each of you. Spicer, you hired me onto your team and gave me an opportunity. You faithfully served our country and didn't let the critics define you or get you down. Raj, you gave me tough love and never let me go out unprepared. I didn't worry when you were handling something because I knew it would probably be done better than if I did it myself. Hogan, you are like a brother to me and always had my back. Your sense of fashion is unmatched in the White House (even by the great Larry Kudlow) and you do an outstanding job speaking on behalf the president. Ditto, who knew how close we would become when we came through the gate on that first day? Your friendship and support helped me endure the toughest moments. Hope, you always had the best one-liners and made me laugh. You are a fundamentally good person and amazing talent. The president and the country are so blessed to have you. Josh, everyone needs a friend like you. You showed us that Democrats and Republicans can set politics aside and work together—and I hope that's the case because I'd never want to go against somebody as formidable as you. Anton, you are a true-life gentleman and a scholar, and you brought serious intellectual fire-power to our team. There is literally no one else like you! Lindsay, you kept us all in line and our office couldn't have functioned without you and your willingness to manage it all. Judd, you are one of the best hires I've ever made. I can't wait to work with you again once I convince you to come home to Arkansas! Sarah F., you are a patriot who admirably served our military and president with distinction. Americans like you are the reason we are the greatest country in the world. Alexa, I can't believe we're still friends after all the times you booked me on CNN during the campaign! You worked so hard and gave it all for the president and our team. Adam, you were often a wet blanket to my hot takes, but invaluable preparing me for every briefing and interview. Ory, some days you were a little more E-ory than Ory but you are smart and strategic and made it look easy. You also had the best DC restaurant recommendations and I never once got kicked out of any of them! Julia, you may be soft-spoken but you have as much fight as anyone in the building. Tony, for a corporate guy from NYC you're really not that bad! Dubke, you throw the best party in Washington and gave me the confidence to take on the job. Mercy, you helped me find work-family balance. You knew what it meant to be a mom first and made sure I never felt like I wasn't enough for my kids. Shine, you never quite got the lighting right or learned how to speak at an appropriate volume, but always nailed being the fiercest defender of our team. Janet, you put up with me every day and protected me and my time better than anyone ever could. Sometimes even I was scared to tell you we needed to change the schedule! Katie, even if you only had five minutes, you made me feel beautiful and confident every day. VP comms (Lotter, Alyssa, and Jarrod), you were always perfectly on message just like your boss! Research, booking, digital, congressional, cabinet, intergovernmental affairs comms, wranglers, and assistant press secretaries, you did all the legwork for none of the credit. Thank you to everyone in White House press and comms for your hard work, loyalty, and friendship.

Additional White House senior staff—Brooke, Pat, Emmet, Johnny, Hagin, Liddell, Shahira, General McMaster, Gary, Kudlow, Waddell, Bossert, Fears, Marc, Justin C., Stepien, Stefan, Hassett, Greenblatt, Kellyanne, Nick, Emma, Zach, Reince, General Kelly, Kirstjen, Mick, Bremberg, McGahn, Annie, Dearborn, Grogan, Reed, KT, among others—each of you made the sacrifice to serve. Many of you paid a personal and financial price to do so and I loved getting to serve alongside you.

Julie and Wynn—you became like family to us in Washington. You didn't mind if my house was a wreck or my kids were screaming in the background. You made doing life together in Washington fun. Your love of the South and jam bands didn't hurt either!

Dina—you're a true pro and mentor who helped me navigate the White House and Washington. I'll be returning to you again and again for good advice in the years ahead.

The White House road team—Scavino, Derek, Walsh, Miller, Tony, Dr. Conley and Dr. Jackson, and the Mil-aides, White House photographers, and military valets—some months we spent more hours in the air than we did at home and I loved every minute of it. From playing cards, working on speeches and statements, and family dinners in the conference room, some of my best memories from the White House I'll always cherish were time I spent with each of you.

White House Advance, Travel Office, and Operations—Clifton, Hannah, Beau, Luna, Jordan F., Bobby, Max, Bethany, Megan, Justin C., Jordan K., Rebecca W., Andrew, Ben W., Alex, Therese, Will, Chang, among others—you made each trip possible, handled every detail, and always made sure I knew where to go and never once left me behind even though I often wasn't in the right place!

FLOTUS team—Lindsay, Grisham, Haley, and Rickie—you

served the first lady exceptionally well and made every event at the White House special and beautiful, and all our foreign trips more fun!

The US Secret Service, the White House Military Office, the Air Force and Marine One flight crews, the White House Communications Agency—you selflessly protect us and faithfully serve our country. America is strong and free because of you, and we are all in your debt.

The many real journalists in the White House Press Corps— even if we often disagreed, you are some of the toughest, smartest reporters in the country, and provide a vital service for the American people. You challenged us and made us stronger every day.

Former White House press secretaries (Marlin, Josh, Ari, and Dana)—you were the voices of previous presidents and paved the way for the rest of us. Your example, advice, and feedback were helpful and encouraging.

Our Arlington neighbors Staci and Cabi—for two and a half years you gave us a social life outside of politics. You brought us into your fold and treated us like lifelong friends.

Our pastors Michael and Heather—you gave us a church home and accepted us the way that God does, just as we are. You were mentors and friends and served as a constant reminder of what really matters.

David Limbaugh—you are the best agent I could have asked for. Patient, calm, and most importantly you believed in me and my story.

Hugh Hewitt—you gave me the title for this book. Any friend of Jan Janura's is a friend of ours!

The team at St. Martin's—you guided me through this process and took a chance on me as a first-time author.

Vice President and Second Lady Pence—you led by example and showed our country what it means to live out your faith and do so unapologetically. You have been a steady and strong force for good in our country.

Don Jr., Ivanka, Eric, Tiffany, Barron, Jared, and Lara—the president couldn't do it without your love, support, and devotion. Very few people fully understand the tremendous sacrifices and contributions you make—but it doesn't go unnoticed or unappreciated. America is better because of each of you.

First Lady Melania Trump—your poise and grace is unrivaled and your love for children is inspiring. You have made a positive, lasting impact on the president and the country.

President Trump—there are no words to describe how much you changed my life. You took a chance on me, let me into your circle, trusted me, and empowered me to carry your message to the world. I will forever be grateful for the opportunity you gave me to serve the American people. I don't care what the critics say—you will go down in history as a great president.

The American People—you make our country good and strong. Thank you to all of you who believed in us, prayed for us, and have taken the time to read my story. I hope you enjoyed it and will encourage your family and friends to read it as well.

And most importantly, thank you to our Creator who gives us purpose and loves us no matter what.

Sarah Huckabee Sanders served as the White House press secretary from 2017 to 2019; she was the third woman and first mother to ever hold the position. The daughter of former Arkansas governor Mike Huckabee, Sanders has worked in leadership roles for US senators, governors, and presidential campaigns. She has been recognized in *Time*'s "40 under 40" as one of the best political operatives of her generation. She is a Fox News contributor, advises major companies, and serves on the Fulbright board as an appointee of President Trump. Sanders lives in Little Rock, Arkansas, with her husband, Bryan; their children, Scarlett, Huck, and George; and their golden retriever, Traveler.